Uneasy Coalition

UNEASY COALITION

The Entente Experience in World War I

JEHUDA L. WALLACH

CONTRIBUTIONS IN MILITARY STUDIES, NUMBER 146

Greenwood Press
WESTPORT, CONNECTICUT • LONDON

Library of Congress Cataloging-in-Publication Data

Wallach, Jehuda Lothar.
    Uneasy coalition : the entente experience in World War I / Jehuda
L. Wallach.
       p. cm.—(Contributions in military studies, ISSN 0883–6884
; no. 146)
    Includes bibliographical references and index.
    ISBN 0–313–28879–8 (alk. paper)
    1. Alliances. 2. World War, 1914–1918. 3. War. I. Title.
II. Series.
    D523.W27 1993
    940.3′1—dc20   93–18144

British Library Cataloguing in Publication Data is available.

Library of Congress Catalog Card Number: 93–18144
ISBN: 0–313–28879–8
ISSN: 0883–6884

First published in 1993

Greenwood Press, 88 Post Road West, Westport, CT 06881
An imprint of Greenwood Publishing Group, Inc.

Printed in the United States of America

The paper used in this book complies with the
Permanent Paper Standard issued by the National
Information Standards Organization (Z39.48–1984).

10 9 8 7 6 5 4 3 2 1

Napoleon was not a great general. He only fought a Coalition.
—Attributed to the French General M. P. E. Sarrail
in David Lloyd George, *War Memoirs*

War, as well as politics, makes strange bedfellows.
—Keith Neilson, *Strategy and Supply*

CONTENTS

INTRODUCTION

Some years ago, I began to investigate the problems of coalition warfare, and was fascinated by the complexity of the subject. I then conducted a postgraduate students' seminar at the School of History of Tel-Aviv University in order to explore this subject further. In this seminar we tried to develop a typology of this particular type of warfare. A short time later, when an international colloquy on military alliances was conducted in Montpellier, France, under the auspices of the International Commission for Military History, I used this opportunity to present the scheme evolved in the seminar to this international audience. Chapter 1 of this book is mainly based on my paper presented in Montpellier. The positive response to this proposal received at the colloquy encouraged me to continue with the research.

Looking for a suitable test case, I soon reached the conclusion that the Entente in World War I would best serve my purpose, to evolve some universal rules for this type of war. In addition, I reached the conclusion that the appropriate vehicle for this research was the memoirs of the personalities involved rather than the official histories of the various countries, which understandably tried to avoid mentioning unpleasant aspects. Because the gist of coalition relations is merely in the sphere of human relations and of the particularistic interests of the various partners, all of them rather delicate issues in the framework of a coalition, these aspects remain normally untouched in official histories.

Coalition wars have many facets. In my seminar, in addition to the aforementioned typology, we concentrated on the following topics:

- Prewar planning, as far as a coalition was in existence prior to the outbreak of war
- Particularistic interests of the coalition partners
- Human relations, on two levels: among soldiers and between statesmen and soldiers
- Frameworks for coordination mechanisms inside the coalition
- General Reserve
- Unified command
- Amalgamation of Allied forces
- Logistical problems in the framework of a coalition
- War finances
- The transition from war to peace, with all its complications. This involves nations not united by identical war aims, or, as Marshal Foch defined it, "the sharing of the plunder, the distribution of the assets." (Charles Bugnet, *Foch Speaks*, New York, 1929, p. 271)

In the concluding chapter there is a brief survey of the development in this field since World War I.

In connection with this research, I would like to touch on the following event: As already mentioned, this study was carried out over the course of several years. In the spring of 1990 I decided to close the list of memoirs consulted and to crystallize my findings. In order to do so, I used a sabbatical leave and went to the Library of Congress in Washington, D.C. Some of my associates considered this a waste of effort, because they thought that in the era of *glasnost* and *perestroika* and the expected dissolving of the opposing world blocs, the Warsaw Pact and NATO, the subject of coalition warfare has lost its relevance. A few months later, in August 1990, the Iraqi invasion of Kuwait led to the formation of a coalition under the auspices of the United Nations that was no less complicated than the one I had investigated. As a matter of fact, my research was able to provide me with some possible scenarios by the time the shooting began. Unfortunately, the issue I was researching is not yet as out-of-date as some of my associates suggested.

I would like to render thanks to all who assisted my work. Above all I am obliged to my students, from whom I received most valuable stimulation. It is always a pleasure to conduct a postgraduate seminar. The necessary financial aid for carrying out research of such a scope, which demands extended stays in libraries abroad, was provided by the Sabbatical Fund of my university. Two libraries which were most helpful should be singled out: the Library of Congress in Washington, D.C., and the Bibliothek für Zeitgeschichte in Stuttgart, Germany. The National Archives in Washington also gave access to the relevant archivalia and provided the necessary microfilms. Zvi Volk has carefully read the manuscript and improved the style of an author who was impudent enough to write in a language other than his native tongue.

Uneasy Coalition

SUGGESTIONS FOR A TYPOLOGY OF WARTIME COALITIONS

It is common knowledge that a large part of the history of mankind is occupied by wars. Even a superficial survey of this history will reveal that most wars were coalition wars. One may be surprised, however, to discover that no clear-cut and satisfactory definition of coalition warfare can be found in either encyclopedias or lexicons (in the East or the West), or in the theoretical works of military thinkers or social scientists. Even the great military thinker Carl von Clausewitz suggested no theoretical definition. The index to his treatise, *On War*, includes only historical examples of actual wars of coalitions under the heading "coalition warfare." There is no theoretical formulation.

It seems, however, that there is no difficulty in evolving a theoretical definition. The word *seems* is used here intentionally, because if one really tries to formulate a satisfactory, all-embracing definition, it soon becomes clear that this is no easy task. At the end of a postgraduates' research seminar conducted some years ago at Tel-Aviv University on the subject of coalition warfare in World War I, the students, both civilians and professional officers, tried to provide such a working definition based on the experience of World War I. They soon realized that it was almost impossible to provide a formula that was likely to cover most of the possible variants. There was the danger of the definition becoming a treatise, which would render it unworkable. On the other hand, a traditional definition would, in fact, not provide a useful analytical tool. It was suddenly understood why the sages had abstained from giving an acceptable definition.

Nevertheless, there is no doubt that military coalitions, both those formed before the actual outbreak of hostilities and those formed during wartime, are of various types. It seems that evolving a typology, a kind of topographical survey or mapping, might be useful for two reasons: first, for the understanding and evaluation of the mechanism of given coalitions in the past, and second, as a device for predicting the function of existing coalitions in any future case.

BASIC PATTERN OF COALITIONS

There are two basic patterns to which coalitions seem to conform.

The first is a coalition between equal partners or, in other words, the case in which all partners are what may be called senior partners.

A second is coalitions between unequal partners. This means that some, either a single participant or several participants, have the status of senior partners, and other participants are, in fact, junior partners in the same coalition.

It should be noted that during the cold war, when massive, international blocs of nations were established, some sources added a third category: satellite partners. The use of this term reflected, of course, a certain weltanschauung.

However, even in a coalition of equals, strange as it may seem, we are likely to find two variations:

First, coalitions of full-fledged, or real equals, as for instance, France and Great Britain in World War I.

The second variant covers coalitions between formally equal, but in fact substantially unequal, partners, as for instance the position of the Russian Empire in World War I. In this case, in the formal sense, France, Great Britain and Russia were all senior partners. In fact, there were never consultations on an equal footing between France and Great Britain on the one hand and Russia on the other. In the memoirs of Maurice Paléologue, the French ambassador to the Court of St. Petersburg, various expressions of the czar can be found that reveal, without a doubt, that he recognized and accepted this fact.[1]

As far as coalitions of unequal partners are concerned, there is a multitude of variants and combinations, resulting from the fact that often junior partners are of different standing. This may be demonstrated by another example taken from World War I. In the coalition of the Central Powers in which Germany was the dominating senior partner, there were tremendous differences in the status of the various junior partners: the Austro-Hungarian Empire, the Ottoman Empire and Bulgaria.

The scheme offered so far seems to be both simple and uncomplicated. However, in reality this is not the case. First of all, one confusing fact must be added. One of the recognized senior partners in both world wars consisted by itself of a coalition of senior and junior partners. The reference here is, of course, to the British Empire, or Commonwealth. Although the British Empire was, in the framework of the alliance, a sovereign and recognized senior partner, it was often hampered in its freedom of action by the very fact that there were domestic pressures in the framework of the Commonwealth with repercussions on the British position in the external coalition. Moreover, there is no doubt that the status of the Commonwealth partners underwent tremendous changes over the time period from World War I to the present, not to mention the change in the specific preeminence of Great Britain itself.

Another confusing fact is that coalitions are seldom monolithic in purpose. More often they differ even as to the ultimate aims to be achieved. Sometimes the partners share only some of the goals to be achieved by the coalition. Suffice it to say that the United States joined the Entente in World War I but confined its participation to the overthrow of Imperial Germany. Therefore, American troops were not available for action in all theaters of war, and under no circumstances in those theaters that were considered by the U.S. government and public opinion colonial theaters. An additional example of limited partnership was provided by the anti-German coalition during World War II, which was united by the desire to destroy the Nazis. From the outset, it differed as to the world order to be established after the Third Reich was defeated. There is a wealth of additional examples of this kind throughout the history of coalition wars. Most recently, the experience of the Gulf War against Iraq and Saddam Hussein again confirmed this peculiar aspect of wartime coalitions.

THE FUNCTIONING OF COALITIONS IN WAR

History provides ample evidence that for the smooth functioning of a war coalition, formal arrangements and proclaimed intentions of governments are not sufficient. What really matters are the personal relations between the military commanders in the field, who are supposed to cooperate. After all, the translation of the formal arrangements and intentions into actions depends on the interpretation given by the man on the spot.

At the outbreak of World War I, and after the British declared war on Germany, British Field Marshal Sir John French was provided by his government with a document defining as precisely as possible his position and mission in the context of the Anglo-French coalition: "The special motive of the Force under your control is to support and cooperate with the French Army . . . to assist the French . . . in preventing or repelling the invasion by Germany of French or Belgian territory and eventually to restore the neutrality of Belgium." But then came in the same document the following statement: "I wish you distinctly to understand that your command is an entirely independent one and that you will in no case come in any sense under the orders of any Allied general."[2] Little wonder that the first real test of this proclaimed cooperation during the phase of the Allied retreat from Belgium on the eve of the First Battle of the Marne, in late August 1914, resulted in Sir John getting the impression that he was cheated by the French generals operating on his flanks, and was both abandoned and sacrificed in order to cover the safe withdrawal of the French army with British troops. The logical result of this attitude was that Field Marshal French put the main emphasis on the second part of the instructions quoted here rather than on the first. Therefore, he decided to leave the line of battle and retreat to the Channel ports in order to save his command.[3] The Secretary of State for War, Field Marshal Lord Horatio H. Kitchener, was compelled to rush to the scene and throw in both his rank and his seniority in order to rescue the coalition. This step was, of course, very much resented by Field Marshal French.[4]

In fact, smooth cooperation was handicapped from the very outset by the fact that Sir John French held his French colleagues in very low regard. After the first meeting with General Charles Louis Lanrezac, he had declared to his aide-de-camp that the French general was not a gentleman, and to Field Marshal Kitchener, the Secretary of State for War, he wrote, hinting at General Joffre, the French commander in chief: "Au fond, they are a low lot and one always has to remember the class these French generals mostly come from."[5] For a member of the British gentry, the source of most of the senior commanders, the issue of cooperation was thus negatively settled, with or without specific instructions from Whitehall.

Examples of this kind are legion throughout the history of all coalitions. Since the official histories of any war tend to evade these facts—because they are seldom reflected in official records, which are the very basis used by the historians writing these official histories—the student of coalition warfare will find much more useful material in the memoirs of the soldiers, and to a certain extent also the statesmen, than in the official histories of the nations involved. For this reason, the current investigation is based principally on the huge body of memoirs, and shuns the official histories.[6]

On the strength of this presentation, one may reach the conclusion that the proper functioning of coalitions depends on the personal relations of the commanders in the field who were called upon to enact mutual cooperation. At the aforementioned research seminar at Tel-Aviv University, a verification of this assumption was attempted. It was found that the smooth and proper functioning of any coalition indeed depended on the amicable relations between the men on the spot. It is most likely that this will continue to be the case in the future. No evidence was found to suggest that a coalition fell apart because of this factor. There is no doubt that strained relations have caused serious friction or even unpleasant situations which resulted in unnecessary casualties, but no more than this. Even in the eighteenth century, the era of the so-called Cabinet Wars, when the composition of coalitions changed frequently, there is no case recorded of a change being caused by tension between commanders in the field. The reason was always a change in political orientation or dynastic interests. One may conclude, therefore, that the proper functioning of any coalition is really based on the sound relations of the men who are called to work together, but that coalitions do not cease to exist when these relations are not assured. In such cases, the coalitions simply face serious handicaps that consume much unnecessary energy and produce ill will instead of cooperation.

NOTES

This chapter is based mainly on the paper I submitted to the International Colloquy of Military History in September 1981 in Montpellier, France. See: Commission Internationale d'Histoire Militaire, *ACTA No. 6*, Montpellier, 1983, pp. 15–20.

1. This is based on the German translation: Maurice Paléologue, *Am Zarenhof während des Weltkrieges*, 2 vols., München, 1925.

2. Brigadier-General James E. Edmonds, *Military Operations, France and Belgium, 1914*, vol. 1, London, 1933, Appendix 8; see also John French, *1914*, Boston, 1919, pp. 14–15 passim. One may be surprised to learn that on December 28, 1915, when Sir Douglas Haig was appointed to succeed Field Marshal French as commander in chief of the British Expeditionary Forces (BEF), almost the same definition was used by the British Secretary of State for War, namely: "I wish you distinctly to understand that your command is an independent one, and that you will in no case come under the orders of any Allied General further than the necessary cooperation with our Allies above referred to" (Field Marshal Sir Douglas Haig, *The Private Papers of Douglas Haig, 1914–1919*, London, 1952, p. 121). No less interesting is the fact that on May 26, 1917, when Major General John J. Pershing of the U.S. Army was appointed by his president to be the commander in chief of the American troops dispatched to Europe, Newton D. Baker, the U.S. Secretary of War, instructed him in writing: "5. In military operations against the Imperial German Government, you are directed to cooperate with the forces of the other countries employed against that enemy; *but in so doing the underlying idea must be kept in view that the forces of the United States are a separate and distinct component of the combined forces, the identity of which must be preserved*" (emphasis added; John J. Pershing, *My Experience in the World War*, vol. 1, New York, 1931, p. 38).

3. Edmonds, p. 241.

4. Ibid., p. 264; French, pp. 101–2.
5. Quoted in Sir Philip Magnus, *Kitchener*, New York, 1959, p. 302.
6. This opinion finds support in Lord Maurice Hankey, *The Supreme Command 1914–18*, vol. 1, London, 1961, p. 3.

2

PREWAR PLANNING BETWEEN ALLIES AND POTENTIAL ALLIES

In his essay "Military Coalitions and Coalition Warfare over the Past Century," the Canadian historian Paul Kennedy remarks that "it is important to understand that many of the difficulties encountered by states in a wartime coalition were themselves consequent upon the circumstances which existed and the decisions which were taken when particular alliances were formed before the conflict."[1] He draws attention to the fact that in the fast-changing European wars of the eighteenth century, coalitions were rather short-term expedients and almost exclusively formed for wartime purposes. In many instances they were even broken off in the course of the conflict, such as in 1762, during the Seven Years' War, when the British abandoned their Prussian coalition partner for their own raison d'état. Another example is the first three coalitions against revolutionary and Napoleonic France, which broke up because some of the partners found the enemy pressure unbearable. It is also a matter of record that the coalition formed during the Crimean War dissolved immediately at the end of the war. The armed conflicts that occurred after this latter war, namely the Austro-Prussian War, the Franco-Prussian War and the Russo-Turkish War, were what Kennedy calls "one-to-one conflicts."

One must therefore ask why this situation changed, and peacetime coalitions began to evolve. It is an established fact that after the signing of the Austro-German Alliance in 1879, Europe was divided into two coalitions whose respective partners pledged to render military support to each other under certain specified circumstances. These coalitions were formed by their members in order to escape from isolation when faced by a hostile and menacing alliance. Therefore, strange as it may seem at first glance, Italy, which was at loggerheads with France, joined the Austro-Germany Alliance even though there was tension between Italy and Austria, which in the end caused Italy to change camps during World War I. On the other hand, France, threatened by isolation after the Franco-Prussian War, and Russia, fearing the same after the dismissal of Bismarck by the German Emperor Wilhelm II, moved toward each other. Thus in the early 1890s, the Dual Alliance of France and Russia was created to face the Triple Alliance of Germany, Austria and Italy.

This explanation places the blame for the phenomenon of peacetime coalitions during the last century on the diplomats, owing to the Austro-German Pact of 1879, in whose wake the threatened parties formed their own alliances. But Kennedy offers an additional explanation for the rise of military coalitions:

The uneven pace of industrialization, strengthening some of the powers more than others, eroded the formerly fairly equal pentarchy of states in the Concert of Europe; in the future, Austria-Hungary alone could not hope to win its Balkan war, nor France alone its Rhineland war. The vast armies mobilized under the Prussian short-service system, and their swift transportation by rail, provoked fears in each country that it was now much more vulnerable to a sudden strike by potential foes. Even the Prussian general staff under Moltke grew nervous: Russian railways could threaten East Prussia just as German railways menaced northeast France.[2]

In addition, the rise of national consciousness transformed the old cabinet style of diplomacy. Though the traditional rulers remained in power, they had to take this new kind of patriotism into account and were also infected by it. As Kennedy observed: "This . . . provided a cement to the peacetime coalitions which simply had not existed a century earlier."[3]

However, this new kind of military alliance on the eve of World War I led to two-edged consequences, as will be analyzed. On one hand, every partner felt reassured by the fact that it would not have to fight against superior adversaries single-handedly. However, the partners began to develop an additional feeling: that they were no longer fully sovereign in their decisions and moves, and that they might eventually be forced to act essentially for the interests of their allies, perhaps even at an unsuitable time. Moreover, whereas every additional ally probably added additional strength to a given coalition, it often also added additional enemies. Any coalition almost always brings with it coercions likely to distort the strategic planning, as is amply demonstrated by the case investigated in this study.

Many historians refer to the Triple Entente, which is dealt with in this work, as if Russia, France and Great Britain were aligned formally with each other both in war and in peace. However, this was not the case. Nevertheless, even French Field Marshal Joseph Jacques Joffre, who was supposed to know the real facts, wrote in his memoirs that "at the beginning of the war in 1914, operations were carried out in accordance with plans which were drawn up by agreement between France, Russia and England."[4] In spite of this statement, he wrote in an earlier part of the same memoirs that none of the Powers that constituted the Entente group estimated the extent of the worldwide character of the conflict. Indeed, none had, in peacetime, taken any measures for preparing and assuring the direction of a wartime coalition.[5] In fact, although France and Russia had been bound by a military convention since August 1892, France and Great Britain were not, despite the staff talks that began in 1905. Moreover, if the military link between Britain and France was tenuous, any Anglo-Russian military convention was nonexistent. It is therefore beneficial to survey the real situation.

FRANCO-RUSSIAN MILITARY CONVENTION— THE DUAL ALLIANCE

As mentioned previously, the Alliance Treaty between Germany and Austria in 1879 and the Triple Alliance between Germany, Austria and Italy in 1882, which were both aimed against Russia, triggered off the Military Convention between Russia and France. In his memoirs, Joffre reveals that this secret document was signed at St. Petersburg on August 17, 1892, by General Obroutcheff, then chief of the Russian General Staff, and General de Boisdeffre, then chief of staff of the French army, who had been sent to Russia for that purpose. The czar and the French government approved this Convention in December 1893. It was agreed that this alliance was to be in effect as long as the Triple Alliance. In 1899 the application of this agreement was considerably extended, and the two governments decided together that the Convention would remain in operation for the same length of time as the diplomatic agreement drawn up for the protection of the interests of the two countries. The agreement states:

France and Russia being animated by a common desire to preserve peace, and having no other object than to make the necessary provisions in case of a defensive war provoked by an attack on the part of the forces of the Triple Alliance directed against one or the other of them, have agreed upon the following dispositions:

(i) If France is attacked by Germany, or by Italy supported by Germany, Russia will employ all her available forces to attack Germany. If Russia is attacked by Germany, or by Austria supported by Germany, France will employ all her available forces to oppose Germany.

(ii) In case the forces of the Triple Alliance, or one of the Powers comprising it, should mobilize, France and Russia, upon the announcement of this event and without it being necessary to come to a previous agreement, will immediately and simultaneously mobilize the totality of their forces and transport them as near as possible to their frontiers.[6]

It was agreed that the forces that would be employed against Germany would be 1,300,000 men on the part of France, and on the part of Russia from 700,000 to 800,000 men, and that these forces would be fully engaged as rapidly as possible in order to oblige Germany to fight in the East and in the West at the same time. Moreover, the General Staffs of the two armies would keep in constant touch. They would, therefore, even in time of peace, exchange information concerning the armies of the Triple Alliance. Thus, the best means for corresponding in time of war would be studied and provided for in advance.[7]

However, the French assumed, as Joffre reports in his memoirs, that the mobilization and concentration of the Russian army would be very slow, because of the paucity of railroads in the country, their limited efficiency and the limited amount of rolling stock. In conformity with paragraph IV of the Military Convention, General Dubail, then chief of staff of the French army, visited Russia in the summer of 1911, conferring with his Russian counterpart. He informed the Russians of the serious inconvenience that would result from the delays caused by their railway deficiency. General Suchumlinov, at that time the Russian Minister for War, provides in his book about the Russian mobilization in 1914 the protocols of this conference, which was held in Krassnoje Sselo on August 11 through 13, 1911.[8] In the preamble to this document it is expressly stated that the term "defensive war" used in the official text of the 1892 Convention does not in any way indicate that the war would be waged in a defensive way. On the contrary, both armies agreed that they would engage in the most energetic offensive. The Russians also agreed not to wait until their armies were completely concentrated before acting. The offensive was to begin the moment the first-line forces were in position, and it was calculated that the Russo-German frontier could be crossed on the sixteenth day after mobilization. Suchumlinov draws attention to the fact that France provided valuable financial assistance for the improvement of both the Russian railroad and Russian heavy industry. But this did not prohibit him from remarking cynically that this assistance was motivated by the purely egoistic French attitude toward Russia. Moreover, this assistance was provided under strict economic viewpoints without any regard for the tremendous political and military advantages for France.

In an angry manner, Suchumlinov wrote that France had no sympathy with Russia and the Russian people, but was only interested in the "Russian cannon-fodder."[9]

Since the two general staffs agreed in principle to meet every year, the following year, General Ivan Shilinski, the chief of the Russian General Staff, went to France. He was accompanied by Admiral Prince Lieven, chief of staff of the Russian navy. On July 16, Admiral Lieven and the chief of staff of the French navy signed a Naval Convention which was analogous to the military one. In the interim some improvements in the Russian railway network had been carried out, and General Shilinski agreed to begin the Russian offensive on the fifteenth day after mobilization.

In August 1913 the meeting of the Russian and French General Staffs was again held in St. Petersburg and Krassnoje Sselo. General Joffre explained to the czar and Grand Duke Nicholas the necessity of speeding up the Russian mobilization and starting an offensive as quickly as possible with that fraction of the Russian armies that had been immediately mobilized. In his memoirs, Joffre explained that the motive underlying his request was the probability that the concentration of the larger part of the German forces would be directed against France.[10] The grand duke assured the French that he fully understood the necessity of the Russian army taking the offensive rapidly and that this request would be satisfied, whatever risks might be involved. Indeed, when the war broke out in August 1914 the Russians honored their commitment. However, Suchumlinov records dryly that at that time he had not entered into elaborations of any operative measures or details.[11] One might wonder how the two Allies intended to maintain communications with each other. The reformulated paragraph 4 of the Convention states that

telegraphic messages between the Russian and the French General Staffs can be maintained with the aid of the English cable. . . . Just now an understanding with England has been achieved; the measures have been taken and the connection is liable to function. Telegrams pass via America, Australia and Sansibar or via South-Africa and Sansibar to reach Odessa.[12]

In spite of the hint of an "understanding" with England, in fact there was no prewar understanding of any kind between Britain and Russia, even though in August 1911 some British statesmen, including Winston Churchill,

foresaw the existence of an alliance between Great Britain, France and
Russia.[13] One has to bear in mind that the Anglo-Russian Entente of
August 31, 1907, in which the relations between Russia and Great Britain
over Persia, Afghanistan and Tibet were regulated, had no impact whatsoever on the problems dealt with in this investigation.

FRANCE AND GREAT BRITAIN

Great Britain, too, was forced to face similar dilemmas concerning
military alliances. In addition to the strengthening of its imperial defense
coalition, an idea that was not always regarded with greatest enthusiasm
by all the self-governing Dominions, it was looking for alliances with other
great powers in order to receive assistance in the event of hostilities. This,
however, also implied the pledge to render assistance to partners, whose
defeat by a mutual enemy might be disastrous to Britain's own interests.
This is the reason behind the Anglo-Japanese Alliance of 1902, which in
fact marked the departure from Britain's "splendid isolation."

As far as Anglo-French relations are concerned, the so-called Entente
Cordiale of 1904 between the two countries removed most of the political
obstacles, but did not include any provisions of a military character in
connection with a future armed conflict involving the partners.

As a matter of fact, first contacts in this direction started in 1905, in a
rather unconventional way. Lord Maurice Hankey, who was closely
acquainted with the events, reveals that in July 1905 Prime Minister Earl
Balfour decided to appoint a subcommittee of the Committee of Imperial
Defence to study combined naval and military operations. At this time
serious trouble arose between France and Germany concerning Morocco.
There were communications between the French and British staffs. In the
case of the Admiralty, these took the form of direct communication
between the First Sea Lord Fisher and the French naval attaché. In the case
of the army they were conducted through Repington, the military corre-
spondent of *The Times*. Field Marshal William Robertson claims that to
some extent there was also direct communication.

Indeed, Hankey mentions that in December 1905 a small group of naval
and military officers began to meet informally to study the proper utiliza-
tion of British forces in the event of becoming involved with France in a
war with Germany. Hankey also discloses that Fisher, who was in principle
opposed to committing the small British army to a Continental campaign,
withdrew the naval representatives, thus boycotting the subcommittee.
The General Staff, however, continued in the work of the subcommittee.
In January 1906, Sir Edward Grey yielded to the French government's

desire for military talks between the General Staffs of the two nations. However, the conversations were to be entirely noncommittal in character and were to involve no promise of support in war. They were not to restrict the liberty of either government to decide whether to provide armed assistance in the event of war. Grey admitted that the authority of the British cabinet was not sought. According to Robertson, these secret conversations were not made known to the cabinet until 1912. The affair was then rectified by means of an exchange of notes with the French government.

At every stage of conversations, the British took the utmost care to ensure that the scheme was not binding on the British government.[14] The British memorandum sent by the foreign secretary to M. Jules M. Cambon stipulated that

if either Government had grave reason to expect an unprovoked attack by a third Power, or something that threatened the general peace, it should immediately discuss with the other whether both Governments should act together to prevent aggression and to preserve peace, and, if so, what measures they would be prepared to take in common. If these measures involved action, the plans of the General Staffs would at once be taken into consideration, and the Governments would then decide what effect should be given to them.[15]

This meant in fact that the French authorities were forced to plan their campaign without knowing whether they would receive British assistance. On the other hand, Robertson says the British were not able to insist upon their right to examine the French plan in return for their cooperation. He correctly points to the fact that "when the crisis arose, there was no time to examine it, and consequently our military policy was for long wholly subordinate to the French policy, of which we knew little."[16]

As mentioned previously, Fisher opposed any military adventure on the Continent. Consequently the Admiralty came forward with a counterproposal relying mainly on economic pressure in the event of war with Germany. In 1908, the British subcommittee unanimously agreed that "in the event of an attack on France by Germany, the expediency of sending a military force abroad, or of relying on naval means only, is a matter of policy which can only be determined, when the occasion arises, by the Government of the day."[17] In fact, the policy of absolute British noncommitment was maintained. The French military attaché in London, Charles J. Huguet, who was appointed liaison officer with the British Expeditionary Forces (BEF) in France at the outbreak of the war, confirms this state of affairs: "It was understood that [the British Government] retained full liberty of action and that—if the likelihood of war between France and Germany were realised—the Government of the day would be the sole judge of the line of action to be taken."[18]

In August 1911, in the wake of the so-called Morocco crisis, Winston Churchill drafted a memorandum on "Military Aspects of the Continental Problem," in which he assumed that "an alliance exists between Great Britain, France, and Russia, and that these Powers are attacked by Germany and Austria." He sketched the way in which the British forces should be deployed and act.[19] In a letter sent to Sir Edward Grey after his memorandum was drafted, Churchill urged the foreign secretary to propose to France and Russia a triple alliance to safeguard (inter alia) the independence of Belgium, Holland and Denmark.[20]

From a memorandum prepared by General Joffre in October the same year, one learns that in fact nothing of a concrete manner happened. On this occasion the French general wrote that he wanted to know whether the relations established between the General Staffs stemmed from a treaty, from written or verbal agreements between the two governments, or, perhaps, from a tacit consent between them. He asked the question whether in all probability Great Britain would support France in a war with Germany.[21]

In August 1912, the British cabinet decided that naval talks should take place between the French and British Admiralties, similar to those that had been held since 1905 between the General Staffs. In these conversations the British made it absolutely clear that if there was a threat of war, the two governments should consult together and coordinate beforehand what common action, if any, they should take.

Churchill stated dryly that the French were obliged to accept the British position that the naval conversations did not involve any obligation of common action. He added: "This was the best we could do for ourselves and for them."[22] However, when Churchill surveyed the naval situation on the eve of the outbreak of the war in July 1914, he observed that the French fleet was on the whole concentrated in the Mediterranean on the assumption that the British fleet would safeguard the northern coasts of France. Though the French had, according to Churchill, made their decision on their own, he nevertheless asked the rhetorical question: "Whatever disclaimers we had made about not being committed, could we, when it came to the point, honourably stand by and see the naked French coasts ravaged and bombarded by German Dreadnoughts under the eyes and within gunshot of our Main Fleet?"[23]

However, at the very moment when the war broke out on August 1,

1914, Gen. Henry Wilson, the main architect of the Franco-British coali-
tion, wrote in his diary that "at 11.30 a.m. Asquith [the British Prime
Minister] wrote to CIGS [Chief of the Imperial General Staff] saying
training was not to be suspended and 'putting on record' the fact that the
Government had never promised the French an Expeditionary Force."[24]
On the following day, Wilson's diary reveals that two quite indecisive
cabinet meetings were held. He believed that a note had been sent to the
French to say that, although Britain was not going to take part in the war,
it would not allow the Germans to descend on the French coast. With a
sigh of despair, he added, "Was ever anything heard like this? What is the
difference between the French coast and the French frontier?"[25] Churchill
recalled Sir Grey's efforts to prevent the war: "He had to try to make the
Germans realize that we were to be reckoned with, *without making the
French and Russians feel they had us in their pockets.*"[26]

A by-product of the wavering British attitude from the French point of
view was connected with the neutrality of Belgium. Joffre rightly remarked that it was the fear of an invasion of Belgium by the Germans that
had led to the military agreements with Great Britain. Therefore, the
French had to be sure that a plan based upon a march of French forces
through Belgium would not result in the withdrawal of British support
from the French. He revealed that in 1906, when the first conversations
took place between the British and French military, the French formally
promised to respect the neutrality of Belgium and that at that time they
had been warned by the British not to let themselves be tempted to enter
Belgium upon a threat from Germany, since it might be in the interest of
that country to push the French toward such a step.[27] Indeed, on July 30,
the French cabinet issued an order that no French troops were under any
circumstances to move within 10 kilometers of the frontier. The troops
were told that this measure was taken to ensure British cooperation.
Edward L. Spears, who was appointed British liaison officer with the
French, maintained that Great Britain was watching events closely since
her leaders were absolutely opposed to war, and she would undoubtedly
have turned from the aggressor.[28] Little wonder that the French were, until
the last moment, rather suspicious of the kind of support the British would
render—the more so, since at staff discussions in early 1912, Joffre, whose
armies were to become assisted by the British troops sent to the Continent,
stated that it was indispensable that before the fourth day of mobilization,
he should be in possession of information concerning the intentions of the
British. The reason was that on this date, the strategic transports of his

troops would start and it would therefore still be possible to alter the center of gravity of the French concentration.[29]

ANGLO-RUSSIAN RELATIONS

It has already been mentioned that there were in fact no military contacts between Great Britain and Russia. However, in his memoirs, Sir Grey hinted that Russia knew of the conversations between the British and French General Staffs. He added that "in order to make Russia feel that she was not kept at arm's length it was desirable that there should be something of the same kind with Russia."[30] But he thought that there was no reason for the General Staffs of the British and Russian armies to communicate, since the geographical separation made it impossible for the two armies to fight side by side in a war against Germany, as the British and French armies could.[31]

As far as Russia was concerned, General Danilov stressed in his memoirs that neither the British relations with France nor those with Russia had reached any binding obligations.[32] He admitted that it was no secret to the Russians that since 1912, France and Great Britain had become closer and their General Staffs had exchanged views in writing in order to explore "the possibility" of Britain rendering assistance to France in case of a German attack. He recalled that in 1913, he observed French maneuvers with British General Wilson, and they were both received as representing friendly powers. This gave him an indication that in the event of a conflict, Russia could count on a favorable British attitude.[33]

In 1913, as the British ambassador to the Court of St. Petersburg reported, Russian Foreign Minister Sazonoff stressed the fact that Germany and Austria were allies, while Great Britain and Russia were only friends. Moreover, if Germany supported Austria, France would make common cause with Russia. However, Sazonoff said, no one knew what Great Britain would do. British Ambassador George William Buchanan explained to his readers that "what really barred the way to an Anglo-Russian alliance was the fact that it would not have been sanctioned by public opinion in England."[34] In an audience with the Russian emperor in April 1914, the emperor said he would like to see a closer bond between England and Russia. When the British ambassador responded that this was impractical at that time, the czar suggested concluding some arrangement similar to the one between France and England. The ambassador replied that for material reasons it would be impossible to send troops to cooperate with the Russian army. To this the czar replied: "I have men enough and to spare, and such an expeditionary force would serve no useful purpose." But he suggested arranging for the cooperation of the British and Russian fleets.[35]

As a matter of fact, Grey saw little, if any, strategic value in this suggestion. He maintained that in a war against Germany, the Russian fleet would not leave the Baltic, and the British fleet would not enter it. As a result, Grey concluded that "to refuse would offend Russia by giving the impression that she was not treated on equal terms with France." Therefore the British government agreed to let the British and Russian naval authorities communicate, after the French had asked for such communications.[36] During April 22 through 24, 1914, King George and Grey visited Paris. At the request of the Russians, the French urged the conclusion of an Anglo-Russian Naval Convention. Discussions were held during the remaining months of the prewar period. However, in his memoirs, Grey took pains to stress the point that these naval arrangements "never had the character of conventions or of anything that had a binding effect on any of the Governments."[37] He further explained that "neither the Franco-British military nor the Anglo-Russian naval conventions compromised the freedom of this country [Great Britain], *but the latter were less intimate and important than the former.*"[38]

POTENTIAL ALLIES

One must bear in mind that certain nations, among them Great Britain, already had treaty obligations, and in particular, the Treaty of 1839, which guaranteed the independence of Belgium. In Churchill's aforementioned letter to Grey on August 30, 1911, he wrote:

Tell Belgium that, if her neutrality is violated, we are prepared to come to her aid and to make an alliance with France and Russia to guarantee her independence. Tell her that we will take whatever military steps will be most effective for that purpose. But the Belgian Army must take the field in concert with the British and French Armies. . . . Offer the same guarantee to Holland and to Denmark contingent upon their making their utmost exertions.[39]

Although Churchill detailed the type of operations he had in mind, in fact no military arrangements whatsoever were undertaken in order to realize these intentions, with the Belgians, the Dutch or Danes. Little wonder, then, that Field Marshal French wrote in his memoirs:

Belgium, however, remained a "dark horse" up to the last, and it is most unfortunate that she could never be persuaded to decide upon her attitude in the

event of a general war. All we ever had in our mind was *defence* against attack
by Germany. We had guaranteed the neutrality of Belgium. . . . What we desired
above all things was that Belgium should realize the danger which subsequently
laid her waste. We were anxious that she should assist and co-operate in her own
defence. The idea of attacking Germany through Belgium or in any other direction
never entered our heads.[40]

When Germany invaded Belgium as expected, the King of the Belgians
invoked the Treaty of 1839, and asked France and Great Britain to help in
conducting "a concerted and common action to repel the invader."[41] But,
as already mentioned, no joint plans for such action existed.

Other potential partners in an alliance with the Entente against the
Central Powers—before the outbreak of the war—included Serbia, Romania,
Bulgaria, Greece, Japan and even Turkey. However, no concrete steps
were taken to have such intentions materialize.

As far as Serbia was concerned, General Danilov drew attention to the
fact that in spite of the blood ties between Russia and Serbia, these two
states had not reached any military agreement. Although the assumption
was that in its hour of need, Russia would hurry to Serbia's rescue, because
of Russia's international position, it was more advantageous not to be
bound by a written agreement. Danilov drew attention to the fact that
although to a certain degree there was a roughly coordinated plan between
the General Staffs of France and Russia for the initial phase of a war, not
even the smallest step in this direction was made between Russia and
Serbia in order to assure a certain unity of operation should Serbia be
attacked.[42]

The case of Japan's participation in the war on the side of the Entente
was even more complicated. There was a serious divergence of interests
of Great Britain (and the British Dominions) and Japan in the Far East. On
the other hand, Great Britain needed Japanese assistance in a worldwide
conflict, although Japanese Minister for Foreign Affairs Baron Kato
Takaaki was careful to let the British know that "Japan has no interest in
a European conflict."[43] The British Admiralty, however, already feeling
the pressure of Britain's worldwide commitment, welcomed the Japanese
readiness to cooperate in the Far East. Moreover, Great Britain not only
appreciated Japanese naval assistance in the Pacific and Indian Oceans,
but also desired its extension to the Mediterranean.[44]

Toward the end of the first year of the war, when it became obvious that
Italy was to join the Entente, actual coordination with this new partner
only began with the Secret Treaty of London on April 26, 1915. A
well-orchestrated military coalition was then still in its infancy.

NOTES

1. Paul Kennedy, "Military Coalitions and Coalition Warfare over the Past Century," in Keith Neilson and Roy A. Prete, eds., *Coalition Warfare: An Uneasy Accord*, Waterloo, Canada, 1983, p. 3.

2. Ibid., p. 5.

3. Ibid.

4. Joseph Jacques Césaire Joffre, *The Personal Memoirs of Joffre, Field Marshal of the French Army*, New York, 1932, p. 379.

5. Ibid., p. 365.

6. Ibid., p. 56.

7. Ibid.

8. Vladimir Aleksandrovic Suchumlinov, *Die rußische Mobilmachung im Lichte amtlicher Urkunden und den Enthüllungen des Prozesses*, Bern, 1917, pp. 255ff.

9. Ibid., pp. 239ff.

10. Joffre, pp. 55ff.

11. Suchumlinov, p. 243. See also: Jurij Nikiforovich Danilov, *Rußland im Weltkriege 1914–1915*, Jena, Germany, 1925, p. 109.

12. Ibid., p. 267.

13. Winston S. Churchill, *The World Crisis 1911–1918*, London, 1964, p. 49.

14. Lord Maurice Hankey, *The Supreme Command 1914–18*, vol. 1, London, 1961, pp. 62–63; William Robertson, *Soldiers and Statesmen 1914–1918*, vol. 1, London, 1926, p. 48.

15. Cited in Edward Grey, *Twenty-five Years, 1892–1916*, New York, 1937, p. 97.

16. Robertson, p. 49.

17. Hankey, vol. 1, p. 70.

18. Charles Julien Huguet, *Britain and the War: A French Indictment*, London, 1928, p. 5.

19. Churchill, pp. 49–51.

20. Ibid., pp. 52–53; see also Grey, pp. 92–93.

21. Joffre, p. 40.

22. Churchill, p. 82.

23. Ibid., p. 121.

24. Sir Charles Edward Callwell, *Field-Marshal Sir Henry Wilson: His Life and Diaries*, vol. 1, New York, 1927, p. 154.

25. Ibid., vol. 1, p. 155.

26. Churchill, p. 120. (Emphasis added.)

27. Joffre, pp. 51–53 passim.

28. Edward L. Spears, *Liaison 1914: A Narrative of the Great Retreat*, London, 1930, p. 11.

29. Joffre, p. 47.

30. Grey, p. 273.

31. Ibid.

32. Danilov, p. 7.

33. Ibid., p. 85.

34. George William Buchanan, *My Mission to Russia and Other Diplomatic Memories*, vol. 1, London, 1923, pp. 138–39.

35. Ibid., p. 183.

36. Grey, pp. 274, 276–77.

37. Ibid., pp. 276–77.

38. Ibid., p. 280. (Emphasis added.)

39. Churchill, pp. 52–53.

40. John French, *1914*, Boston, 1919, pp. 8–9.

41. Albert I, *The War Diaries of Albert I, King of the Belgians*, London, 1954, p. xv.

42. Danilov, pp. 90, 229.

43. Madelaine Chi-Sung-Chun, *The Chinese Question during the First World War*, Ann Arbor, Mich., 1977, p. 18.

44. Ibid., pp. 21, 26.

3

PARTICULARISTIC INTERESTS
IN THE COALITION

In December 1922, American General T. H. Bliss, who was a close observer of the Entente's coordination efforts, analyzed them in a brilliant essay published in *Foreign Affairs*.[1] Drawing attention to the Allies' enormous sacrifices in money, material and men, he pointed out that their adversaries, in spite of their acknowledged mistakes, were far more unified in their purpose and efforts. As a result, they almost realized their war aims:

In a nutshell, the cause of this failure—for failure it was—was the manifest absence of *unity of purpose on the part of the Entente Powers*. They were allied little more than in the sense that each found itself fighting, at the same time with the others, its own war against one enemy, and too largely *for separate ends*.[2]

Many years later, and after another great coalition war, another American maintained that

cooperation among allies is difficult to achieve and sustain because the nations who compose given coalitions rarely fight for exactly the same purposes. Although the members of a coalition may be joined by antagonism toward a common enemy, they often disagree on the proper strategy to defeat that enemy. Although interallied controversies develop from many sources of irritation, the most important usually is divergence in political aims.[3]

David Trask's opinion, quoted above, was already supported by the important French statesman Raymond Poincaré, who wrote in his memoirs that "the diplomatic coalition seems but little easier to manage than the military."[4] Therefore, it seems to be worthwhile to investigate the political and military aims of the various partners in the Entente coalition.

FRANCE

From the outbreak of the war, it was obvious that France bore the main brunt of the German onslaught and was compelled to bear heavy sacrifices in human life and in territory. Little wonder, therefore, that very early in the war the conservation of France's manpower became one of the main features of French war policy. This was so pronounced that France's allies were always suspicious of its intention to shift the burden onto their shoulders. For instance, on March 29, 1916, Field Marshal Haig wrote in his diary that "the French spoke freely and said: 'They had lost severely in men and it was now time for the British to play their part,' and a good deal more." Haig also revealed that Lord Kitchener held the opinion that this "shows the real French intentions" and had warned him "to beware of the French, and to husband the strength of the British army in France."[5]

Moreover, the British liaison officer with the French army, Brig. Gen. Edward L. Spears, disclosed in his memoirs the strange fact that in General Joffre's *Instruction Générale No. 4*, to the French Third, Fourth and Fifth Armies and to the BEF, issued on September 1, 1914, certain passages were omitted in the copy sent to the British. In the copy forwarded to Field Marshal French, all mention of an immediate French offensive was omitted, as was the limit of retreat. (One must bear in mind that this order was prior to the Battle of the Marne.) Most significantly, there was no indication that the copy the British received was not the complete version.[6]

French politicians were aware of the fact that in spite of controversies between the Allied generals, amicable relations were necessary in order to insure their aim of conserving French forces. In March 1915, Poincaré reminded General Joffre that "if we do not come to amicable terms with the English they may send their new armies elsewhere than to France."[7]

It is important to remember that in 1814, 1815 and 1871, enemy forces paraded in the French capital after the defeat of France. The recollection of this fact influenced the minds of the French politicians and generals. Preventing the recurrence of such a trauma became an important war aim. Thus, in September 1914 and again in the spring of 1918, the deployment of French troops for the defense of Paris was carried out solely for this reason, and without regard for the overall operative Allied aspects. It is not surprising that on September 2, 1914, Field Marshal French mentioned that "the safety of the Capital was the paramount thought in the minds of the French generals."[8] Haig got the same impression in the spring of 1918, in the wake of initial German successes during their Spring Offensive.

It is not surprising that there were extreme controversies between the various Allies concerning the war aims in different parts of the world. For instance, it can be learned from Poincaré's memoirs that in 1915, when Lord Kitchener proposed to land a British force at Alexandretta, the French ministers were quite unwilling, "for military reasons."[9] It is quite obvious that the real reason was the French insistence that Alexandretta, which bordered Syria, was considered part of the French sphere of influence in the Near East, and could by no means be "abandoned" to the British.

A similar attitude was revealed by the French when they learned from their ambassador in St. Petersburg (Petrograd, after 1914) about Russian intentions to make Constantinople and southern Thrace part of the Russian Empire. In a personal letter to the French ambassador, Poincaré wrote quite frankly that the assignment of Constantinople, Thrace, the Narrows and the coast of the Sea of Marmora to Russia would mean the division of the Ottoman Empire. There was no reason for France to want this. Should it nevertheless happen, there was no reason why it should be at the expense of France. Therefore an arrangement should be found to enable France to reassure her Mussulman subjects in Algiers and Tunis as to the ultimate independence of the Commander of the Faithful. Moreover, the preservation of France's holdings in the Near East and the safeguarding of her economic interests in Asia Minor—the recognition of her rights in Syria, Alexandretta and the *vilayet* of Adana—must be secured. Poincaré also reasoned that the possession of Constantinople would not only give Russia privileges as to the line of succession in the Ottoman Empire but would also bring her within the concert of Western nations and might enable her to become a great naval power. Thus the equilibrium of Europe would be upset. France could only accept such an increase of Russian strength if she were to derive equivalent advantages from the war. France could only back up Russia's wishes in proportion to what she would gather herself.[10]

As was to be expected, the very moment the end of the war neared, the particularistic interests of all the victorious partners emerged without any "making up." As Special Commissioner to the United States André Tardieu wrote in his memoirs,

As soon as the armistice was signed, a dual tendency became manifest: the weakening of centripedal and the strengthening of centrifugal forces. The end of the war, the disruption of war organizations, the awakening of economic interests, the conflict of political ideals, the restoration of the empire of old habits, were the underlying causes of the phenomena. The mistakes of men did the rest.[11]

GREAT BRITAIN

One must recognize that, contrary to most other nations at the time, England maintained only a small professional army intended mainly for police purposes throughout its empire. For a prolonged period, it continued to base its military power on volunteers. It was therefore natural that it considered the conservation and preservation of this precious military force imperative. This is evident from the previously quoted instructions issued to the commander in chief of the BEF.[12] The Secretary of State for War, Field Marshal Lord Kitchener, stressed explicitly: "It must be recognized from the outset that the numerical strength of the British force and its contingent reinforcement is strictly limited, and with this consideration kept steadily in view it will be obvious that the greatest care must be exercised towards a minimum of losses and wastage." He continued:

Therefore, while every effort must be made to coincide most sympathetically with the plans and wishes of our ally, the gravest consideration will devolve upon you as to participation in forward movements where large bodies of French troops are not engaged and where your force may be unduly exposed to attack.[13]

Little wonder that when war broke out, there were British statesmen who were not eager to involve England. Even when the die was cast and Great Britain declared war on Germany, a controversy erupted as to whether to dispatch all the divisions earmarked for France or perhaps to withhold some for the defense of the British Isles. Strong objections were raised in the government to the dispatch of the BEF to France, although this had been agreed upon between the General Staffs. British politician Lord Beaverbrook revealed in his memoirs that some ministers were in favor of keeping the entire British army at home.[14] From a July 24, 1914, entry in the memoirs of the British ambassador in Russia, one learns that even though the outbreak of the war was imminent, in a conversation with Russian Foreign Minister Sazonoff, the British diplomat was not yet sure whether his country would unconditionally "support France and Russia by force of arms *on behalf of a country like Serbia, where no direct British interests were involved.*"[15]

It has been mentioned previously that the scales were tipped in favor of British participation in the war when the Germans invaded Belgium. However, the fear of leaving the British Isles without military forces led to the strange request to the Russians, forwarded by the British ambassador, to dispatch a Russian army corps to London. The purpose of this Russian force was to defend the British capital. The transport of this corps would be carried out by English ships via Archangelsk. Suchumlinov

called this an example of "characteristic British super-selfishness."[16] The
scarcity of British armed forces at the beginning of the war and the desire
to enlarge them brought Field Marshal French to suggest an amalgamation
of the Belgian army with the BEF in December 1914, although he was
aware of the fact that the King of the Belgians was unable to gain the
consent of his government and that the French would not agree to this
plan.[17] In this context, it is interesting to learn from Spears, the British
liaison officer with the French, that in 1917, the British war cabinet was
pleased with the plan of General Nivelle, the French commander in chief,
in sharp contrast to the British General Staff and the British commanders
in France, because "the French were to have the chief role and *bear the
main burden of the attack.*"[18]

The British attitude concerning its role in the coalition was clearly
defined by Lloyd George, namely, that Britain had always visualized
playing her traditional role in Continental wars: her navy would keep the
seas open for her allies, and her wealth would help them to finance their
foreign purchases, but her army would play a subordinate part in the
struggle.[19] This same approach is reflected in a Memorandum on the
General Strategic and Military Situation prepared in April 1917 by South
African General Jan C. Smuts in his capacity as adviser to the Imperial
War Cabinet. The relevant passages read:

We entered the War in a very small way with a small military force and not as a
principal combatant but rather as an auxiliary to France. This fact was reflected
in our general military policy which was of necessity one of great modesty and
almost complete subordination to that of France. Our Army took its position side
by side with the French Army in defence of French soil. . . . During the last two
years the whole situation has been transformed and we are now the principal
opponent of the Central Empires and the financial, naval, and, to a large extent,
the military mainstay of the Entente. This anomalous situation is now reflected
in three curious respects.

1. While our Army is defending the soil of France as if it were part of the French
Forces, the French have taken the military and diplomatic lead in the Balkans and
Greece and are either making mistakes which are seriously embarrassing the
success of the War in those parts, or, if success is achieved, are after the War
going to enjoy all the prestige in the Balkans which should legitimately have gone
to the most powerful and disinterested member of the Entente.[20]

Some months earlier, in January 1917, on the occasion of the Allied
Conference in Rome, General Wilson wrote in his diary:

We are now the most important of the Allies, in money, in fleets, in shipping, in
coal and (almost) in armies, and yet we allow our Allies to do things of which we

entirely disapprove, and, although it is quite true that we cannot dictate, still we can get our own way to a great extent by bargaining.[21]

Returning to the situation in the theater of operations in France, it will be seen to be analogous to the French concern for the safety of Paris. The British forces in France were anxious to assure the protection of the Channel ports. German forces reaching them would not only prevent the logistic support for the BEF and block its route of escape from the Continent, but would also create a direct threat to the British Isles. It is therefore not surprising that during the so-called Great Retreat on the eve of the Battle of the Marne in 1914, while the French generals were anxious to protect Paris, the commander in chief of the BEF was mesmerized by the Channel ports.[22]

After the Battle of the Marne, when the military situation in northern France stabilized, Sir John French was still haunted by the possible German menace to these ports. He revealed in his memoirs that "from this time I sent constant and urgent warnings to London . . . to look out for the safety of the same ports."[23] Moreover, he remembered that at about this time he began to conceive the idea of disengaging from the Aisne and moving to a position in the north, for the main purpose of defending the Channel ports. In addition, he admitted that this would also have provided him with a better position for combined action and cooperation with the Royal Navy.

Quite frankly, he confessed that his fear for the Channel ports began to lay a strong hold upon his mind, and even affected his dispositions throughout the rest of the time during which he took part in the Battle of the Aisne. Indeed, he admitted, he was strongly convinced that his proper sphere of action was on the Belgian frontier in the north.[24] As a matter of fact, these were the reasons behind the Battle of Ypres in 1914 (and behind all the following Battles of Ypres).[25] By the end of September 1914, during a visit by Winston Churchill, then First Lord of the Admiralty, to Sir John's headquarters in France, they discussed the advisability of joint action by the army and navy. It was at this juncture that they sketched the plans for an offensive with one flank toward the sea.[26]

Accordingly, on September 29, 1914, Sir John sent a letter to General Joffre demanding to have his forces relieved from the Aisne front and transported to the left wing of the French armies.[27] Joffre was less than delighted with this development, which prompted him to record in his memoirs:

I am obliged to say that the precipitation with which the British army got itself relieved from the Aisne front caused, as I had predicted when the question arose, the almost complete interruption during ten days of the transport of the French troops towards the northern theatre of operations. The definite loss of the rich region centering in Lille was due, in my opinion, to this operation, my consent which was accorded only with the greatest regret.[28]

What a sharp criticism this was of the handicaps of particularistic currents in a wartime coalition.

In the spring of 1918, when German General Erich Ludendorff's Spring Offensive almost broke through the Allied front in France, the phenomenon of summer and fall 1914 was repeated: the French forces retreated in order to cover Paris, and Field Marshal Haig was worried about his communications with the Channel coast. In a conversation between Haig and General Pétain on March 24, 1918, after the initial German onslaught, Haig understood that the latter had attended a cabinet meeting in Paris and this his orders from his government were to "cover Paris at all costs." In fact, this meant the separation of the French from the British right flank, which would allow the enemy to penetrate between the two armies. Therefore, it was obvious that maintaining contact with the British army was no longer the basic principle of French strategy.[29]

In June of the same year, after additional German blows and successes, and after the appointment of General Foch as generalissimo, the same controversy remained. At the end of a meeting held in Paris in the prime minister's office, Foch reported that General Wilson reverted to the question that had already been raised at the time of the Battle of Flanders: if the development of the German offensive should threaten both Paris and the British sea bases, what would the line of conduct be? From Foch's response, it seems that his intention to ensure the defense of Paris and the protection of the ports at the same time was not too convincing to the British. The instructions of British Secretary of State for War Milner to Haig, dated June 22, 1918, were to carry out loyally any instructions issued by the C in C, Allied forces. But at the same time, if any order given by him appeared to imperil the British army, Haig should appeal to the British government before executing such order.[30]

Another bone of contention between the British and French emerged when both nations competed in attracting the arriving American forces to provide, either temporarily or permanently, replacements for their depleted formations. At a certain juncture, agreements were reached between U.S. Secretary for War Baker and Lord Reading, the British representative in the United States, and in England, between General Pershing, the American commander in chief in Europe, and British Secretary of State for War Milner. The French suspected a deal to their disadvantage. Fowler reports that Foch and Georges E. B. Clemenceau violently condemned the Pershing-Milner agreement because it appeared to loan American soldiers exclusively to Britain. However, "after two days of often uninhibited debating, the French had to submit to an Anglo-American settlement." As Fowler cynically recalled, "They [the French], after all, had only the supreme commander, whereas the Americans had the manpower, and the British the ships [to bring the troops over]."[31]

In an earlier section of this chapter, the conflicting French and British views concerning the Russian claims for the incorporation of certain parts of the Ottoman Empire into the Russian Empire were mentioned. The extent of the British ambivalence to these claims can be learned from a memorandum of the British Embassy in St. Petersburg dated February 27 (March 12), 1915.[32]

As was to be expected, the future peace settlement increased the tension between the Allies. The memoirs of Huguet, the French liaison officer with the BEF, are informative in this matter. Huguet was in close touch with the British during the duration of the war and understood their aims toward a peace settlement. He stated:

Already during the war strange self-interest had shown itself several times and asserted itself with still greater force once victory was assured. . . . The will to defeat Germany was definitely and strongly proclaimed, but this did not preclude the "powers that be" in London from seeking more immediate and more profitable ends.[33]

He also gave an explanation for the British reluctance to participate in the Salonika Expedition: "Since for a long time the Salonika Expedition had appeared to offer to England no immediate or direct advantages—she only agreed to co-operate to a limited extent, with small numbers of men and still smaller objectives." Moreover,

one of England's aims in taking part in the war had been to weaken both Germany's Navy and mercantile marine. From the moment of the Armistice she wished to realise the first and demanded the immediate surrender of the Fleet. Marshall Foch was opposed to this, saying that such a move would be both useless and dangerous. . . . But he had to give way to the demands of our Allies, and the surrender of the enemy Fleet was made one of the conditions of the Armistice.[34]

These facts led the Frenchman to state that "from then on the self-interest of England showed itself without reserve." He continued that the only question, as far as England was concerned, was to make a profit as quickly as possible out of the fruits of victory, by giving new life to her trade and her industries, which their privileged position appeared to assure for them hereafter.[35] This was a harsh verdict, indeed, from the pen of a close observer of the events. On the other hand, from Haig's papers of October 1918, it is clear that the British field marshal and commander in chief of the BEF was struck by the insistence of the French generals that French troops should seize the left bank of the Rhine, which meant not only the regaining of Alsace-Lorraine, but also French occupation of the Palatinate. Haig wrote that Pétain spoke of taking a huge indemnity from Germany, so that she would not be able to pay it. In the meantime, French troops would hold the left bank of the Rhine as a pledge.[36]

In Chapter 1, the fact that the British Empire was by itself a coalition in the framework of the international coalition was discussed.[37] The British government was therefore very often forced to make compromises with the demands of its Dominions. These demands were not always in line with British policy and intentions. This was particularly apparent in connection with the attitude of Australia and New Zealand toward Japanese participation in the war. Japan's aspirations to annex the German colonies in the South Pacific were resented and opposed by the British Dominions. Grey admitted that

in the early days the Japanese Alliance was a matter of some embarrassment. . . . Japan was ready to take her part in the war as our Ally; the Far East and the whole of the Pacific Ocean lay open to her and were her natural sphere of operations. But the prospect of unlimited Japanese action was repugnant to Australia and New Zealand. . . . [T]hey would have viewed the substitution of Japan for Germany with positive alarm. . . . It was unthinkable that we should not have the most scrupulous care for the interest and the feelings of British Dominions that were taking their part in the war, ready to face danger and to make sacrifices with so much patriotism.[38]

The British dilemma was, therefore, how to explain to Japan that her help would be welcome, but, on the other hand, that her action must be limited and her acquisition of German territory must not extend beyond certain bounds. Grey lamented that it was hard to explain to an Ally that its help would be welcome but that you hoped it would not be made inconvenient. This was, however, not only politic but essential for Great Britain and for the Allies.[39] Lord Hankey quoted the criticism aired by then Australian Prime Minister William M. Hughes in connection with the peace treaties. Hughes wanted to know what Australia was to get for the sacrifices she had made. Hinting at U.S. President Wilson's proposal of the establishment of a League of Nations, he continued, "When we had secured what we wanted, the freedom of the seas as we knew it and meant to have it, and necessary guaranties for the security and development of the Empire and reparation and indemnities, then we would have no objection to handing over other matters to a League of Nations."

Referring to President Wilson's rejection of the annexation of the German colonies, Hughes remarked sarcastically that President Wilson was talking of a problem he did not really understand. Since New Guinea was only eighty miles from Australia, the people of Australia were united on the retention of these islands.[40] On the same occasion, the Canadians proclaimed as future policy that "as an Empire we should keep clear, as far as possible, of European complications and alliances."[41]

RUSSIA

One must bear in mind that Russia did not wage its war on a joint front with its Allies. However, the latter, assuming that the main enemy onslaught of the Central Powers would be directed against France at the beginning of the war, expected Russia to tie up a considerable number of hostile forces because of the abundance of manpower at its disposal. Although the Russians fulfilled these expectations, very soon their Western allies discovered a poverty in all sorts of war material prevailing in the Russian army, especially the lack of rifles and ammunition of all types. The outstanding feature was that the Russian authorities, both civilian and military, withheld from their Allies necessary information as to the real condition of the Russian armed forces. In his memoirs, Joffre mentions that "the Allies were very poorly aided by the Russian representatives in France, who were constantly endeavouring to conceal the truth."[42] He provided an example, in which the Russian representatives at an Allied conference presented intentionally false numbers of the Russian effectives and made it clear that a lack of confidence reigned between the Russian and French General Staffs. Moreover, he complained that at the *Stavka* (the Russian General Staff) the French liaison officers were politely ignored and that they found it most difficult to learn about the plans of the Russian High Command.[43] The British ambassador to the Court of St. Petersburg reported similar instances.[44]

From a random utterance in General Danilov's memoirs, one may conclude that because of the differences in the social system between the autocratic czarist regime and Western democracies, the Russian ruling class was not interested in providing the Westerners any insight into their domestic affairs. Danilov explained the reasons for Russia joining the Entente and pointed out the advantages it gained from its previous close connections with Germany: "The loyal clinging to the German alliance provided Russia with a long period of peace . . . and thus gave her the opportunity to keep to her traditional way of life, which kept the people outside any active participation in the national life of the country."[45] A by-product of these peculiar relations between Allies was that the Russian government ordered munitions in the United States, not only independently from its Allies, but actually in direct competition with the British.[46]

For various reasons, Russia had reservations about increasing the Allies' scope. Danilov criticized the efforts of the Entente governments to draw additional states into the coalition, particularly the small states. He reasoned that preference should have been given to a neutral benevolent attitude of the small states toward the Entente Powers. Any addition of coalition partners would aggravate not only the food situation, but also material and technical resources. The incorporation of these small states was not advantageous, and in addition, it would complicate the already difficult joint conduct of operations.[47] In this connection, Lord Balfour wrote to Lloyd George on March 5, 1915, that the Russian Foreign Office "are not only indifferent to the augmentation of the Allied Forces by the adhesion of fresh states to the Entente: they appear positively to dislike it."[48]

Becoming convinced that it was in the Allies' best interest to add Romania to the Entente camp and that Russian-Romanian military cooperation was therefore essential, neither country could overcome its mutual suspicion. Russia would not agree to the integration of the Russian population of Bukovina into the Romanian orbit, nor to the extension of the Romanian frontier into the Banat, almost to the outskirts of Belgrade.[49] On the other hand, when the Russians proposed to take upon themselves the defense of Bucharest, the Romanian capital, this offer was turned down by the Romanians,[50] probably because they feared that the Russians might not evacuate the city after the war. Moreover, the Romanian government did not accept the Russian offer to occupy the Banat, fearing that a temporary occupation might become a permanent one.[51] Joffre hit the nail on the head when he wrote in his memoirs that the Russian plan inspired Romania with an invincible suspicion and that on the other hand the Romanian plan was distasteful to Russia, which looked upon her neighbor as an insignificant vassal power.[52]

At first glance, it may be surprising that Russia was opposed to any participation of Greek forces in the Dardanelles campaign, which was launched in order to open a new supply route to Russia. On March 3, 1915, Winston Churchill reported that the Russian foreign minister had informed the British ambassador that the Russian government could not consent to a Greek participation in operations in the Dardanelles. Sazonoff also added that "the Emperor had in an audience with him yesterday declared he could not in any circumstances consent to Greek co-operation in the Dardanelles."[53] Three days later, Prime Minister Earl Herbert Henry Asquith mentioned in his memoirs: "Russia, despite all our representations and remonstrances, declines absolutely to allow the Greeks to have any part in the Dardanelles business or the subsequent advance on Constantinople." He also explained why the Russians were so obstinate: "The other question is the future of Constantinople and the Straits. It has become quite clear that Russia means to incorporate them in her own Empire. That is the secret of her intense and obstinate hostility to the idea of allowing the Greeks to take any share in the present operations."[54]

No less surprising is the fact that Russia had severe reservations concerning Italy's participation in the war as a partner in the Entente camp. On March 1, 1915, Asquith reported that

there are significant indications that before long Italy may come in on the side of the Allies. That seems natural enough, but what is strange is that Russia strongly objects. She thinks that as Italy kept out from the stress of the War she will demand an exorbitant territorial prize, and that the three Allies should continue to keep the thing entirely in their own hands.[55]

Danilov tried to explain this strange Russian position. He reasoned that since the French and British were not ready to give in to Italian demands in their spheres of interest, the only way to satisfy the Italians was at the expense of Serbia and the Slavdom, whose natural protector was Russia. Thus, during the entire period of negotiations, Russia was in a rather awkward position, the more so since these negotiations were conducted in London in the absence of high-ranking Russian officials. In the long run, Russia was to face a final arrangement without much input.[56]

One can learn about the Russian aspirations toward a peace agreement from a letter the Grand Duke Nikolai Mikhailovich wrote to the czar on October 4, 1916. In this letter he outlined the problems confronting Russia in a future peace settlement:

1. What territory should Russia acquire in Europe and the East? . . .
3. How can we assist in the territorial restoration of Serbia, Montenegro, and Belgium?
4. Poland???
5. Acquisitions in Asia Minor—the formulation of the Armenian question.
6. Future fate of Persia.
7. Promises to Romania?

8. How shall we treat Bulgaria?
9. The same about Greece.[57]

BELGIUM

While keeping in mind that England entered the war only when it was obvious that Belgian neutrality had been violated by the Germans, one will not be surprised to learn from the memoirs of Albert I, King of the Belgians, that in his view, particularistic interests ranked higher than those held in common with his rescuers.

It has already been mentioned that early in the war, when the British contribution to the Belgian-French front was relatively insignificant, it was suggested that the Belgian army be amalgamated with French or British forces. At the time, the Allies had the impression that the Belgian high commanders lacked ability and energy. In his memoirs, the king revealed that on November 19, 1914, General Foch used this argument when he proposed to transfer four Belgian divisions to the Ypres sector or to distribute Belgian units among the French forces in the proportion of one brigade per division. The king reported that he "would neither agree to being deprived of his constitutional prerogatives, nor let his Army be split up, nor deliver the fate of his soldiers to decisions of foreign authorities beyond his control." His reply to Foch's demand was: "The Belgian Army must remain intact, master of its own operations and absolute master of its organisation."[58]

Several days later, Field Marshal French transmitted a similar proposal: to incorporate the Belgian army into the British army, one Belgian brigade per British division. This time the king's reply included, inter alia, the warning that Belgian "officers and soldiers would be reluctant to obey foreign leaders," with the explanation that "my country can only make its existence felt through its Army and it would never understand a change which would be equivalent to suppressing the latter." As was to be expected, the Allies agreed.[59]

Allied intentions to amalgamate were not the only bone of contention, however. The King of the Belgians was at variance with his Allies as far as both operations on Belgian territory and the use of Belgian troops were concerned. "The blood of our soldiers, that precious capital, was not to be shed except to good purpose."[60] He stated that in the domain of general politics Belgian ambitions must not be confused with those of the Allies. These, with their immense resources, could strive for revenges, conquests and annexations. Belgium, however, was fighting only for her honor and independence. Being reduced to her little army, she could not afford to gamble with it other than parsimoniously. Furthermore, Belgium had every right to fear a reconquest foot by foot, which would lay her country in ruins.[61]

This reasoning was a common thread in all future discussions of operational plans with the Allies. In the fall of 1915 the king recorded in his diary that the inviolability of the territory remaining in Belgian hands must be a principle admitted by the Allies.[62] He was not without mistrust of England when he wrote on November 3:

Countries like France and Belgium, which have been dragged into the conflict in spite of themselves and against their wishes, have everything to lose in being chained to an indestructible power like the British Empire. They take all the blows which were not intended for them. . . . Belgium must be no one's vassal, neither England's nor France's. She was neutral before the war. The mass of the people does not want to be tied up with any of its neighbours.[63]

In July 1916 Albert I sharpened this observation: "We must never lose sight of the fact that any engagement with a Great Power, particularly Great Britain or France, invariably ends in an interference by that Power in our military, political and economic regime."[64] At the end of the same year he stated that the Belgian war aim was not the same as Great Britain's; Belgium was not under arms to destroy Germany. She would not take part in unrealizable undertakings. The king stressed that he would not sacrifice his men in operations in whose success he did not have any faith.[65] At the same time, Belgium was not admitted to the Allied conference in Paris. The king explained why he took offense: "This means that we are excluded from deliberations on the conduct of a war, from the effects of which our Army and our people suffer so harshly. Decisions upon which perhaps the conditions of our liberation and our future existence depend, are taken without us being in a position to discuss them."[66] This was a most cogent definition of a junior coalition partner.

As already indicated, the king was worried about the risks to Belgian territory and population from Allied operations carried out in his country, in both the sectors that were occupied by the enemy and those that were not. In 1915 he was unhappy with the direction of the Allied attack in progress because it "exposes Belgium to all the horrors of war. The center of the country risks being completely ravaged."[67] In an argument with General Foch over this Allied intention, Foch agreed "that Belgium will suffer the horrors of war," but he saw no means of avoiding them, although he promised the king that "there will be no siege of Brussels."[68] In

December 1916, when the king learned that the British were planning an advance along the Belgian coast in order to secure the communications of the BEF and to reduce the German submarine menace to British shipping, he drew the attention of his cabinet to the dangers Belgium was running. He argued that her liberation by arms was tantamount to her destruction, by being towed in the wake of the Great Powers. He stressed the point that the moment had come to defend the Belgian point of view before her Allies and, without requiring an impossible separate peace, at least to define clearly the Belgian war aims. He stated that his cabinet was unanimous in declaring it impossible and inadmissible that the country should be reconquered foot by foot and thus destroyed.

This posture involved a dilemma. Several Belgian ministers were haunted by fear of their Allies. They thought that the alliance could not survive any discussion, in spite of their conviction that the Allies needed Belgium for moral reasons.[69]

The king reached the conclusion that the struggle, which the Great Powers wanted to wage to the bitter end, bore for the Belgian people— almost entirely in the hands of the enemy—only increased suffering resulting from the ruthless character of the present war, of which the invaded countries were to bear the brunt. Therefore, anybody responsible for safeguarding the interests of the Belgian nation could not subscribe to a war policy that exposed Belgium to total destruction.[70]

Two months later, Field Marshal Haig again suggested an operation on the Belgian coast. The king maintained again his opinion that the recapture of the coast would serve the interests of England rather than those of Belgium. He argued that small countries must beware of the big ones, even when these call themselves Allies![71] In the spring of 1918, the British again wanted to move into Belgium by evicting the enemy from the Belgian coast, which it occupied. Even this late in the war, the Belgians rejected this move for the same reasons.

Besides the problem of amalgamation, which has been discussed, a question arose repeatedly in connection with independent command over the Belgian army. In early 1917 the Allies planned an operation on the Flemish coast with the participation of twenty English and three to four French divisions as well as the Belgian army, with the cooperation of the French and British fleets. The combined forces were to be led by Field Marshal Haig. In order to convince the Belgians to agree to this arrangement, the example of the mixed Salonika army under French command was presented. Nevertheless, the Belgian Army Command considered it a humiliation.[72]

On May 15, 1917, General Pétain wrote a letter to the King of the

Belgians mentioning that the forthcoming operation in Flanders was to be carried out by about thirty British divisions. In his letter, he tried to entice the king to agree to Belgian participation for two reasons: the front was also occupied by Belgian troops, and prospects were thus opened for the reoccupation of Belgian territory.

The French army would participate, too. Under these conditions, it seemed natural that the conduct of the operations should be in the hands of the British army. Nevertheless, the minor part to be taken by Belgian and French forces required that the troops of these two nations should be united under a single command. It was suggested to offer to the King of the Belgians the command of the French participating divisions for the duration of operations.

The king, who was insulted, replied through his chief of staff that he would not accept a situation where in fact he would be abdicating his authority over the Belgian army. He stressed that he held the command of the army from the Belgian constitution, or in other words, by the will of the Belgian people. He was not allowed to relinquish a part of this command, which had been entrusted to him by the nation. He was therefore obliged to decline the offer to command the French-Belgian army and would thus retain the effective and exclusive command of the Belgian army.

During a visit of the commander in chief of the BEF, the king protested a plan to which he was asked to contribute although it was conceived without his knowledge.[73]

After the establishment of a unified command under General Foch in 1918, this issue emerged again. A puzzled General Pershing reported a session of the Supreme War Council in which the only question discussed was whether the Belgian army would be under the Allied commander in chief. Pershing recalled that the Belgian chief of staff objected to Foch on the grounds that a king could not be placed under the command of a major general. He thought that the point was not well taken, as Haig and Pétain and he himself were senior in rank to Foch, who, after all, held his place by common agreement.[74] It is obvious that the American general, representing the greatest power, was not aware that the problem of royalty in a coalition composed from countries of different regimes was an additional handicap in the delicate fabric of a wartime coalition. Identical problems emerged with the king of Italy.

JAPAN

Because of the Anglo-Japanese Alliance of 1902, which was mentioned previously,[75] it was obvious that Japan could not remain neutral should the war spread to the Far East. Moreover, Japan had its own interests, and was thus certain that it would take part in the war. Indeed, on August 19, 1914, the Japanese chargé d'affaires in Berlin presented an ultimatum to the German foreign minister with reference to the Anglo-Japanese Alliance. It demanded the removal or disarmament of all German naval vessels from Japanese and Chinese waters as well as the unconditional surrender of the German colony Kiautchou in China to the Japanese authorities. These demands were explained as a necessity in order for Japan to remove from the area all possible impediments to peace. The German government reacted to this ultimatum by recalling the German ambassador to Tokyo on August 23 and by expelling the Japanese chargé d'affaires from Berlin. This meant that a state of war existed between the two countries.

However, as already mentioned,[76] Japan was not at all inclined to participate in the war in Europe, which disappointed the Entente. At the end of December 1914, Joffre suggested to the French Minister of War that Japan should be approached with the idea of sending some of its forces to the European theater. Some months later, he was informed that negotiations with Tokyo on this subject had begun. However, this suggestion ran counter to the wishes of the Japanese people. Their army was the product of compulsory military service, submitted to in order to assure the country's defense. The Japanese people objected to sending their army to a distant land to play the role of mercenaries for the advancement of foreign interests.

The Japanese government later objected to the plan because of the logistics involved in transportation. But Joffre soon discovered the real cause of Japan's refusal to intervene militarily. The government of Tokyo had taken possession of the German colony of Tsing Tao; it now addressed a series of demands to China, which, under pretext of solving the Shantung question, sought to obtain from this power a series of decisions so advantageous in their nature as to secure for Japan a predominating situation in the country.

Joffre admitted that from the Japanese viewpoint, the moment was well chosen, because France, Great Britain and Russia were occupied in Europe and the United States was absorbed in watching the affairs of the Old World. None of these governments felt disposed to involve themselves in any Chinese complication. The French foreign minister hoped that after a final settlement of this problem in Japan's favor, it would accede to the French request. This never materialized, however.[77] As late as October 1917 the discussion of Japanese intervention in Europe was renewed in official French circles. But the Japanese Minister for Foreign Affairs replied that "the question of the dispatch of troops had been decided once and for all, and the Government would not change its mind."[78]

The situation was quite different in regard to Japan's naval participation in the war. In her study of Chinese participation in World War I, Madelaine Chi-Sung-Chun records four British requests for naval assistance from Japan. She stresses that "for Japan the war was a mercantile venture. Each British request fulfilled had its price, and Japan refused to comply when it did not suit her interest."[79] On September 2, 1914, the British foreign office requested Japanese naval assistance in the Mediterranean, trying to attract the Japanese by offering their Navy "every facility for supplies and repairs in His Majesty's arsenals and dockyards" as well as financial remuneration. But these offers failed to attract the Japanese foreign minister, who told the British ambassador that the "Japanese Navy was founded primarily for the defence of its country."[80]

In early 1917, the Allies were in desperate need of reinforcement. Therefore on January 9, the British foreign office once again requested Japanese naval assistance. It wanted the Japanese Admiralty to send two light cruisers from Singapore to the Cape, and an additional flotilla of destroyers to cooperate with the British forces in the Mediterranean. The foreign secretary informed the British ambassador in Tokyo that if the Japanese government appeared reluctant to accede to this request, he was to stress the point that the British "would supply fuel to those vessels at the expense of His Majesty's Government."[81] Chi-Sung-Chun remarks, "Once assured of her reward, Japan showed less reluctance towards participation in the war."[82]

Indeed, in May 1917, four more Japanese destroyers were dispatched to Europe. In his excellent study, Sir Frederick Maurice reports on a certain difficulty in the wake of this Japanese contribution:

Some relief was obtained by the arrival of eight Japanese destroyers in the Mediterranean, but this added a fresh complication to the problem of command, for the Japanese insisted that their ships must not be under British or French orders, and, while they promised co-operation, they sent a Japanese admiral flying his flag in a light cruiser to command their destroyers.[83]

Chi-Sung-Chun observed that

by 1917 Japan clearly felt uneasy about her peripheral position in the allied camp and her possible isolation after the war; she knew, too, that her half-hearted co-operation had not endeared her to the Entente Powers. Hence she became less reluctant to comply with British requests for naval assistance.[84]

In connection with the problems of the Allied intervention in Russia after the revolution there, it became obvious that the question of Japanese participation in this intervention caused much tension between the partners, in particular with the United States, which was not pleased by the Japanese invasion of Russia from the Far East.

ITALY

Although Italy was originally a member of the Triple Alliance of the Central Powers, it managed by means of legal interpretation of its obligations to stay out of the war. Being at loggerheads with the Austro-Hungarian Empire over various territorial issues, it sent out feelers to the Entente camp once the fighting began. Toward the end of the first year of the war, Italy became aware of the precarious situation of the Entente and of the desire of the members to attract new partners to their camp. Thus Italy was in a position to put forward exaggerated demands for its future services, which were not all acceptable by some of the Entente Powers. This bargaining position was strengthened by the very fact that Germany was aware of the Italians' wavering attitude and exerted pressure on its Austrian ally to yield to the Italian demands.

As one learns from the diary entries of Aldrovandi Luigi Marescotti, negotiations in Vienna continued until the very day on which the secret treaty between Britain, France, Russia and Italy was signed in London. After haggling over almost every minor island on the Dalmatian coast, the concessions that Italy wrestled from its new partners were so superlative that the Allies had indeed every reason to keep the treaty secret.[85] General Bliss's biographer remarks that the treaty was not published around the world because "it would have been bad propaganda in America."[86]

During the entire course of the war, there was an uninterrupted tug-of-war between the Allies operating in the Mediterranean over the question of a joint command over the Allied fleets. In his memoirs, Poincaré mentioned that as early as May 1915, Italy wanted to entrust the command of the Allied fleets in the Mediterranean to the Duke of Abruzzi. The French marine minister threatened that "he would rather resign than allow our [French] squadrons to come under the orders of a foreign Admiral even if it were only to be in the Adriatic."[87] At the Versailles meeting on May 1, 1918, the appointment of a Supreme Commander to the Allied fleets in the Mediterranean was again discussed. This time the Italians objected. Field Marshal Haig, a participant in this meeting, maintained that "their object seemed to be to stay in port and keep their fleet safe." He added: "I was disgusted with their attitude."[88] Although the British First Sea Lord,

Admiral Wemyss, was in agreement with the French admiral, the Italian objection could not be overcome.[89]

Following the same meeting, General Wilson reported that "after a prolonged and heated discussion, it was decided that Jellicoe should go as Admiralissimo in the Mediterranean." However, the next day this decision was cancelled "because the Italian Admiral said he might be ordered to sea."[90] Palmer, again quoting General Bliss, recalls that in June 1918 Clemenceau called for the reexamination of the naval situation in the Mediterranean. Reports from Russia, where chaos reigned, suggested that the Germans were going to take over the Russian Black Sea fleet and pass into the Mediterranean together with the Turks. The French and British wanted the Italians to send battleships to join the French Mediterranean fleet in preparation for meeting the combined fleets of Turkey and Germany. The Italian admiral saw no reason for this. He said that according to the pact by which Italy agreed to enter the war, the British and French obligated themselves to give Italy naval support until Austrian battleships were destroyed or peace was concluded. Now, in negation of this pledge, the Allies were asking for naval assistance from Italy.

The French and British admirals considered the Italian objections secondary because Italy was stronger at sea than Austria and, more important, would not have to fight Austria single-handedly. The Italian admiral responded that "the Italian Fleet would never serve under the French, accepting their command, tactics and fire control."[91] He had a low opinion of the French navy, and accused the British of having broken the agreement. It became obvious that, in Bliss's words, "no cozening, no baiting, no storming would lead Orlando [the Italian Prime Minister] to agree to fight the Turco-German-Russian Fleet. Italy had only five battleships, he said, and she proposed to keep them safe in harbor as long as one Austrian battleship was afloat."[92] Sir Frederick Maurice concludes this issue: "While the [British] relations with the Italian Navy were never satisfactory, those with the French Navy were with some exceptions good, and there was never the least friction with the American Navy when the United States came into the war."[93]

On the other hand, since the Italians badly needed reinforcements of British and French divisions from the western front after the Caporetto disaster, they had no other choice but to swallow their pride and yield to Allied demands. As a result, at the Rapallo Conference in November 1917, the Italian commander in chief and his chief of staff were dismissed and replaced.[94]

When American troops arrived in France, the Italians were arguing over the transfer of Americans to the Italian front. Though the French and

British had given military assistance to the Italian front without reservation, the Italian military representative in Versailles told General Bliss that the Italians disliked the French very much, and the French reciprocated this feeling.[95] In an official letter, Bliss later tried to explain the reasons why the Italians wanted a large force of Americans in their country: The first reason was fear. They were mortally afraid of the Germans, even though their reports of large numbers of Germans massing against them were unverified. The second reason was money. The Italians had heard of the large sums the Americans were spending in France, and Italian politicians were blamed for not getting their share. The third reason was ambition. The Italians wanted to strike a major blow for territorial gains and future power. Bliss added a more substantial reason: "There is a general undercurrent of belief here that the Allies will not even give Italy that which they specifically promised. Italy knows this. Therefore she would like to have the decisive blow struck from Italy rather than France, with her army as the predominant factor."[96]

UNITED STATES

The United States only entered the war on the side of the Entente toward the fourth year. Its war aims were not completely identical with those of the other Entente partners, as was already obvious from the instructions given to General Pershing. The United States was not immediately prepared to play an active role in the fighting. Even in mid-October 1918, Field Marshal Haig rated the American army as "not yet organised: it is ill-equipped, half-trained, with insufficient supply services. Experienced officers and NCOs are lacking."[97] But there was no doubt that without the Americans, the latecomers and the "rich uncle," the war could not have been won. This particular issue will be dealt with in subsequent chapters.

The principal expedients to overcome the obstacles of particularistic tendencies in the coalition were conducting coordination conferences and establishing a unified command. These expedients are the subjects of Chapters 5 and 6. But before embarking on these investigations, another handicap of coalition warfare will be discussed: the impact of personal factors and rivalries on the conduct of war.

NOTES

    1. Tasker H. Bliss, "The Evolution of the Unified Command," *Foreign Affairs* 1, no. 2, Dec. 15, 1922, pp. 1–30.

2. Ibid., p. 2. (Emphasis added.)

3. David F. Trask, *The United States in the Supreme War Council. American War Aims and Inter-Allied Strategy 1917–1918*, Middletown, Conn., 1961, p. 3.

4. Raymond Poincaré, *The Memoirs of Raymond Poincaré*, vol. 4, New York, 1931, p. 243.

5. Field Marshal Sir Douglas Haig, *The Private Papers of Douglas Haig, 1914–1919*, London, 1952, p. 223.

6. Edward L. Spears, *Liaison 1914*, London, 1930, p. 343 n, pp. 543–44.

7. Poincaré, vol. 4, pp. 68–69.

8. John French, *1914*, Boston, 1919, p. 105.

9. Poincaré, vol. 4, p. 287.

10. Ibid., p. 55.

11. André Tardieu, *France and America: Some Experience in Cooperation*, Boston, 1927, p. 239.

12. Supra, pp. 4; 5, n.2.

13. French, pp. 13–15.

14. William Maxwell Aitken Beaverbrook, *Politicians and the War 1914–1918*, London, 1960, pp. 36–37; also Edward Grey, *Twenty-five Years 1892–1916*, New York, 1937, p. 66.

15. George William Buchanan, *My Mission to Russia and Other Diplomatic Memories*, vol. 1, London, 1923, p. 190. (Emphasis added.)

16. Vladimir Aleksandrovic Suchumlinov, *Die rußische Mobilmachung im Lichte amtlicher Urkunden und den Enthüllungen des Prozesses*, Bern, 1917, p. 381.

17. French, pp. 350–52 passim.

18. Edward L. Spears, *Prelude to Victory*, London, 1939, p. 44. (Emphasis added.)

19. David Lloyd George, *War Memoirs of David Lloyd George*, vol. 1, London, 1936, p. 426.

20. W. K. Hancock and Jean van der Poel, eds., *Selections from the Smuts Papers*, vol. 3, Cambridge, England, 1966, p. 488.

21. Charles Edward Callwell, *Field-Marshal Sir Henry Wilson*, vol. 1, New York, 1927, p. 307.

22. French, pp. 75, 95.

23. Ibid., p. 159.

24. Ibid., p. 165.

25. Ibid., pp. 218–19.

26. Ibid., p. 166; also: Charles Julien Huguet, *Britain and the War*, London, 1928, p. 159.

27. Joseph Jacques Césaire Joffre, *The Personal Memoirs of Joffre*, vol. 1, New York, 1932, pp. 299–300.

28. Ibid., pp. 303–4.

29. Haig, pp. 296–300 passim.

30. Ibid., pp. 314–15; Ferdinand Foch, *The Memoirs of Marshal Foch*, New York, 1931, p. 325.

31. W. B. Fowler, *British-American Relations 1917–1918. The Role of Sir William Wiseman*, Princeton, N.J., 1969, p. 148; also Haig, p. 227; Callwell, vol. 2, pp. 53–54.

32. Frank Alfred Golder, *Documents of Russian History, 1914–1917*, New York, 1927, pp. 60–62.

33. Huguet, p. 208.

34. Ibid., p. 209.

35. Ibid., pp. 209–10 passim.

36. Haig, p. 336.

37. Supra, p. 3.

38. Grey, vol. 2, pp. 103–4 passim.

39. Ibid., vol. 2, p. 104.

40. Lord Maurice Hankey, *The Supreme Control at the Paris Peace Conference 1919; A Commentary*, London, 1963, p. 18.

41. Ibid., p. 19.

42. Joffre, vol. 1, p. 419.

43. Ibid., p. 422.

44. Buchanan, vol. 1, p. 219.

45. Jurij Nikiforovich Danilov, *Rußland im Weltkriege 1914–1915*, Jena, Germany, 1925, pp. 33–34.

46. Keith Neilson, *Strategy and Supply: The Anglo-Russian Alliance 1914–1917*, London, 1984, p. 52.

47. Danilov, pp. 401–3 passim.

48. Neilson, pp. 72–73.

49. Danilov, pp. 509–10.

50. C. Shumsky-Solomonov, *Russia's Part in the World War*, New York, 1920, p. 29.

51. Vassilij Iasifovic Gurko, *Rußland 1914–1917. Erinnerungen an Krieg und Revolution*, Berlin, 1921, pp. 130–31.

52. Joffre, p. 433.

53. Cited in Winston S. Churchill, *The World Crisis 1911–1918*, London, 1964, p. 429.

54. Earl of Oxford and Asquith, *Memoirs and Reflections*, vol. 2, London, 1927, pp. 77–78.

55. Ibid.

56. Danilov, pp. 479–82 passim.

57. Golder, pp. 74–77 passim.

58. Albert I, *The War Diaries of Albert I, King of the Belgians*, London, 1954, p. 25.

59. Ibid., pp. 26–28 passim.

60. Ibid., p. xix.

61. Ibid., pp. xix–xx.

62. Ibid., p. 63.

63. Ibid., p. 73.

64. Ibid., p. 118.

65. Ibid., pp. 130–31.

66. Ibid., p. 132.

67. Ibid., p. 42.

68. Ibid., p. 45.

69. Ibid., pp. 136–37.

70. Ibid., pp. 142–43.

71. Ibid., p. 156.

72. Ibid., p. 155.

73. Ibid., pp. 165–68 passim.

74. John J. Pershing, *My Experience in the World War*, vol. 2, New York, 1931, p. 134.

75. Supra, p. 12.

76. Supra, p. 18.

77. Joffre, p. 324; also Poincaré, vol. 4, pp. 57–58.

78. Madelaine Chi-Sung-Chun, *The Chinese Question during the First World War*, Ann Arbor, Mich., 1977, p. 213.

79. Ibid., p. 233.

80. Ibid., pp. 233–34.

81. Ibid., pp. 241–42.

82. Ibid., p. 250.

83. Sir Frederick Maurice, *Lessons of Allied Cooperation: Naval, Military and Air: 1914–1918*, London, 1942, p. 94.

84. Chi-Sung-Chun, p. 253.

85. Aldrovandi Luigi Marescotti, *Der Krieg der Diplomaten: Erinnerungen und Tagebuchauszüge 1914–1919*, München, 1940, pp. 76ff.

86. Frederick Palmer, *Bliss, Peacemaker: The Life and Letters of General Tasker Howard Bliss*, New York, 1934, p. 233.

87. Poincaré, vol. 4, pp. 96–97.

88. Haig, p. 313.

89. Ibid.

90. Callwell, vol. 2, p. 104.

91. Palmer, p. 272.

92. Ibid., p. 273.

93. Maurice, p. 177.

94. Marescotti, pp. 164ff.

95. Palmer, pp. 312–13.

96. Ibid.

97. Haig, p. 334.

4

HUMAN RELATIONS

SOLDIER-SOLDIER RELATIONSHIPS

War, like every other human endeavor, is strongly influenced by human relations. How much more so, if the war is waged by a multinational coalition in which the different national characteristics clash and there is a language barrier as well.

Little wonder that Huguet, the French liaison officer with the British Expeditionary Forces in France, who was constantly confronted with these problems, was quite aware of them. In his memoirs he wrote that he had learned for the first time how insignificant little details often influence the big events of this world. Moreover, it was difficult for some natures to get outside themselves and to rise to the height of the circumstances in which they were placed. He added that this experience was repeated many times in the course of the war.[1]

Referring to the language barrier, he wrote that it is difficult for men who cannot speak the same language to make themselves understood, even with the help of interpreters. He observed that it was not always easy to sense exactly the meaning of words, even when the conversation was between people of the same nationality; it was much more difficult when the speakers were foreign to each other! Therefore, not only were misunderstandings of this kind inevitable in war, but they equally arose also in postwar conferences, so many in number and so polyglot in character. They did account in some degree for the divergences of opinion that have so frequently shown themselves later on.[2]

One should not be surprised that the close relations between the different partners of a coalition and their interdependence might create a certain amount of hatred toward foreigners. In his memoirs, Lloyd George reveals that the Chief of Imperial General Staff, Robertson, who was the British government's highest-ranking military adviser,

had a profound and disturbing suspicion of all foreigners; if I may use a fruit grower's vocabulary, Robertson had the canker of xenophobia in his very sap and that vitiated the quality of his product. In a war conducted by an alliance of several nations it was essential to victory that there should be a sound and broad interpretation of the policy of the single front. In order of his distrust came Frenchmen, first and deepest of all, then Italians, Serbians, Greeks, Celts, and last of all—if at all—Germans. The Austrians had no existence for him except in his arithmetical tables. They were not near the Western Front and did not otherwise obtrude their hostile presence into his strategical conceptions. The French always irritated him and brought out all his stubbornness. That is why they called him "General Non-non"; that represented his first impulse towards all their requests and proposals. Briand once said to me: "Rob-berrt-son says 'Non' before he has heard what your proposal is about."[3]

At the time the Americans joined the Allied camp, Lloyd George revealed that Robertson added the Americans to his xenophobic list, though in this case there was no language barrier.[4]

F. M. John French and the French Generals

In Chapter 1 it was discussed that from the beginning, the relationship between the British C in C in France, Field Marshal Sir John French, and his French colleagues was not the most cordial.[5] Although the transfer of the BEF to the Continent was ahead of the timetable agreed on between the two General Staffs, the hard-pressed French commanders were not too impressed by this. On the other hand, French C in C General Joffre was in fact formally junior in rank to the British field marshal, despite the fact that French had only six divisions, organized into three army corps under his command, whereas Joffre commanded five armies. At their first meeting in Paris, on August 16, 1914, Joffre learned that in accordance with the instructions of the British Secretary of State for War referred to previously,[6] his British ally considered himself wholly independent, and that he could only offer the collaboration of his army.[7] More disastrous for the ensuing battle, however, was the meeting scheduled to take place the following day in Rethel between Sir John and General Lanrezac, commander of the French Fifth Army. The BEF was to form up on the left of General Lanrezac's forces. General Wilson, a member of Sir John's staff, reported, in what turned out to be a gross understatement, that this meeting did not pass off altogether satisfactorily, since neither of the distinguished commanders formed a high opinion of the other.[8]

Wilson's biographer explained in a footnote that Lanrezac knew no English and Sir John's French was not of a kind readily intelligible to a Frenchman; therefore, the discussion was carried out mainly through Wilson, acting as an interpreter. Field Marshal French wrote in his memoirs that Lanrezac's personality did not convey the idea of a great leader and his manner did not strike him as being very courteous. He added that he had left General Lanrezac's headquarters believing that Joffre, the commander in chief, had overrated Lanrezac's ability. French was therefore not surprised when he afterward turned out to be the most complete example of the Staff College "pedant" whose "superior education" had given him little idea of how to conduct war.[9]

Spears, the British liaison officer with the French, reported this unfortunate meeting in great detail. His verdict was that in fact, it was a dialogue of the deaf and mute. He recalled that no interview between two individuals similarly situated led by its sheer negative results to such serious, such disastrous consequences.[10] Adding some personal characteristics of Sir John, he explained:

If he had once lost confidence in a man, justly or unjustly, that man could do no right in his eyes. . . . [H]e judged both French and British by the same standards, and when, at the time of Mons, he came to the conclusion that General Lanrezac was not playing the game with him, it was finished. Once he had lost confidence in the Commander of the Fifth Army he ignored him and acted as if he and his Army did not exist.[11]

Moreover, Spears observed that

the staffs of both armies were not slow to realize that the two men had not taken to each other. General Lanrezac did not disguise from his entourage his feelings towards Sir John, and I learnt a few days later at Le Cateau that Sir John had not liked Lanrezac. The interview had resulted in a complete fiasco.[12]

Another misunderstanding, among many others in this fateful meeting, happened when these two officers exchanged views on tactical matters, and in particular, on the employment of the cavalry. Due to translation difficulties, Lanrezac got the impression that his British counterpart would not use his cavalry as cavalry, but rather as mounted infantry.[13] Thus, Lanrezac reported immediately to Joffre that the British cavalry would only be employed as mounted infantry, and could not be counted upon for any other purpose.[14] In retrospect, Spears lamented:

That such a misunderstanding should ever have arisen is strange enough, but what is quite extraordinary is that it was not cleared up. It was certainly never mentioned to me either by General Lanrezac or by his Chief of Staff. If General Lanrezac had had a further conversation with Sir John, or had maintained any sort of personal contact with the British, his mistake would have been swiftly corrected.

Spears subsequently offered his analysis of Lanrezac's personality:

Like so many Frenchmen, he had by training and tradition an instinctive mistrust of foreigners, and, in common with the rest of mankind, disliked what he did not know. That the British should be difficult and unreliable was just what such a man would expect. That an English Commander should not know his job was taken as a matter of course. . . . What he [Lanrezac] had gathered of Sir John's intentions fitted in so well with his preconceived ideas that he made no attempt to dispel the misconceptions upon which his impressions were based.[15]

Spears stressed the fact that General Lanrezac never returned French's calls. The two generals did not see each other again until their meeting on August 26 at St. Quentin, after the battles of Charleroi and Mons had been fought and lost. When they finally met, it was not on their own initiative. They were summoned by General Joffre to confer with him. Spears concluded that the Allied cause suffered an injury, as the result of the Rethel interview. Philosophically he added that men and their characters are what count in war. Thus their smaller defects turned the scale against the Allies that day.[16]

The days following this unlucky meeting were, as might be expected, a chain of uncoordinated actions of two armies which were supposed to act in harmony. Nevertheless, on August 22, Sir John tried to visit Lanrezac again at his headquarters. In his memoirs, French reported that after entering the area of the Fifth French Army, he discovered that columns of infantry and artillery from this army were moving south, which meant in fact that they were retreating. Since there appeared to be some difficulty in finding General Lanrezac, the field marshal decided to return to his headquarters. The first indication of the French army's retreat reached the British commander in chief through an officer dispatched from Lanrezac's staff, who wanted to know if the British would attack the flank of the German columns that were pressing him back. In his memoirs, Sir John noted that it was very difficult to realize what was in Lanrezac's mind when he made such a request.[17] This reflects exactly his judgment of his French colleague. Moreover, the British commander realized on August 25 that his allies were in fact a day's march in rear of the British and that every report indicated continual retreat.[18] A day earlier, this fact led the British liaison officer with Lanrezac to hurl the pathetic accusation and warning at the French general that if by his action the British army would be annihilated, England would never pardon France and France would not be able to afford to pardon him.[19]

On August 26, 1914, the previously mentioned meeting in French's headquarters in St. Quentin added to this "tragedy of errors." General Joffre reported that he arranged for an interview with Sir John French at his headquarters and that he also summoned General Lanrezac to this meeting, because he considered it important to make arrangements in the presence of the British commander in chief.[20]

Spears's report reflects the dense atmosphere of this meeting. General Joffre turned to Sir John, who seemed to be irritated by the very presence of Lanrezac, to whom he attributed so many of his difficulties. Sir John pointed out the dangerous situation of the British army, since it had been ceaselessly attacked by overwhelming numbers, whereas the Fifth Army, attacked by an enemy inferior in strength, had continuously held back behind his own, and had finally retired headlong without giving any warning or explanation. Sir John did not speak long. Realizing that he was not understood, since most of the Frenchmen present spoke no English, he asked General Wilson to translate. Wilson modified and softened somewhat his chief's presentation. However, this bowdlerized translation did not efface the impression Sir John's tone had made on General Lanrezac. The latter sensed the deep resentment of the British commander against himself. However, he only shrugged his shoulders slightly and made a few remarks that neither answered the British field marshal's claims nor explained his own actions.[21]

French's own impression of Lanrezac's reaction was that Lanrezac appeared to treat the whole affair as quite normal. He had in fact not offered any explanation, and also gave no reason for the very unexpected moves he had made. It seemed that the discussion was distasteful to him. He remained only a short time at French's headquarters, and left before any understanding as to future plans and dispositions had been arrived at.[22]

Spears continued his report by drawing attention to the pointed way in which French's remarks were ignored and brushed aside. French told Spears after the war how profoundly galling this was to him, whereas General Joffre looked hard at his subordinate but said nothing.[23] Spears also stressed the point that neither Sir John nor General Lanrezac addressed each other directly.[24]

It is interesting to compare the final conclusions of the two liaison officers, Huguet and Spears, concerning the St. Quentin Conference.

Spears maintained that in one sense the conference at St. Quentin was useful since it brought General Joffre and Sir John French closer together and also led each to a better comprehension of the other's point of view. Sir John told Spears much later that after Lanrezac had left, Joffre made it clear that he was anything but satisfied with the way the Fifth Army was being led. An additional result of this conference was that Joffre realized for the first time the exasperation of the British commander in chief and his staff at the way in which the expeditionary force had been treated.[25]

On the other hand, Huguet's observations were much more critical. In his opinion, though the St. Quentin Conference had achieved no military result, it might have effected a rapprochement between Sir John French and the French generals if only a few words of sympathy and confidence had been used. The extreme coolness that reigned and the lack of cordiality shown throughout emphasized the differences of opinion and the disparity of character of those present. Huguet reached the impression that Sir John French left with a full and bitter heart and that what little confidence he had left, vanished. French wrote to Lord Kitchener the same day that he had not been generously treated by the French command. From then on, he considered himself isolated and thrown back on himself, and only one idea obsessed him, namely, that of a quick retreat in order to escape from the dangers oppressing him. In accordance with the instructions received, he strove to keep as intact as possible the little army entrusted to his care. Huguet regretted that this state of mind was, unfortunately, to continue.[26]

In the sequel, and after the repeated retreat of the Allied forces, a point was reached when the British field marshal almost decided to disengage his army from the fighting line. On August 30, 1914, he sent a letter to Lord Kitchener in which he indicated his pessimistic outlook as to the further progress of the campaign in France, and added that his confidence in the ability of the leaders of the French army to carry this campaign to a successful conclusion was fast waning, and this was the reason for the decision he had taken to move the British forces so far back.

Spears tried to justify Sir John's step by explaining that that point in British psychology had been reached where complete and blissful confidence was replaced by almost irremediable suspicion and mistrust. Everybody who had to negotiate with Englishmen knew how difficult it was ever to retrieve ground thus lost and to reestablish confidence.[27]

However, Spears was forced to admit previously that both sides had a case. The French considered the British were running away at the critical moment, while the British were convinced that they had been treated so badly that they could place no further reliance on their Allies.[28]

Into the tense entanglement of personal relations between alien commanders, an additional factor, tension between two British field marshals, was added. Lord Kitchener, the British Secretary of State for War, was very disturbed by Sir John's letter of August 30, and wired French to urge him to conform as much as possible with General Joffre's plans in the conduct of the campaign. Sir John replied with a long telegram that included this passage:

If the French go on with their present tactics, which are practically to fall back right and left on me, usually without notice, and to abandon all idea of offensive operations, of course then the gap in the French line will remain, and the consequences must be borne by them. . . . An effective offensive movement now appears to be open to the French, which will probably close the gap by uniting their inner flanks. But as they will not take such an opportunity *I do not see why I should be called upon again to run the risk of absolute disaster in order a second time to save them.*[29]

French explained in his memoirs that he could not forget that the Fifth French Army had commenced to retreat from the Sambre at least twenty-four hours before he had been given any official intimation that Joffre's offensive plan had been abandoned. It was therefore his duty to his country that demanded that he should risk no recurrence of such a situation.[30]

It is not my intention to choose sides in this situation. What is most important is to draw attention to the dangerous situation the alliance faced because of this state of affairs. Little wonder that the British cabinet decided that evening that Lord Kitchener should go to France to see the commander in chief. Kitchener rushed to the Continent, met Field Marshal French at the British Embassy in Paris, and as the result of this meeting, achieved a more cooperative attitude toward the French conduct of the campaign. However, French resented the fact that for this meeting, Lord Kitchener wore his field marshal's uniform. French accused Kitchener of exploiting his seniority in rank and of assuming the air of a commander in chief rather than the civilian Secretary of State for War. There was great tension centering around Kitchener's intention to inspect British troops in the field, a step that was avoided by the clever intervention of British ambassador Sir Francis Bertie. The relations between the two British field marshals remained strained after French's removal from the command of the BEF. He continued his vendetta against Kitchener even after Kitchener's tragic death, and French's son, Gerald, persevered after his father's death.[31] Huguet's verdict was that "on that day Lord Kitchener rendered . . . an inestimable service to the Allies in reestablishing an uninterrupted front and in so doing making possible the resumption of the offensive which was to end in the battle of the Marne."[32]

To paraphrase, General Joffre realized that Lanrezac's unpleasant personal relations with Sir John French had compromised the cooperation of the British army with the French army and removed Lanrezac from the command of the Fifth French Army. The following day he noted that the initiative taken by General Franchet d'Esperey, the new commander of the Fifth Army, had reestablished good relations between his army and the British.[33] The process of the removal of Sir John from the command of the BEF took much longer.

As far as the relations between Joffre and French are concerned, they remained rather ambivalent. Joffre recorded that on September 7 he had requested the Minister of War to express to Lord Kitchener the warmest thanks for the constant support that the British forces had brought to the French armies. He also sent a personal letter to French to tell him of his gratitude. French answered the same day, thanking Joffre for his message.[34]

However, French's diary entry of September 30 does not reflect such a rosy picture. He thought that he could get on much better if the French commander in chief would tell him more of his general plans.[35] It is not without interest that Huguet, this keen observer of British-French relations due to his position as liaison officer, did not put the blame solely on Sir John. Summing up the events of 1914, he wrote that the differences were unfortunately accentuated on the French side by the character of Joffre, the commander in chief, who was little skilled in the management of men and in overcoming difficulties. When, as a result of the victory of the Marne, General Joffre had seen his confidence, prestige and authority grow bigger, he laid claim—in the name of unity of command—to exercise over the British army a control to which Sir John French submitted with increasing difficulty. It thus happened that success, instead of bringing the two men closer together, had only marked more plainly the contrasts in their characters. Huguet observed that from then on opportunities for difficulties and quarrels arose at every turn, and their relations, which had never been confident or cordial, became colder and colder.[36]

The clever General Wilson, with his fluent command of French, advised Joffre to give the British orders without appearing to do so, never to refer to their numbers and dispositions but to refer to Sir John's loyalty and to leave the rest to his good heart—and to Wilson.[37]

When Foch was appointed to coordinate operations of the French, Belgians and British Allies on the northern front, making him an army group commander, Wilson noted that Sir John's initial reaction was that he would not take orders from a junior. But after Wilson, who was on friendly terms with Foch, told him that it was a tonic to have a talk with Foch, he accepted the inevitable.[38] Indeed, Huguet reported that the feelings of sympathy and confidence that the qualities of Foch had inspired in Sir John French were noticeable from the first. Whereas General Joffre's welcome was always cold, constrained and full of reserve, General Foch was, on the contrary, remarkable for his warmth, gaiety, and good humor, to which he added perfect tact and a deference that was particularly pleasing to Sir John French.[39]

Haig, Nivelle and Others

After assuming his post as commander in chief of the BEF, Sir Douglas Haig held a position vis-à-vis his Allies that was different from his predecessor's. Joffre admitted that it should not be forgotten that at the outbreak of the war, the BEF brought to France by Sir John French consisted of only 70,000 men, whereas in the middle of August 1916, General Haig had under his orders 1,439,000 soldiers, of whom 1,200,000 were combatants.[40]

From a letter sent by General Robertson, Chief of the Imperial General Staff, to Field Marshal Haig on January 5, 1916, it is clear that Haig liked Joffre, although the xenophobic CIGS felt compelled to warn his colleague that "as a whole, the French Commanders and Staff are a peculiar lot. . . . The great thing to remember in dealing with them is that they are Frenchmen and not Englishmen, and do not and never will look at things in the way we look at them."[41]

Joffre recalled an incident that Haig related to Colonel des Vallières, Chief of the French Mission at British General Headquarters. On May 4, 1916, M. Clemenceau, president of the French Senate Military Committee, visited Sir Douglas and asked whether he was under General Joffre's command. Haig replied that he was solely responsible to the British government for the employment of his troops and the conduct of operations, but that he nevertheless believed that there could not be two commanders in chief in the same theater of operations and that therefore the French and British forces constituted one single army. As a consequence, he guided himself absolutely by the directions issued by General Joffre and had complete confidence in him and a high appreciation of the ability of the officers commanding his armies.[42]

Three weeks later, on May 26, Haig wrote about the French that they were, indeed, difficult Allies to deal with. He later added in a condescending manner: "But there is no doubt that the nearest way to the hearts of many of them, including that of the 'Generalissimo' [Joffre], is down their throats, and some 1840 brandy had a surprisingly soothing effect on both him and Castelnau!"[43]

Haig's papers show that there were ups and downs in his relations with Joffre during the remainder of Joffre's command, centering on the question of Sir Douglas's position relative to Joffre as the "Generalissimo."[44]

This relative calm ended when General Robert G. Nivelle, with his ambitious operative plans, was appointed commander in chief of the French armed forces in the western theater. Spears, highly experienced in inter-Allied affairs, observed, justifiably, that General Nivelle failed to perceive that as a junior and new commander he should have to be especially careful in dealing with an officer senior to himself like Sir Douglas Haig.[45] Matters came to a head at the Calais Conference in February 1917, at which operations for 1917 were discussed. A decision was reached putting Haig under Nivelle for the anticipated combat.

Haig noted in his diary that the following evening he received a letter from Nivelle. Its language was couched in very commanding tones. He asked for a copy of Haig's orders to his armies for the forthcoming offensive. In Haig's opinion it was a letter that no gentleman could have drafted. Above all it also was one that certainly no C in C of the British army should receive without protest.[46]

Even before receiving this letter, Haig, who was offended by the Calais decision, dispatched a secret letter to the king without informing the CIGS and the government. In his letter, he complained about what had taken place, which was quite an unusual step.[47] The tension between Nivelle and Haig continued unabated until Nivelle's dismissal as the result of his unsuccessful offensive.

Haig's xenophobic character also revealed itself in relations with other Allies. After a meeting with General Ruquoy, the new Belgian chief of staff, he wrote in his diary: "I felt it was a waste of time to talk to this fellow. He talked a great deal with a Walloon accent, and seemed very ignorant of a soldier's work. He gave me the impression that he is a funk of the Germans. . . . I formed a poor opinion of the man as a soldier and of his determination as a man."[48]

On the Romanians he wrote that he would not believe that such chickenhearted creatures would ever fight until he saw them actually engaged.[49] And on the Portuguese he reported that a battalion refused to go into the trenches. However, the British did not want to quarrel with Portugal because it had many suitable submarine bases for the enemy. He considered the Portuguese troops with their Portuguese officers useless for this class of fighting.[50]

On May 1, 1918, when the Americans arrived in France, Haig attended a conference in which the American commander in chief, General Pershing, participated; Haig thought that Pershing was very obstinate, stupid, and seemingly unaware of the urgency of the situation.[51]

The Americans

In reference to his instructions, which were mentioned previously,[52] Pershing was afraid that his Allies would not let him carry out these instructions. In his memoirs he noted that the apparent indifference of the Allies to the specific American problems gave further color to the suspicion that perhaps an American army as such was not wanted.[53] In a later section of his memoirs he focused on the French in particular:

There is no denying the fact that the French as a whole regard themselves as a superior people in many aspects. . . . In any event they never gave up the idea of regarding us as only an associated power, that had come into the war late, to be used as they might dictate.[54]

Pershing's suspicious mind perceived concealed Allied intentions everywhere:

The missions with us, especially those of the French and British, did not always confine their activities to normal lines, but often took occasion to advance their ideas regarding the training and use of our army. . . . Knowing this attitude, it was necessary to be on the lookout to avoid commitments to suggestions that might eventually involve the question of amalgamation.[55]

Even before becoming actively involved in the fighting, Pershing evolved a low opinion of the fighting qualities of his coalition partners:

The organization of our army was radically different from that of any of the Allied armies and we could not become imitators of methods which applied especially to armies in which initiative was more or less repressed by infinite attention to detail in directives prepared for their guidance. It was my belief . . . that efficiency could be attained only by adherence to our own doctrines based upon thorough appreciation of the American temperament, qualifications and deficiencies. I recommended the withdrawal of all instruction in the United States from the hands of Allied instructors.[56]

The Allies were aware that special care was required to develop cordial relations with the Americans. General Pétain issued special instructions to the French liaison officers with the American Expeditionary Force. Entitled "In Their Relations with American Officers the French Officers Must Always Use the Greatest Tact," the instruction stressed that one should not forget that America is a great nation and that the Americans have a national self-respect developed and justified by the breadth of vision that they bring to bear upon all the questions that they consider. Furthermore, it was explicitly stated that French officers should treat the officers of their grade or of a subordinate grade as little as possible as a master does a scholar. Concerning officers who are of a higher grade than the French officers, the French should wait to give advice until such advice is requested.[57]

South African General Smuts, who was sent by the British prime minister to investigate the front in France in June 1918, expressed a low opinion of General Pershing, considering him very commonplace, without real war experience, and already overwhelmed by the initial difficulties of a job too big for him. Furthermore, Smuts aired doubts whether he would loyally cooperate with the Allied Higher Commands. Above all, Pershing could not get together a first-class staff. Smuts feared very much that with the present Higher Command the American army would not be used to the best advantage. Smuts therefore proposed to suggest to President Wilson a reorganization of the American command. He added that this, however, was a very delicate matter, as every risk of hurting American pride should be avoided.[58]

In the biography of American Secretary of War Newton D. Baker, a memorandum is quoted from Sir William Robertson, the British CIGS. Robertson described Pershing as looking "older and rather tired, and I doubt if he has yet an intelligent and considered view of his task." Robertson concluded: "My general impression is that America's power to help win the War . . . is a very weak reed to lean upon."[59]

An entry in Haig's papers in April 1919, after the termination of the war, suggests Pershing's feelings toward his Allies:

Pershing thanked me afterwards most gratefully for the remarks which I had made and he mentioned that the French had never once said a word of thanks or complimented the American troops on what they had done. . . . Pershing assured me that it would be impossible for any officer or man of the American Army ever to forget the bad treatment which they had received from the French and that it was difficult to exaggerate the feeling of dislike for the French which existed in the American army.[60]

The British Empire

It has already been mentioned that in fact, the British Empire constituted a coalition in the framework of an international coalition. Therefore, it is not surprising that the internal relations in the Empire were infected with almost the same problems as the external relations. British relations with the Australian Dominion, which did not differ from those with the other Dominions, will prove the point.

The letters of Australian General John Monash shed some light on this issue. From the start of the war, the higher echelons of the Australian contingent were made up of British career officers, because Australia had no regular armed forces. As Australian officers became more experienced and yet the propensity for having British officers continued, the Australians, both military and civilians, resented the matter. Monash, who proved himself an outstanding soldier and was even considered by the British prime minister as the possible successor to Field Marshal Haig to command the BEF, wrote in March 1916: "If Australia chooses to let her forces be exploited to find jobs for unemployed senior British officers that is not my affair."[61] In a subsequent letter, he wrote:

There are constant rumours of a regrouping of the Australian divisions, and I happen to know that the Commonwealth Government is making strenuous efforts to get rid of the 2nd Anzac Corps H.Q., because they are all English, and have no Australian staff at all, but this is not very popular with the Army Council.[62]

In a letter in September 1917, he continued: "There has been strong pressure from Australia, for a considerable time past, to remove from the A.I.F. all those officers of the British Army who hold command and staff appointments, and to replace them by Australians."[63] Finally, on May 31, 1918, he wrote: "But for all practical purposes I am now the supreme Australian commander, and thus at long last the Australian nation has achieved its ambition of having its own Commander-in-Chief, a native born Australian—for the first time in its history."[64]

A different facet of the relations within the Commonwealth is also illuminated in Monash's letters. On October 18, 1917, he wrote from France:

Our men are being put into the hottest fighting and are being sacrificed in hair-brained ventures . . . and there is no one in the War Cabinet to lift a voice in protest. It all arises from the fact that Australia is not represented in the War Cabinet, owing to Hughes [the Australian Prime Minister], for political reasons, having been unable to come to England. So Australian interests are suffering badly, and Australia is not getting anything like the recognition it deserves.[65]

About a year later he wrote:

The question of the adequate recognition of the work done in the war by the Australian troops, and indeed by all Dominion troops of the Empire, is a very burning one. Far from it being the case that Dominion troops have in the past received more than their fair share of recognition, the exact contrary is the case. For some time past the German propaganda has been trying to represent Lloyd George as climbing to victory over the corpses of Canadians and Australians and putting them in wherever the fighting has been hottest. The Imperial Government and also G.H.Q. have been rather afraid of the effect of such propaganda, and they have rather erred on the side of unduly suppressing references to the deeds of the Australians.[66]

To conclude this part of the investigation it is fitting to quote Marshal Foch, who managed to conduct the final stage of the war as "Generalissimo." After referring to General Nivelle's blunders in 1917, he told one of his biographers:

One must know how to lead the Allies—one does not command them. Some must be treated differently from the others. The English are English, the Americans are another matter, and similarly with the Belgians and Italians. I could not deal with the Allied generals as I did with our own. . . . [A]lthough they loyally accepted the situation, a mere trifle might have upset them and dislocated the whole scheme. I could not give them orders in an imperative manner. . . . Anything might have happened. It was necessary to hear their views, otherwise they would have kicked. . . . Accordingly, when important decisions were involved, I used to see them, or asked them to see me. We talked and discussed questions between ourselves, and, without seeming to do so, I gradually won them over to my point of view. I provided them with a solution, but I did not force it upon them. They were satisfied.[67]

RELATIONSHIPS BETWEEN SOLDIERS AND POLITICIANS

Often in this connection, French Prime Minister Briand's bon mot is quoted: "War is much too serious a matter to be left to soldiers and sailors." Almost a century earlier, General Carl von Clausewitz, the German military philosopher who was himself a soldier, investigated the relationship of war and politics and presented his findings in his monumental book *On War*: "The assertion that a major military development, or the plan for one, should be a matter for *purely military* opinion is unacceptable and can be damaging. Nor indeed is it sensible to summon soldiers, as many governments do when they are planning a war, and ask them for *purely military advice*."[68] He also violently rejected as a complete absurdity the theorists' widespread demand that all available means should be at the disposal of the military commanders, to draw up a purely military war plan.

Clausewitz believed that war and its general outlines had always been determined by political institutions and not by the military. Therefore, one should not speak, as was often done, of the harmful influence of policy on the conduct of war. It was not this influence but the policy itself that was at fault. Conversely, if the policy was correct, it could only affect war favorably. To avoid friction between politicians and generals and for smoother coordination of policy and military actions, Clausewitz suggested that the commander in chief become a cabinet member. In cases where the statesman and the soldier were not the same person, as happened in ancient times, in absolutistic regimes, such as that of Alexander the Great, the Kings of the Absolutism and even Napoleon, this enabled the commander to participate in the principal decisions affecting the politician's actions. If the conduct of war is really dominated by politics, then it is the government that decides on the size of the army, thereby determining a vital part of strategy. The commanding general must regard this absolute strength as a given quantity.

It was therefore natural that Raymond Poincaré, the president of the French Republic, pondered the relationship of warfare and politics and investigated the situation in the various countries of the coalition. He reached the conclusion that "it is a matter which has to be considered especially, as in no belligerent country, whatever its constitutional conditions, are the relations sufficiently defined between the civil power and the military command." He compared the procedures of the different nations:

In Great Britain it is a Cabinet consisting of twenty-two members which, almost entirely independently of the King, has the political control of the war; Lord Kitchener ... only considers himself as the Minister for raising the troops and supplying and equipping them for the field; he gives no orders to Sir John French, who, as he is not on British soil, receives scarcely any from the British Government, and considers himself more and more independent.[69]

Turning his attention to other countries, Poincaré wrote:

In Belgium the King commands the armies, but day by day he needs all his tact and all his personal authority to bring what his Government does into line with what his military staff want to do. In Russia the Czar passes for being all powerful, but he is at times the plaything of his Ministers, who themselves are constantly and sulkily opposing the Grand Duke. In Italy General Cadorna is Commander-in-Chief; the Ministers are responsible for sending him men, arms and ammunition, but they seem to leave him entire freedom as to strategy, a freedom on which Victor Emanuel never trespasses.[70]

Turning to the situation of France, he observed that in France ever since the outbreak of the war the commander in chief had apparently assumed that everything centered on him. But then he concluded that little by little the nation had quite obviously asked the government to resume all responsibility. He added the important observation that in a coalition campaign, strategy and politics never functioned in two separate worlds.[71]

French Politicians and French Generals

This passage from Poincaré's memoirs, alluding to General Joffre's position vis-à-vis the French government, sheds light on the relationship between them. This state of affairs explains why Joffre "exploded" when he received a telegram from the government on August 25, 1914, ordering him to switch three army corps for the defense of Paris. Arriving during the so-called Great Retreat, he reacted as might be expected. He maintained that this telegram caused him intense surprise, for he saw here taking shape the menace of governmental interference in the conduct of operations—an interference which, if the eventualities envisaged were realized, bid fair to hamper considerably his liberty of action at the very moment when it was most essential that it should be entire and complete.[72] Since both sides involved felt the necessity to evolve a mechanism to avoid friction as much as possible, liaison officers between the government and General Headquarters were instituted.[73]

However, from a conversation between President Poincaré and Prime Minister Viviani, one sees that Viviani was annoyed by the fact that Joffre bypassed the Minister of War and wrote directly to the president. Poincaré stressed that there was something wrong as to the relationship between the military command and the civil government. Viviani's complaints that the generalissimo wrote to the president directly and not through the war minister were reasonable. However, the liaison officers explained to the president that General Headquarters considered themselves wholly independent of the government in time of war, and regarded as superior only the nominal and irresponsible authority of the president of the Republic. The president agreed that such a theory, if it were to materialize, would run contrary to the spirit of the Republican institution. But he was also quite sure that the irreproachable loyalty of Joffre would never allow such to be sustained. However, Poincaré admitted that there was considerable risk in these circumstances of uncertainty. He concluded that General Headquarters must not shut themselves up in an ivory tower and strip themselves of all control. It would have been as dangerous as it would have been ridiculous for the government to interfere in the conduct of military operations, but by all means government officials ought to have been better informed than they had been up to then.[74]

In April 1915 a new controversy erupted between Joffre and the government surrounding the possible transfer of divisions from the western theater of operations. In this context, Poincaré wrote in his diary that he had also reminded Joffre that he was not generalissimo of the whole French army but only of the forces on the western front and that it was for the government to decide on the distribution of troops on other fronts. Poincaré insisted that this point be made clear for the future.[75]

In spite of Joffre's principal insistence on his independence in military matters, he did not abstain from invoking political interference from the French government in order to force the participation of the BEF in the manner he desired in the Battle of the Marne. In his memoirs, he recorded that he had evolved the idea of seeking diplomatic support for bringing pressure to bear upon Field Marshal French. Therefore, in spite of his great objection to talking in advance to anyone concerning his plans, he decided to convey to Minister of War M. Millerand, in whose tact and patriotism he had perfect confidence, the exact situation and the necessity of an intervention by the government for the purpose of fortifying the request to the British commander in chief. He sent Millerand a personal letter asking him to act "through diplomatic channels."

Millerand informed Joffre that he had broached the matter with the Minister of Foreign Affairs, who would contact the British ambassador for the purpose of urging him to make representations to his government in the desired sense.[76] A year later, in March 1915, Joffre again wrote a long letter to the Minister of War with complaints against the British C in C and a request for political interference. The president, in fact, intervened, and asked the relevant French ministers to remind England what risks were incurred with the existing conditions.[77] From Joffre's memoirs it is evident that a year later, he still used the same method after he understood that the British cabinet was not in agreement with his operational plans. He kept the French cabinet informed and tried in every way to bring pressure to bear on the London government. If the views of the British government prevailed, the effect upon the projected offensives would have been very serious. He concluded that the intervention of the French government had its effect.[78]

In the spring of 1917, when General Foch was sent to Italy following the disaster in the Italian theater of operations, Painlevé, who was then French Minister of War, outlined to the British that General Foch had gone to Italy not as the emissary of the French General Staff but as the representative of the French government.[79]

The Sarrail affair elucidates the complicated relationship between military and domestic political matters. As C in C of the French front, General Joffre decided to remove General Sarrail from the command of the Third French Army. In his memoirs, Joffre wrote that this caused the government much embarrassment for political reasons.[80] Hankey, the secretary of the British war cabinet, made it clear that Sarrail was "an important person in the Republican party" and therefore "he could not be completely *degomme*, and was even reputed to be an aspirant to Joffre's place."[81]

Therefore, for political reasons it was necessary to find a job for Sarrail that was out of Joffre's sphere of influence. Joffre remarked dryly that the politicians decided to entrust Sarrail with the command of the Expeditionary Corps of the East in Salonika.[82] However, since this force was a multinational one, the consent of the partners was necessary, and this was difficult to obtain. On December 28, 1915, President Poincaré recorded that the cabinet in London agreed to Lord Kitchener's proposal that a French general should be in supreme control at Salonika, but on the condition that this should not be Sarrail. Sarrail, like General Mahon, the commanding officer of the British contingent, should come under the orders of the new chief. Not surprisingly, Joffre quite smiled on this idea, and would have liked to send other French generals, but Painlevé and Léon Bourgeois strongly opposed it, protesting that it was not for the English to select the French generals. The British government were therefore thanked for their consent in principle, but were told that Sarrail would remain in command of the expeditionary force.[83]

However, from General Robertson it is understood that although General Sarrail was theoretically in supreme command of the whole Macedonian theater of war, no important measure could be taken without reference to the governments concerned.[84]

General Pershing drew attention to the complicated position of General Foch, who was finally appointed Allied commander in chief. The overall conduct of the war was in the hands of a Supreme War Council. Nevertheless, as Chairman of the Supreme War Council, Clemenceau had not been granted authority to issue directions to the Allied commander in chief. But in his capacity as the French prime minister he had the authority over

Marshal Foch as an officer of the French army. It was obvious that the marshal realized this, and although he had been chosen by the Allied governments and was responsible to them jointly, his tenure of office naturally depended upon their pleasure, and especially upon that of his own prime minister. This would readily account for any action he might have taken at the suggestion of the latter.[85] Little wonder, then, that, as Foch revealed in his memoirs, Clemenceau did not abstain from complaining to him in a lengthy letter that the American army was "marking time." In fact, he had nothing less in view than a change in the chief command of the American army.[86]

Great Britain

The memoirs of the British leaders, both civilian and military, reflect a permanent state of tension between the two sectors. For instance, Lloyd George's *War Memoirs* displays a constant disregard, and even suspicion, of military leaders. On the other hand, Field Marshal Sir Henry Wilson, one of the soldiers almost always in direct contact with the civilian authorities, referred to them with the most contemptuous phrases (e.g., "The Frock Coats"). It is therefore not surprising to find the following in the memoirs of Field Marshal William Robertson, who served for a long period as Chief of the Imperial General Staff:

Throughout the war, ministers never seemed able to understand what educated soldiers well know, that the employment of troops of different armies in the same operation is attended with many difficulties and complications. . . . Military salads of this kind are sometimes justifiable and may be unavoidable, but it must be remembered that the mere counting of heads may give a wrong impression of the capabilities of the force, and that the appointment of an Allied Commander-in-Chief does not entirely remove the disadvantages incurred, though in some respects it may perhaps mitigate them.[87]

These were correct observations by themselves, but the term "educated soldiers" seems to indicate that the ministers referred to were uneducated.

Field Marshal Douglas Haig also pondered the relationship between soldiers and politicians. He considered it both "a great conflict" and "strained." Moreover, the outbreak of the war had produced a series of problems that strained relations still further. He maintained that in the old days of small-scale wars fought on principles of limited liability, the spheres of the army and the government were fairly easy to distinguish. But the new epoch of mass armies and total warfare, which began in 1914, produced new problems. Military decisions now involved political issues such as civilian morale, the use of resources, and the distribution of manpower. These problems could not be answered by soldiers alone. Difficult constitutional questions also arose. For instance, how could the ultimate responsibility of the cabinet be reconciled with the need to give military experts freedom to make military decisions? Moreover, what should be the relationship between the prime minister, the cabinet, the Secretary of State for War, the Chief of the Imperial General Staff and the commander in chief of the expeditionary force? Haig stated that all these problems faced the government of a nation with a strong antimilitary tradition, a nation that had not fought a major war since the Battle of Waterloo. He concluded pessimistically that it was not surprising that even to the end no real solution was found.[88] In a letter to Lady Haig written in October 1916, he mentioned a conversation with Prime Minister Lloyd George in which Lloyd George was quite aware of the danger that a wedge could be driven between him and the soldiers. Lloyd George also complained that the General Staff at the War Office did not let him know *everything*, but only fed him with what they thought was suitable for him to know.[89]

From the outbreak of the war, not only was there a controversy concerning how, where and when to deploy the BEF, as mentioned previously,[90] but when the danger of a German conquest of Antwerp was realized by the British government, the traditional British tendency against admitting the possession of Antwerp by any Continental power led to a decision to switch British forces to defend Antwerp. This decision was resented not only by the French, who did not like the idea of reducing the Allied forces in northern France, but also by the C in C of the BEF, who was expecting reinforcements from home that might now be switched to Belgium and thereby separated from his command.

Winston Churchill, the First Lord of the Admiralty, directed 8,000 marines to Antwerp. He was sent there by the cabinet in order to assess the situation. He had just arrived when he offered to take command of the British forces operating in Antwerp, an offer that was received with chagrin by the soldiers in France and at home, and was not accepted by the government. From Joffre's memoirs it is clear that he was opposed to sending any of the British reinforcements arriving on the Continent to Antwerp. His explanation sheds light on the relationship between the Secretary of State for War and the C in C of the BEF. Sir John French thought that Lord Kitchener wished in this way to create a new British army that would be outside the authority of the commander in chief of the British Expeditionary Force. On the other hand, Joffre considered it dangerous for Allied troops to go wandering off into a divergent theater of operations.[91]

Nevertheless, shortly afterwards, Sir John and Churchill cooperated in developing the idea of a joint army-navy operation along the Belgian coast. This no doubt also suited the personal interests of Sir John, who wanted to concentrate the BEF on the left wing of the western front.[92]

Field Marshal French also resented the direct communications between the British Secretary of State for War with General Joffre and the French government; since Lord Kitchener did not communicate through French, the field marshal was quite unaware of what was passing between them.[93] In the wake of the aforementioned Kitchener-French controversy,[94] French emphasized in his memoirs that he was anxious to lay particular stress on a principle that seemed to be of the utmost importance, namely, the danger of undue interference by the government at home with the commander of an army in the field.[95]

In November 1916, when the statesmen decided to convene a conference in Paris in order to discuss future military operations, Lloyd George resented the fact that the military chiefs were proposing to hold their meeting at Chantilly, the seat of the French commander in chief, a week before the Paris conference could be held. He considered it to be undesirable, for, as he pointed out to the committee, there would be a tendency among the generals to commit themselves as to their strategical views before the responsible heads of the governments had been able to reach a decision as to what they felt was necessary in the way of preliminary consultation with the Eastern Allies, and there might be difficulty subsequently in inducing the generals to modify or reconsider their opinions.[96] He was obviously correct.

As mentioned previously in this chapter, the tension between Haig and Nivelle on the eve of and during the so-called Nivelle Offensive was mainly due to the fact that the British government, particularly the prime minister, had given consent to subordinate Haig under Nivelle's command. From Lloyd George's memoirs it is evident that the prime minister held Field Marshal Haig in low esteem. This is also reported by General Robertson, then CIGS.[97] On the other hand, Haig not only disliked British politicians, he also disdained politicians of other nations. A diary entry from March 16, 1917, related to a possible change in the French War Ministry. He mentioned two candidates who were both revolutionary socialists. He added that these were the people under whom the British army had been placed for the forthcoming offensive operations. In describing General Lyautey, the retiring Minister of War, he hinted that he must have had a most difficult position in a government of political jugglers with a chamber of semilunatics.[98]

In 1917, General Robertson reported that two new governmental bodies were created: the Imperial War Committee, including representatives of the Dominions, and the War Policy Committee of the Cabinet, which was formed of members of the war cabinet and dealt with the general conduct of operations and war policy. However, Robertson stressed the fact that it was composed entirely of ministers and that the military and naval chiefs attached to it were only acting as advisers and executive agents and never as members.[99] This new arrangement may perhaps explain Robertson's writing to Haig on June 13, 1917, that one had to remember that the government carried the chief responsibility and that in a war of this kind many things besides the actual army had to be considered. Remembering this, however, one was entitled to make sure that unsound military plans were not adopted—or all other plans might come to nought.[100]

Referring to the inter-Allied conference in Rome in January 1917, General Wilson not only ridiculed the statesmen ("the Frock Coats are being led by the French into war with Greece, and we soldiers are in clear disagreement"), but he also resented the fact that the soldiers were not allowed in at the conference.[101] In the spring of 1918, Winston Churchill was sent by Prime Minister Lloyd George to meet General Foch in France. General Wilson, already Chief of the Imperial General Staff, went to see Churchill at the Charing Cross railway station en route to France and told him that he could not agree and must have this changed, that Churchill must go to Clemenceau and not to any soldier.[102]

When Wilson succeeded Robertson as CIGS, this was also due to Robertson's strained relations with the prime minister. The Secretary of State for War, Lord Derby, told Robertson that the prime minister could not "get on" with him. Bearing in mind that the office of the CIGS was part of the War Office, Robertson presented his view of the situation:

I was not surprised . . . at the decision to remove me from the War Office, for . . . I had been unable to agree with some of the strategical plans the Prime Minister wished to see adopted, and my opposition to the Palestine plan a few days before was the culminating point of previous refusals to lend my authority and name to acts which, I was convinced, were unsound and a danger to the Empire.[103]

Field Marshal Sir Henry Wilson's biographer pointed out that toward the end of the war, as might have been expected, the then CIGS took an active part in the political deliberations concerning the moves of U.S. President Wilson. On October 15, 1918, he wrote in his diary: "At War

Cabinet we considered Wilson's last answer to the Boche. It really is a complete usurpation of power of negotiation. . . . He is now taking charge in a way that terrifies me, as he is only a super-Gladstone—and a dangerous visionary at that."[104]

United States

The instructions given by Newton D. Baker, the American Secretary of War, to General Pershing when he left for Europe on May 26, 1917, stated in section 5 that "until the forces of the United States are in your judgement sufficiently strong to warrant operations as an independent command, it is understood that you will co-operate as a component of whatever army you may be assigned by the French Government."[105] At the same time, Pershing received a letter from Major General Tasker H. Bliss, the acting chief of staff of the American army, ordering that upon his arrival in France, he should establish relations with the French government and the military representatives of the British government now serving in France.[106]

Both documents indicate that Pershing was not only supposed to act as the commander in chief of the American Expeditionary Force in Europe and to be in touch with the corresponding military authorities, but he was also expected to establish contact with the governmental authorities, particularly the French. It is therefore not surprising to learn from Pershing's memoirs that he proposed procedural suggestions to Clemenceau to convene the commanders in chief and chiefs of staff to examine the situation and if possible determine a general program of combined action. According to Pershing, Clemenceau thought that would be a good thing to do and at once approved his suggestion.[107] On the other hand, Pershing was quite annoyed when U.S. Ambassador Walter H. Page suggested sending a few American divisions to aid the Italians. Pershing made it quite clear that he was strongly opposed to the use of American troops anywhere except on the western front, and as components of an American army.[108]

After the establishment of the Supreme War Council at the Rapallo Conference in November 1917, the Allies assumed that the U.S. president would become a fourth member of the council, accompanied by his Secretary of War, if time and distance would permit. At the December session, the U.S. president's advisor, Edward M. House, acted for Wilson. Pershing and Bliss hoped that he would remain, but Wilson wanted him nearer Washington than Versailles. After some time, General Bliss became the State Department representative on the council as well as its military representative. On February 19, 1918, in a letter to Frank L. Polk, the State Department's councilor, Bliss explained the function of the Supreme War Council, namely, that it was a bench of judges consisting of the political heads of three of the Allied governments before whom the military men urged the pros and cons of each case, and each case was submitted to the decision of these judges.[109] However, from W. B. Fowler's biography of British diplomat Sir William Wiseman, it is clear that "President Wilson, although he authorized House, and Bliss as military representative, to sit on the council, . . . did not recognize any capacity on the part of the council to bind the United States to any diplomatic or political position."[110]

Pershing reacted angrily to attempts by French leaders, both civilian and military, to lodge complaints with the president or with House against him. He called these actions "back-door methods," reaching the conclusion that these complaints were made for the purpose of finding out the exact extent of his independent authority.[111] Pershing became even more furious when he discovered that Clemenceau had sent a long cable to his ambassador in Washington on January 3, 1918, urging him to approach the U.S. Secretary of War to accede to the French demand to incorporate American companies or battalions into French units and to recommend this to General Pershing. Indeed, the French ambassador went to the War Department and read the dispatch to Secretary Baker. Baker then cabled its substance to Pershing.

This new effort to go behind Pershing's back and reach him through Washington prompted Pershing to send a sharp letter to Clemenceau ending with the angry phrase: "May I not suggest to you, Mr. President, the inexpediency of cabling such matters to Washington."[112] T. B. Mott, the American military attaché, in recalling this incident, added:

Clemenceau was furious. It was bad enough to have his plans miscarry, but to be called down by a mere soldier was gall and wormwood to a person who had so little liking for military men. Accustomed as he was to seeing generals bent to the will of politicians, it was a new experience to find that Wilson and Baker told their commander everything that was going behind his back and trusted his judgement more than that of a prime minister.[113]

Mott aired his suspicion that the aforementioned letter to Foch,[114] in which Clemenceau complained about the conduct of the American forces and suggested a change in their commander in chief, was in fact the result of this incident, for which the French politician never forgave the American general.[115]

Controversies over war aims between the Americans and other Allies never ceased. At the height of the German Spring Offensive in 1918, General Belin, the French military representative, gave a document to his American colleague, General Bliss. Prepared in the political branch of the French military section, it suggested that Bulgaria should be offered territorial compensation at the expense of Allies Serbia and Greece. Serbia had been heroic to the Allies at the time of the Austrian invasion in 1914, and the Greek statesman Eleutherios Venizelos brought Greece into the war. But at this point, Serbia had lost its value as a military factor, while Venizelos had difficulties with mutinies in the Greek army and had brought precious little material military aid to bear. It seemed to Bliss that the French plan served both French and Italian interests in the Mediterranean.

In a letter to the American Secretary of War dated May 11, 1918, Bliss wrote:

The policy may commend itself to diplomats who play with territories and peoples as we do with pawns on a chessboard, and it may appeal to some military men who may grasp at it as a means of beating the enemy, but to me it is repugnant. After leading up to the rather naive declaration that the time has come to "jettison cargo" or "throw out ballast" (by which he means Serbia and Greece), he [General Belin] suggests that this task might be assigned to our President "who has no engagements of any kind with respect to Serbia." I cannot think that this idea will take very strongly in the United States.

His conclusion was straightforward:

One thing is certain, that if we surrender our principles we will soon be floundering deeper and deeper in a very nasty mire. I doubt whether England will take kindly to General Belin's proposed policy. But it is hard to tell what nations will do in these days if they think that their straits are desperate enough.[116]

It is fitting to close this chapter with a statement made by General Bliss in his final report to the Secretary of State:

Napoleon was a great psychologist. He thoroughly understood the inherent weaknesses of national human nature. . . . He, himself, toward the end fought coalitions with coalitions. In some of his campaigns he brought together under his single control a group of peoples naturally hostile to each other, heterogeneous and dissimilar in national instincts and longings, but not so heterogeneous and dissimilar as the forces recently gathered from the ends of the earth—white, black, yellow and brown—to defeat the Central Powers. When he was successful in the

management of such a coalition, his success was due to absolute unity of
command, and, as a consequence of this unity, co-ordination of effort. He had
both political and military control.[117]

This investigation of these issues forms the basis for the following
chapters.

NOTES

1. Charles Julien Huguet, *Britain and the War*, London, 1928, p. 52.
2. Ibid., p. 67.
3. David Lloyd George, *War Memoirs of David Lloyd George*, vol. 1, London, 1936, p. 467.
4. Ibid., vol. 2, p. 1806.
5. Supra, p. 4.
6. Supra, pp. 3-4.
7. Joseph Jacques Césaire Joffre, *The Personal Memoirs of Joffre*, vol. 1, New York, 1932, p. 161.
8. Charles Edward Callwell, *Field-Marshal Sir Henry Wilson*, New York, 1927, p. 164.
9. John French, *1914*, Boston, 1919, pp. 36-37.
10. Edward L. Spears, *Liaison 1914*, London, 1930, p. 72.
11. Ibid., p. 73.
12. Ibid., p. 75.
13. Ibid., pp. 77-78.
14. Ibid., p. 503.
15. Ibid., p. 78.
16. Ibid., p. 79.
17. French, pp. 57-60.
18. Ibid., p. 75.
19. Spears, p. 201.
20. Joffre, p. 194.
21. Spears, p. 234.
22. French, p. 85.
23. Spears, p. 234.
24. Ibid., p. 236.
25. Ibid., pp. 237-38.
26. Huguet, pp. 67-68.
27. Spears, p. 298.
28. Ibid., p. 257.
29. Ibid., pp. 321-22; Huguet, pp. 80-81 (emphasis added).
30. French, p. 96.
31. The main sources for this controversy are: French; Spears; Huguet; Lord Maurice Hankey, *The Supreme Command 1914-18*, London, 1961; also the books published by Gerald French: *The Life of Field-Marshal Sir John French, First Earl of Ypres*, London, 1931; *French Replies to Haig*, London, 1936; and *Some War Diaries, Addresses and Correspondence of the Field-Marshal the Earl of Ypres*, London, 1937.

32. Huguet, p. 85.

33. Joffre, pp. 236, 250.

34. Ibid., p. 267.

35. Gerald French, *The Life*, p. 245.

36. Huguet, p. 156.

37. Callwell, vol. 1, pp. 216–17.

38. Ibid., p. 184.

39. Huguet, pp. 128–29 passim.

40. Joffre, p. 478.

41. Field Marshal Sir Douglas Haig, *The Private Papers of Douglas Haig, 1914–1919*, London, 1952, p. 122.

42. Joffre, p. 468.

43. Haig, p. 145.

44. Vide, e.g.: ibid., pp. 154, 171–73.

45. Edward L. Spears, *Prelude to Victory*, London, 1939, p. 61.

46. Haig, p. 203.

47. For the correspondence with the king, vide: ibid., pp. 203ff. As for reports of the Calais Conference and its aftermath, vide: Haig, pp. 198ff; Spears, *Prelude*, pp. 132ff, 546ff; Callwell, vol. 1, p. 324 (Wilson was not present).

48. Haig, p. 194.

49. Ibid., p. 162.

50. Ibid., p. 302.

51. Ibid., p. 307.

52. Supra, p. 5, n.2.

53. John J. Pershing, *My Experience in the World War*, vol. 1, New York, 1931, p. 95.

54. Ibid., vol. 2, pp. 119–20.

55. Ibid., vol. 1, p. 165.

56. Ibid., vol. 2, pp. 237–38.

57. Ibid., vol. 2, pp. 68–69.

58. W. K. Hancock and Jean van der Poel, eds., *Selections from the Smuts Papers*, vol. 3, Cambridge, England, 1966, pp. 661–62.

59. Frederick Palmer, *Newton D. Baker: America at War*, vol. 2, New York, 1931, p. 111.

60. Haig, p. 361.

61. John Monash, *War Letters of General Monash*, Sydney, 1934, pp. 107–8.

62. Ibid., p. 188.

63. Ibid.

64. Ibid., p. 245.

65. Ibid., p. 201.

66. Ibid., pp. 267–68.

67. Charles Bugnet, *Foch Speaks*, New York, 1929, p. 250.

68. Carl von Clausewitz, *On War*, Princeton, N.J., 1976, p. 607; see also: Jehuda L. Wallach, *The Dogma of the Battle of Annihilation*, Westport, Conn., 1986, pp. 12–16.

69. Raymond Poincaré, *The Memoirs of Raymond Poincaré*, vol. 4, New York, 1931, pp. 144–45.

70. Ibid., p. 145.

71. Ibid.

72. Joffre, p. 193.

73. Ibid., p. 178.

74. Poincaré, vol. 3, pp. 92–93.

75. Ibid., vol. 4, p. 74.

76. Joffre, pp. 243–45 passim.

77. Poincaré, vol. 4, pp. 50–51.

78. Joffre, p. 418.

79. Spears, *Prelude*, p. 443.

80. Joffre, p. 372.

81. Hankey, p. 411.

82. Joffre, p. 372.

83. Poincaré, vol. 4, p. 329.

84. William Robertson, *From Private to Fieldmarshal*, London, 1921, p. 278.

85. Pershing, vol. 2, p. 307.

86. Ferdinand Foch, *The Memoirs of Marshal Foch*, New York, 1931, pp. 434ff. The complexity of the relationship between the military and the politicians in France during World War I is investigated in detail by Jere Clemens King, *Generals and Politicians: Conflict between France's High Command, Parliament and Government, 1914–1918*, Berkeley, Calif., 1951.

87. Robertson, p. 279.

88. Haig, pp. 32–33.

89. Ibid., p. 172.

90. Supra, p. 24.

91. Joffre, p. 305.

92. John French, pp. 166ff; also Gerald French, *The Life*, p. 264.

93. John French, p. 180.

94. Supra, pp. 51–52.

95. John French, p. 112.

96. Lloyd George, vol. 1, p. 543.

97. William Robertson, *Soldiers and Statesmen 1914–1918*, vol. 1, London, 1926, p. 213.

98. Haig, p. 214.

99. Robertson, *Soldiers*, vol. 1, p. 180.

100. Haig, p. 239.

101. Callwell, vol. 1, p. 309.

102. Ibid., vol. 2, p. 79.

103. Robertson, *From Private*, pp. 334–35; also Winston S. Churchill, *The World Crisis 1911–1918*, London, 1964, p. 855.

104. Callwell, vol. 2, pp. 136–37.

105. Pershing, vol. 1, p. 39.

106. Ibid., pp. 39–40.

107. Ibid., p. 300. Entry of January 24, 1918.

108. Ibid., p. 106.

109. Frederick Palmer, *Bliss, Peacemaker*, New York, 1934, p. 220.

110. W. B. Fowler, *British-American Relations 1917–1918*, Princeton, N.J., 1969, p. 102.

111. Pershing, vol. 1, p. 257.

112. Thomas Bentley Mott, *Twenty Years as Military Attaché*, New York, 1979, p. 238.

113. Ibid.

114. Supra, p. 63.

115. Mott, p. 238.
116. Palmer, *Bliss*, pp. 306–7.
117. Ibid., p. 239.

5

COORDINATION CONFERENCES AND COORDINATION BODIES

In spite of agreements that were made before the war began, as described in Chapter 2, no practical measures were taken by the potential alliance partners to ensure that the coalition would function properly. In this context, General Joffre's critical afterthought has already been mentioned.[1] The lack of coordination in the initial phase of the war was criticized more precisely by Winston Churchill, then First Lord of the Admiralty. His analysis defined the full extent of the problem: The alliance suffered grievously at the beginning of the war from the want of a common clearing house where the different relative values of politics and strategy could be established and exchanged. He maintained that a single prolonged conference between the Allied chiefs, civil and martial, in January 1915 might have saved the alliance from inestimable misfortunes. Things could never be thrashed out by correspondence. Principals must meet, and plans must be concerted in common. Instead, each Allied state pursued more or less its own course, keeping the others informed. Armies and navies dwelt in every country in separate compartments. The war problem, which was all one, was approached from many different and disconnected standpoints. He stressed that war, which knows no rigid divisions between French, Russian and British Allies, between land, sea and air, between gaining victories and alliances, between supplies and fighting men, between propaganda and machinery, was in fact simply the sum of all forces and pressures operative at a given period, and was dealt with piecemeal. Therefore years of hard learning were necessary before even imperfect unifications of study, thought, command and action were achieved.[2]

Lord Hankey, the secretary of the British war cabinet, who was closely associated with the steps taken to assure a coordinated war effort, offered a verdict that was short and sharp: "No Power engaged in the war had thought out the problem of the Supreme Command and everyone blundered in this respect."[3]

FIRST STEPS TOWARD COORDINATION

Though the two Western Allies—France and Britain—exchanged liaison officers between their armies from the outset, General Joffre felt it necessary to convene a meeting between the commanders of the forces, particularly as he became aware of the strained relations between Field Marshal Sir John French and General Charles Louis Lanrezac, discussed in Chapter 4. The St. Quentin Conference was convened on August 26, 1914. The first of its kind, this conference is also dealt with in detail in Chapter 4 of this volume.[4] Although the results of the conference were, at the time, not too encouraging, it set the pattern for future meetings. Indeed, General Foch reported in his memoirs that on November 1, 1914, a conference was called in Dunkirk, which was attended by the French president, the Ministers of War and Finance, General Joffre, General Foch, Colonel Weygand (General Foch's chief of staff), British Secretary of State for War Lord Kitchener and the French ambassador to Great Britain. Due to the heavy losses sustained by France and Great Britain to this point, the main topic of this conference was the question of British reinforcements.[5]

On the political-strategic level, the three senior coalition partners considered it necessary to reinforce their alliance with an agreement not to conclude any separate peace with enemy powers. Although such a clause was already included in the Franco-Russian Military Convention of 1892, the British entry into the Allied camp led to the signing of the Pact of London on September 5, 1914, in which the British, French and Russian governments pledged themselves to make no separate peace.[6] As mentioned previously, Japan joined the Allies by declaring war on Germany, although for the time being no new coordination channels were created.

1915: GROPING FOR A SOLUTION

In 1915 Churchill lamented the lack of inter-Allied meetings. This sentiment is sustained by a remark in Lord Hankey's treatise on the Supreme Command. Relating to arguments in the British War Council on January 28, 1915, dealing with inter-Allied problems concerning support to Serbia, he wrote: "In later days, Ministers would at once have repaired to Paris, or, later still, to the Supreme War Council to have the matter sorted out."[7] However, from Lloyd George's memoirs it is apparent that in this very meeting referred to by Hankey, "Lord Kitchener had one more of those flashes which now and again cast their rays deep into the gloom of the stormy problems which were raging around us."[8] Lloyd George reported that Kitchener suggested that there should be a central authority where all the Allies were represented and full information was available. Moreover, attacks should be arranged to take place simultaneously.

The British War Council decided that while attending a meeting of Allied finance ministers in Paris, Lloyd George should avail himself of any favorable opportunity that might present itself to initiate the idea of a central body to provide the Allies with facilities for consultation. The purpose was greater coordination efforts. However, a disappointed Lloyd George reported that nothing came of the discussions at the time, since the French military authorities were obsessed with the notion that their Great Headquarters had, and ought to have, the supreme control of the land war. They were prepared to leave the naval direction to the British. However, their view was that as far as the Continent was concerned, the British had neither the forces nor the experience that entitled them to equality of authority in the strategy of the war. Lloyd George stated that Joffre was at that time the unchallenged dictator as far as the war direction was concerned.[9] From the diary of Lord Bertie, the British ambassador in Paris, and from Poincaré's memoirs, it is evident that in early February Lloyd George, in his capacity as Chancellor of the Exchequer, had not only met with the finance ministers of France and Russia (one of the rare occasions of meeting with high-ranking Russian officials), but had also discussed the problem of sending an inter-Allied military expedition to Salonika. As decided by the British government, he informed the French president of the advisability of setting up a council in France with representatives of the French, Russian and British commanders in chief. As already mentioned, the response to this suggestion was negative.[10]

In the meantime, the scope of the Entente was to become enlarged when Italy joined the Allies. The secret diplomatic negotiations were conducted in London. At first it was assumed that Italy would declare war only on Austria, during the second part of May. In order to straighten out the necessary military and naval arrangements for Italy's entry into the war, a conference was convened in Paris at the end of April between French, Russian and British naval and military experts on one side, and Italian naval and military delegates on the other side. The conference was presided over by the French war minister. The French were represented by General Joffre's chief of staff, the British by officers from the Admi-

ralty and the War Office, the Russians by their military attaché in Paris
and the Italians by a colonel of their armed forces.[11] In spite of this
meeting, Italy was not invited to any inter-Allied conference until May
1916.

In the meantime, a crisis erupted in connection with the unexpected
increased need for weapons and ammunition. The British War Council
decided to arrange a conference at the earliest moment between the French
military authorities and Minister of Munitions on the one hand and the
British military authorities and Minister of Munitions on the other with a
view to arriving at a common basis for computing the number and caliber
of guns and the quantity and natures of ammunition necessary to ensure
the success of the next great offensive operation on the western front.

This conference was scheduled for June 19, 1915, at Boulogne. Lloyd
George commented that this turned out to be a momentous decision, for
in the sequel it undoubtedly revolutionized the whole of ideas as to the
scale and character of the requirements of the British army. He added that
the situation that had arisen abroad was illustrated in the lack of contact
between the Allies on vital matters. In fact, each of the Allied countries
was running its own war on and behind the various fronts.[12]

The next important step to improve coordination of war effort was made
on July 7 in a meeting of the Allies at Chantilly, the seat of the French
Great Headquarters (GQG). This meeting was partly the result of a
memorandum of July 3 that was presented to the British cabinet:

(i) To discuss the whole policy of the war as soon as possible with French.
To bring about a consultation with representatives (statesmen as well as soldiers)
of the French government, with a view to an early round-table conference at
which all the Allies will be represented.

(ii) An inquiry should be set on foot as soon as possible on the means for
financing a long war . . .

(iii) A definite establishment for our military effort should be arranged after
consultation with the French.[13]

Indeed, on July 6, an inter-Allied conference was held in Calais (instead
of in Paris, as planned). It was attended by the British and French prime
ministers and their chief colleagues, General Joffre and Sir John French.
In retrospect, Hankey, who participated in almost all the conferences, felt
that this was not one of the more fruitful reunions of its kind. Nevertheless,
he commented that it marked an important point in the development of the
Supreme Command of the Allies, as it was the first formal conference to
be attended by the prime ministers and some of their leading colleagues.

The next day, the first inter-Allied military conference of the war was held at Joffre's headquarters at Chantilly. Alexandre Millerand, the French War Minister, presided. In addition to General Joffre, Field Marshal French and their chief staff officers, there were representatives of the Belgian, Italian, Russian and Serbian armies.[14]

After the meeting, the French ambassador in St. Petersburg revealed how the decisions of this conference were understood in Russia. In his diary he quoted General Joffre's demand that if one Allied army faced the main enemy onslaught, the other partners at their fronts would be compelled to rush to the aid of the one who was under attack. He praised the Russians for taking the offensive in August and September 1914 in order to ease the enemy pressure on the French and British forces in France. Now it was the turn of the other partners to render assistance to the hard-pressed Russian armies. Joffre then enumerated the tasks of the different Allies, in particular at the French and Balkan fronts, and concluded that it was an unavoidable matter of honor for the Franco-British and the Serbo-Italian armies to start their offensives as soon as possible. This resolution was unanimously agreed upon by the conference.[15]

In October 1915, General Henry Wilson suggested that the British cabinet adopt a resolution stating that the British and French governments should agree not to repeat ventures like Antwerp, the Dardanelles, Asia Minor or Salonika until the problem had been thoroughly discussed at a meeting of six persons—the two foreign ministers, the two war ministers and the two commanders in chief. But this step was not taken.[16] It may be assumed, however, that Wilson's suggestion triggered the speech British Prime Minister Herbert Asquith gave in the House of Commons on November 2, 1915. He attached great importance to a more complete and intimate coordination between the staffs of the Allied powers. He felt there should also be a more intimate and regular interchange by some combination not only with the staffs of the War Office and the Admiralty, but with those who conducted diplomatic affairs. He stressed that it was impossible to carry on these things in watertight compartments. There had to be coordination of contact—close, constant, practical, continuing.[17]

An important step in the right direction was taken in the fall of 1915. French War Minister Alexandre Millerand established a direct, personal relationship with British Secretary of War Lord Kitchener by appointing as liaison officer a very able young captain, who soon won the confidence of all those he came in contact with. After a change in the French government, the same officer was promoted by Prime Minister Aristide Briand to act as liaison officer not merely between the two war ministers but also between the two prime ministers.[18]

On September 11, a conference convened in Calais that was attended by the French and British war ministers, French Generals Joffre and Sarrail, and British Field Marshal French and General Wilson. The issue was the dispatch of four French divisions to the Dardanelles.[19]

In early November, General Robertson, who was not yet appointed CIGS, recommended to the prime minister that the British government assume a more prominent role in the war policy. He claimed that until then the French had had it all their own way and without full reflection had embarked on an expedition in the Balkans.[20]

On November 16, 1915, the British War Committee went to Paris to discuss the question of the evacuation of Gallipoli and the landing at Alexandretta. Kitchener recommended both actions. The situation on the Salonika front was also investigated. Hankey reported that a positive result of this meeting was the approval in principle of a sort of embryo constitution for future conferences. The British prime minister was invited to work out the details. Hankey brought the draft for the approval of the War Committee after the delegation's return from France. It was then sent to the French prime minister via the French liaison officer. After a considerable interchange of views, it was adopted and initialled by both prime ministers at a conference in January 1916.[21]

Meanwhile, in early December, representatives of the two governments met again at Calais to discuss the British demand to evacuate Salonika. The decisions that were reached caused a serious political crisis in France, and then in Great Britain. As the next step, a military conference was convened at Chantilly December 6 through 8. In fact, this conference was the first effort by all the Allies to establish some sort of framework for the future conduct of the war. Joffre considered this attempt to be all the more pressing because it was during the course of these autumn months that the profound divergencies of view had manifested, especially in regard to the Orient. In Joffre's memoirs, he recorded that those present at this three-day meeting included Field Marshal French, Lieutenant General Murray (the CIGS), General Shilinski (Chief of the Russian Military Mission at the French Great Headquarters), General Porro (Assistant Chief of the Italian Army), General Wielemans (Chief of the General Staff of the Belgian Army) and Colonel Stephanovitch (Serbian Military Attaché in France). During these meetings all the problems were studied, and Joffre suggested a plan of action that was accepted unanimously except for the principle of the retention of forces at Salonika, which was contested by the British representatives.

Later, the participants unanimously affirmed the necessity of establishing a defensive posture in Salonika. According to Joffre, the outcome of these conversations was to draw up a document that in fact constituted the charter of the coalition during the winter of 1915–1916 and the summer campaign of 1916. Nevertheless, while these decisions revealed general agreement on many issues, the conference emphasized the fact that each of the Allies had interests that were particularly vital to them. At Chantilly, general agreement was also reached on the need to provide munitions for Russia. The preliminary work for this decision had been accomplished at an inter-Allied munitions conference that met in London from November 23 to December 1.[22]

In Poincaré's diary, the entry for the last day of 1915 indicated that Prime Minister Briand wanted to create a diplomatic organization with periodical sessions of the Allies, to take place at Paris, similar to the military conference over which Joffre presided in December. He wrote that London and Petrograd had accepted the idea but there was as yet no reply from Rome. He asked the question whether the materialization of the project would contribute to the unanimity in decisions and to greater rapidity in actions. He hoped so. But he added that a conference was far from being the same thing as unity of command.[23]

Thus at the end of 1915, the solution for a coordinated war effort was still a long way off.

1916: STILL NO SOLUTION

Following the Chantilly Conference in December 1915, Joffre called another inter-Allied military conference for March 12, 1916, and convinced Prime Minister Briand to convene an Allied conference to be held in Paris on March 27. This conference was attended by political and military representatives of all the Allies and was by far the largest to that date. Joffre communicated to the conference the proceedings and conclusions of the military conference. His recommendations were accepted by the conference without discussion. It then proceeded to deal with the problems of munitions, labor for factories and transportation. It was decided to establish a permanent committee to coordinate economic matters and to organize an international freight bureau. These were definite steps toward international cooperation.[24]

Nevertheless, in the meantime, Robertson, who had advanced to the position of Chief of the Imperial General Staff, was not very satisfied with this procedure of inter-Allied conferences. "The conferences were assembled on no kind of system," he maintained, either as to time, place, or purpose, while all the attempts to regularize them failed because so many people were concerned that it was impossible to make arrangements to suit the convenience of everybody. When arranged, they had more than once to be deferred, adjourned, or abandoned altogether, because some unforeseen event, such as the sudden irruption of political troubles at home, made it undesirable for the Ministers of one country or another to be absent from their posts. . . . The number of people present rendered the preservation of secrecy and the prompt dispatch of business impossible. It was seldom that less than a score would attend, and when all countries were represented the number might amount to as many as a hundred, made up of Prime Ministers, Ministers for Foreign Affairs, Army, Navy, Munitions, and Finance, Ambassadors, Commanders-in-Chief, and other technical delegates, secretaries, assistant secretaries, and interpreters.

Robertson's final verdict was: "No body less suitable to be entrusted with the supreme management of the war could have been devised."[25]

As mentioned previously, Italy declared war on Austria-Hungary on May 23, 1915, but not on Germany. The Italians felt somewhat left out because they were not invited to all the conferences between France and Great Britain. There was still no definite liaison between these three countries. The British wanted to improve relations with the new partner, especially since Italian CIGS General Cadorna had visited London during the second half of March 1916. The British prime minister therefore decided to utilize the Allied conference in Paris, in which the Italians participated, and to continue his journey to Rome and also to accept Cadorna's invitation to visit the Italian army. In spite of serious domestic troubles at home, Asquith visited Italy from March 31 until April 4. However, Italy only declared war on Germany on August 28, 1916.

During all of 1916, a series of meetings between the French and British were conducted concerning the controversial issue of the Balkan front. In addition to the Allies' continued deliberations at Joffre's headquarters, meetings that included the Russian representative, the question was aired at a special Anglo-French conference held in London on June 9 at which the British prime minister was accompanied by almost the entire War Committee.[26] On August 27, 1916, Romania joined the Entente, declaring war on Austria-Hungary. Additional conferences dealing with the war in the Balkans were held in Boulogne between French and British statesmen and soldiers on October 20, and again in Paris on November 15 and 16. The controversies were vaguely settled by compromise.

Another subject that occupied the Western Allies during the first half of 1916 was the supply of war material to Russia. For the planned Allied offensives, it was absolutely essential to properly equip the Russian multitudes. However, Russia's own supplies were totally inadequate. In April it became clear that the shortage was more serious than had been assumed. The French government sent two ministers to make inquiries. They arrived in Russia in May. Although Alfred W. Knox, the British liaison officer with the Russian army, wrote in his memoirs that "the French visit undoubtedly did good,"[27] the situation did not improve substantially. The tragic sequel was, as Knox reported, that "early in May Lord Kitchener told Count Benkendorf [the Russian Ambassador in London] that he would like to visit Russia if given an official invitation. The Emperor, when informed by M. Sazonoff, said he could receive him after June 10."[28] Although Kitchener's biographer presents the story in reverse, namely that "in early May the Emperor caused it to be known that he had long cherished the wish that Lord Kitchener should pay a visit to Russia,"[29] it is obvious from Knox's memoirs, as well as from those of Samuel Hoare, the new British ambassador in St. Petersburg, that this visit was in fact imposed on the Russians and that the British representatives in Russia recommended dropping the idea.[30]

However, because Kitchener drowned en route to Russia, one can only speculate what the outcome of this mission might have been. The subject of the relationship between the Western and the Eastern Allies remained on the agenda of the conferences, and in November Lloyd George urged progress. He suggested that the statesmen and generals of the great Western powers should confer with the statesmen and generals of the eastern front, taking for their program the examination of the situation in its entirety, and more particularly the military situation in the East. He stressed that the object of this conference had to be to determine what it was possible to do on the eastern front and the nature and importance of the help that was judged to be necessary. Above all, the statesmen and generals of the West ought to explain clearly to the statesmen and generals of the East the limits that were imposed on the possible efforts in the Salonika region. Lloyd George maintained that since the dismissal of M. Sazonoff in Russia, only two men there could speak with authority: the emperor and General Alexeieff. Since at that moment it was impossible for either of them to come to the West, it was of capital importance that the generals and statesmen competent to represent the Western powers with the fullest authority should go to Russia as promptly as possible in order to discuss these questions, which were vital for the conduct of the war.[31] However, this proposition was only to materialize later, when it was already too late.

On November 15 and 16, an additional conference on the situation in the Balkans was convened in Chantilly. In this context it is interesting to compare the reports in the memoirs of Haig and Joffre. While their reports are not identical, the discrepancies are certainly not simply the result of language differences. They reflect different approaches to the problems discussed. Among the joint resolutions was the paragraph on mutual support. The members of the conference renewed the undertaking for mutual assistance adopted by the conference on December 5, 1915, and fully observed by all throughout the course of the present year, namely, that if one of the powers was attacked, the others should come immediately to its help to the full limit of their resources, whether indirectly by attacks that the armies not assaulted by the enemy would carry out upon prepared zones, or directly by means of the dispatch of forces between theaters of operations linked by easy communications. For this latter eventuality, studies of transport and of the employment of combined forces were to be undertaken between the French, English and Italian headquarters staffs.[32]

It was also decided that the conclusions of this conference were to be ratified by another conference that was to take place at the czar's headquarters in Russia. From an entry in General Wilson's diary of November 26, it is clear that Lloyd George told him that a meeting was to be held in Petrograd in a fortnight or so, at which the next year's plan of campaign was to be decided. The French would send Castelnau and others, and the choice of the British representatives was either Wilson or Lord French. Grey would also go. The delegation was assured a carte blanche.[33]

In the interim, there were personnel changes in the political and the military arena: in Britain, Lloyd George became prime minister; in France, General Nivelle was appointed commander in chief of the French forces on the western front. He immediately caused tension between the two commanders in chief: Haig and himself. Churchill explained the source of this tension in December 1916.

These discussions—not to say disputes—between the French and British Headquarters upon the share which each should assume upon the front, were continuous throughout the war. All followed the same course: the French dwelt on the number of kilometers they guarded, the British on the number of German divisions by which they were confronted, and each reinforced these potent considerations by reminding their Ally that they were about to deliver or sustain a major offensive.[34]

To summarize the nondecisive coordination efforts in 1916, it should be mentioned that at the end of February, the admirals of the navies operating in the Mediterranean—French, British and Italian—were ordered to confer in Malta, to attempt to solve the naval problems in this theater of operations. British Admiral Sir Roger Keyes summed up this conference by saying rather optimistically, "After ten days we parted company the best of friends, having improved the Allied cooperation in the Mediterranean very considerably."[35]

Keyes's optimism notwithstanding, Robertson's critical presentation of the handicaps of the inter-Allied conferences has already been presented. Nevertheless, one more critical observation emphasizes his view. He explained that the proceedings were prolonged, or rather tedious, because they usually had to be conducted in two languages, in French and in English. It was obvious that some of the English representatives could neither speak nor understand French, whilst most of the French and the other foreign representatives had little or no knowledge of English. Therefore, not only did the greater part of the discussions have to be duplicated, but while it was being interpreted for those who had not understood the original, those who had understood it were usually engaging in whispered conversation amongst themselves and thus distracted the attention of those who were trying to listen to the translation. Moreover, the translation, as was usually the case, did not always convey the intended meaning. Therefore, often further explanation had to be made in order to clear away possible misunderstandings. There was no doubt that ministers and others were at a great disadvantage if they did not possess a fair working knowledge of French—the language used by practically all the Allied representatives except the British and the Americans.[36]

1917: ITALIAN DISASTER PAVES THE WAY FOR A SOLUTION

Lloyd George was not the only one to feel that when the Russians attended the inter-Allied conferences that were convened in the West, they were not represented by top-level, authoritative statesmen and soldiers. In fact, the Russians felt this themselves.[37] On the other hand, from Hoare's memoirs, one understands that whereas the czar was prepared to accept advice from a great and esteemed general like Kitchener, neither he, the Russian government nor the Russian people wanted an Allied mission to give them advice. True, they needed munitions, and they even needed some advice from distinguished officers like Kitchener or Foch. However, when it came to the gathering of the British, French and Italian politicians—officers and experts flocked into Petrograd on January 29, 1917— the Russians saw only an insulting annoyance at this trying time. Hoare maintained that the Russians were too polite not to accept the Allied offer of a conference in Russia. However, as he recorded rather cynically: let the delegation come; the Russians would see to it that the delegation did not cause any damage. The simplest way to achieve this was by not allowing the delegates to do anything, by the polite strategy of involving them in a series of receptions and banquets.[38]

This is more or less what happened between January 29 and February 21. The conference had been split up into three commissions: political, military and technical. From the beginning it was obvious that the delegates, in spite of the carte blanche mentioned by General Wilson, had no power to decide on vital issues.[39] Even if the outcome of this conference had been more decisive, it would not have prevented the Russian Revolution, the first waves of which erupted a fortnight after the departure of the Western delegates from Petrograd.

A meeting to discuss the Macedonian theater of war was held in London at the end of December 1916. The delegates, representatives of the French cabinet and their British counterparts, reached no decision. As a result, Lloyd George proposed an additional meeting to be held in Italy. In fact, this meeting preceded the Petrograd Conference. After the first plenary session of the Rome Conference, the participants were divided into two groups: one for politicians, the other for soldiers. In his diary, General Wilson recorded that Lloyd George had prepared a Memorandum on Strategy with regard to the Romanian, Salonikan and Italian fronts. The interesting fact is, this document was written without either consultation with or the knowledge or approval of Robertson, the CIGS. "Robertson very cross," Wilson recalled.[40]

Indeed, Lloyd George proposed a massive attack on the Austrian front rather than renewing the offensive in France. This was to be waged mainly by Italian troops supported by an enormous concentration of Anglo-French batteries. The French, already under Nivelle's influence, opposed the plan, as did Robertson. In his memoirs, Aldrovandi Luigi Marescotti, the Italian diplomat who participated in the conference, regretted that the Italians, too, had not accepted Lloyd George's offer of military support for the Italian front.[41] In fact, the Rome Conference of January 1917 also ended with a compromise, a fact that is reflected in the first paragraph of the final conclusions: "The Conference agrees in principle that in the future there should be closer co-operation between the Allies than in the past. They further agree that in the future more frequent conferences are necessary."[42]

The next event in these inter-Allied relations was rather surprising. As the train taking Lloyd George home from Rome waited at the Gare du Nord in Paris, General Nivelle boarded it and presented his plan for the future offensive in France. Churchill recalled that the first impressions on both sides were favorable. As a result, Nivelle was invited to London to meet with the war cabinet on January 15. Churchill remarked that Lloyd George's resistance to the new offensive plan melted rapidly after the meeting at the Gare du Nord. He soon transformed into an ardent supporter.[43]

For this meeting, Haig and Robertson were summoned to London. A memorandum formally approving a renewed offensive on the western front to begin not later than April 1 was drawn up and signed by all three generals. Haig recorded that these conclusions were hastily considered by the War Committee.[44]

In order to understand further developments, it is necessary to follow Churchill's analysis of the decision. He hinted that so far all had been harmonious. However, the prime minister, in the process of becoming converted from his previous opposition to the offensive, had evolved a further design. He was already set upon his great and simple conception of a united command. He believed that better war direction could be obtained from the French. He also believed—and in this case with more justification—that one single commanding hand ought to prevail on the whole of the western front. Churchill quoted Lloyd George, who later in the war had said: "It is not that one General is better than another, but that one General is better than two."[45] As a matter of fact, Nivelle returned to Chantilly carrying the promise of the prime minister that Haig and the British army would be subordinated to his directions. However, "these important additional developments were not at this stage imparted by the Prime Minister or the War Cabinet to either Robertson or Haig."[46] This important fact sets the stage for the next dramatic event, which was mentioned in another context:[47] the Calais Conference of February 26.

This conference was convened ostensibly as a meeting between the Allied political and military leaders to discuss problems of transportation. No hint was given to Haig beforehand that the question of command in the coming offensive was even under consideration. Nor was the CIGS any better informed. In fact, the decision to place Haig under Nivelle had been secretly agreed upon between Lloyd George, Briand and Nivelle some days earlier, and was confirmed on February 24 at a meeting of the British war cabinet, which the CIGS was not invited to. For some reason Lord Derby, the Secretary for War, was also not informed of this decision, and only learned what had happened at the cabinet after the end of the Calais Conference. It is hardly surprising that when they found themselves confronted at Calais by proposals drastically changing the status of the British army, Haig and Robertson regarded themselves as having been double-crossed by their prime minister. After extreme tension among the

British and between the British and the French, the sharp-witted Hankey produced a document that was finally signed by all concerned: British and French, statesmen and soldiers. This "formula," as Hankey called it, provided that because the object of the forthcoming operations was to drive the enemy from French soil, and as the French army was larger than the British, the general direction of the campaign should be in the hands of the French C in C. The British war cabinet would endeavor to direct their C in C to have his plans conform with the general strategy of the French C in C. This measure was to apply both during the period of preparation for the operations and during their execution.

If Haig felt that Nivelle's instructions were endangering either the safety of his army or the prospects of success, he could have refused to conform, but in that event he was to report immediately to the British government. He was to be free to choose the means he would employ and the method of using his troops in the sector allotted to him by Nivelle. An addition, agreed to at the final meeting, provided that each government was to judge when its army's operations should be considered terminated. When the operations were, in fact, terminated, the agreement was no longer in force. In other words, the agreement applied only for this particular battle.[48] Thus, this conference ended with a compromise, and resulted in bad feeling on both sides. Churchill concluded this episode by recording that the intimate cooperation that had existed so long between the British and the French staffs had undergone a noticeable decline.[49]

In spite of the compromise reached in Calais, the controversies between Haig and Nivelle gained momentum. It was therefore essential to convene another conference, this time in London, to iron out all the difficulties. On March 12 and 13, Lloyd George employed all his diplomatic abilities, partly in private conversations with Haig and with Nivelle, to reach additional compromises.[50] However, Haig added the following amendment to the document he finally signed:

I agree with the above on the understanding that, while I am fully determined to carry out the Calais Agreement in spirit and in letter, the British Army and its Commander-in-Chief will be regarded by General Nivelle as allies and not as subordinates, except during the particular operations which he explained at the Calais Conference.[51]

The disappointing results of the so-called Nivelle Offensive are well known, and generated further delay in attempts to coordinate the war effort.

When the United States entered the war on the side of the Entente, and declared war on Germany on April 6, 1917, the scope of the Allied camp was considerably enlarged. In fact, until the end of the war, this alliance numbered thirty-four members (including six members from the British Commonwealth).[52] This addition of a new and important partner, rich in resources and manpower, demanded new approaches in the coordination process. Tasker H. Bliss's essay, which was discussed in Chapter 3,[53] states that "shortly after April 6, 1917, there began to arrive and to establish themselves in Washington military, naval and financial missions from the Allied governments in Europe with whom we had, from that date, associated ourselves in war against the Central Powers."[54] However, the actual integration of the Americans into the common war effort was rather slow.

The unsuccessful Allied offensives on the western front in the spring of 1917 and the unexpected disaster of Caporetto on the Italian front in October 1917 led Lloyd George to consider more seriously a better way to conduct the Allied war effort. In order to understand the new developments, it is of interest to trace his train of thought. He reached the conclusion that a mere change in commanders and War Office advisers would not alter the intrinsic defect that led to the failures in Allied strategy. He observed that the French had changed their commanders in chief and their chiefs of staff repeatedly, but nothing had happened except a change in the signature appended to War Office documents. He concluded, therefore, that the removal of Haig and Robertson would not touch the real problem, but that there should be a more thorough and essential change in the whole method of conduct of Allied strategy if the war was to be won. His opinion was that the only way out of the impasse was to set up an authoritative inter-Allied body that would have its own staff and its own Intelligence Department who, working together, would review the battle-field as a whole and select the most promising sector for concentrated action. The essential conditions for the efficacious working of such a body would be constant touch between the various GHQs, but it should be entirely independent of their control. The experts chosen for the task should be men of unquestioned ability and mastery of their respective professions. Ministers should be represented on that body so that they could be consulted on questions of policy while plans were being considered. Until this time campaign plans had been submitted to the governments only after they had been formulated and fashioned and agreed to by the military staffs in every detail. But it was the governments alone who could decide such vital questions as the available manpower, shipping, finance, blockade and diplomatic expedients. In fact, hitherto plans had been prepared to the last details without the governments ever being consulted. Lloyd George's verdict was that no sound plans could be formed by such methods. Moreover, naval experts must also constitute an integral element in the composition of the inter-Allied staff, since sea power was the decisive factor in the end. He observed that up to 1917 there had not even been one inter-Allied naval conference. Lloyd George was amazed by the fact that with full knowledge of the importance of sea power, statesmen and naval experts had not to this date been called into effective consultation when campaigns for the coming year were being settled by the military chiefs. They were consulted only when a particular operation was dependent on the active cooperation of the navy—as for instance, in the case of Gallipoli and the battle for clearing the Flanders coast. He pointed out that this was taking much too narrow a view of the vast battle area of the war, since the sea front was as essential to victory as the western or any other front. It was impossible to rightly judge the wisdom or other aspects of the general campaign without thoroughly understanding how the command of the sea would affect the military situation and especially the economic conditions that determined the equipment and morale of the various belligerents. His conclusion was straightforward, that campaigns must therefore be prepared taking the naval situation into account as an essential element.[55]

He also reached the conclusion that the real weakness of Allied strategy was that it never existed! Instead of one single great war with united fronts, there were at least six separate and distinct wars, with a separate, distinct and independent strategy for each. There was a lack of unity of concept, coordination of effort or pooling of resources in order to deal the enemy the hardest knocks at his weakest point.

The prime minister had also a severe view of the military conferences conducted to date. These two-day conferences of great generals, which were held late each autumn to determine the campaign for the ensuing year, were in his opinion only an elaborate handshaking reunion. All of them had come to the meetings with their plans in their pockets. Nothing was discussed.[56]

From the moment Lloyd George reached these conclusions, he asked Field Marshal John French to formulate recommendations for the creation of an independent inter-Allied body to direct the war. French emphasized the extreme desirability of establishing at once a Superior Council of the Allies, because only such a body could thoroughly examine a joint scheme of action in all its bearings. He recommended that the representatives of the Allied powers should meet together without delay to discuss the immediate formation and establishment of a Superior War Council. He suggested that this body be comprised of the prime ministers or their selected representatives and one or more general from each Allied country. This Supreme Council was to begin immediately, first to assess the general situation and then to formulate plans.[57]

Lloyd George wasted no time, and urged the British war cabinet to discuss this matter and make a decision. On November 2, the cabinet decided to accept in principle the proposal for the establishment of a Supreme Inter-Allied War Council consisting of the prime minister and one other minister, who would meet at frequent intervals together with a Permanent Inter-Allied Advisory General Staff composed of one general officer from each of the principal Allies. On this occasion the cabinet also decided that the British military representative would be General Wilson.[58]

Under the impact of the collapse of the Italian front, the statesmen and generals from France, Great Britain and Italy met on November 7, 1917, in the small Italian town of Rapallo and signed the final draft for the formation of a Supreme Inter-Allied War Council, based on the British cabinet decision made five days earlier:

I. The representatives of the British, French and Italian Governments assembled at Rapallo on the 7th November, 1917, have agreed on the scheme for the organisation of a Supreme War Council with a Permanent Military Representative from each Power, contained in the following paragraph.

SCHEME OF ORGANISATION OF A SUPREME WAR COUNCIL

II. (1) With a view to the better co-ordination of military action on the Western Front a Supreme War Council is created, composed of the Prime Minister and a Member of the Government of each of the Great Powers whose armies are fighting on that front. The extension of the scope of the Council to other fronts is reserved for discussion with other Great Powers.

(2) The Supreme War Council has for its mission to watch over the general conduct of the War. It prepares recommendations for the decision of the Governments, and keeps itself informed of their execution and reports thereon to the respective Governments.

(3) The General Staffs and Military Commands of the Armies of each Power charged with the conduct of military operations remain responsible to their respective Governments.

(4) The general war plans drawn up by the competent Military Authorities are submitted to the Supreme War Council, which under the high authority of the Governments, ensures their concordance, and submits, if need be, any necessary changes.

(5) Each Power delegates to the Supreme War Council one Permanent Military Representative whose executive function is to act as technical adviser to the Council.

(6) The Military Representatives receive from the Government and the competent Military Authorities of their country all the proposals, information and documents relating to the conduct of the War.

(7) The Military Representatives watch day by day the situation of the forces, and of the means of all kinds of which the Allied Armies and the enemy armies dispose.

(8) The Supreme War Council meets normally at Versailles, where the Permanent Military Representatives and their Staffs are established. They may meet at other places as may be agreed upon, according to circumstances. The meetings of the Supreme War Council will take place at least once a month.

III. The Permanent Military Representatives will be as follows:

For France	General Foch
For Great Britain	General Wilson
For Italy	General Cadorna

Rapallo, 7th November, 1917.[59]

In order to integrate the United States into the decision-making process after it joined the Allied camp, on September 26, 1917, Sir William Wiseman wrote a letter to Colonel House, President Wilson's personal adviser. In it he asked whether the president would consider sending envoys to London and Paris, "with the object of taking part in the next great Allied Council . . . and also to arrange . . . for some machinery to bridge over the distance between Washington and the theatre of War."[60] On October 15, Lord Reading, British special envoy to the United States, informed the president that "I am now authorized by the French and British Governments to express their earnest hope that it will prove possible for your Government to send a representative to Europe to discuss important military and other questions of vital interest to co-belligerents."[61] From Bliss's biography, it is evident that after the Rapallo Conference, Lloyd George appealed to Colonel House to assist in gaining the president's support for America to join the Supreme War Council. General Bliss vigorously pressed House to cable to President Wilson to ask for his agreement. Wilson replied that he not only favored the plan, but insisted on it. He also asked House to attend the next council session, with Bliss as military adviser.[62]

It is apparent from General Pershing's memoirs that the soldiers were not pleased with this new organization. Pershing drew attention to subparagraph (4), which indicated that the British "Prime Minister had it in mind to assume greater control of operations. . . . While the Commanders-in-Chief of the armies concerned were expected to attend meetings of the Council . . . they were not members and had no vote."[63] Pershing also revealed that the creation of the Supreme War Council did not enjoy universal approval. In particular the commanders of the British and French armies opposed it. Pershing reported that the British army viewed it with considerable suspicion, thinking it might substitute politicians for professional soldiers in formulating strategy. He concluded his presentation saying that the formation of this council indicated a realization that Allied success in the future would depend upon better coordination of effort. The action of the prime ministers was a step in the direction of unified command. However, he added, somewhat cynically, that this was without any doubt one reason why most British as well as French officers, and a considerable number of those in high civil positions, were lukewarm toward it.[64]

The Supreme War Council (SWC) created at Rapallo on November 7, 1917, convened in eighteen sessions until March 1919.[65] Secretary Baker's biographer remarked that "the only practical goal as the result of the latest disaster [Caporetto] was *unity of policy under several leaders.* Unity of command was not to be attained until after another disaster."[66] Attention should be given to the fact that in the SWC only the great partners of the coalition were represented: Great Britain, France, Italy and the United States. All other partners in the alliance were not included.

1918: THE ENEMY IMPOSES UNIFIED COMMAND

As already indicated, the creation of the SWC was undoubtedly an important step toward a satisfactory solution of a well-concerted Allied war effort. However, this new system was still affected by many weaknesses, in particular by the covert and overt opposition of Robertson, the British CIGS, and Haig, the C in C of the BEF. In the introduction to Haig's papers, his editor states that both British soldiers considered the new arrangement principally to be a means for Lloyd George to bypass them, because he profoundly mistrusted their advice. Up to this point, however, he had not dared to dismiss them. As a result, he was faced with a dilemma. Lloyd George either had to accept their strategic advice, which he did not believe, or he had to reject it and incur the reproach of being an ignorant civilian who disregarded the advice of military experts. Haig and Robertson reasoned that the new committee at Versailles provided an alternative source of military advice, which Lloyd George *could* consult. To ensure that this advice would be more congenial than that which came from the CIGS, Lloyd George appointed General Sir Henry Wilson as the British military representative. He was known to be Haig's and

Robertson's opponent, and his promotion was a direct insult to the High Command.

At the end of January 1918, the prime minister made a decision that brought this state of affairs to a head. Together with Clemenceau, the new French premier, he decided to give executive as well as advisory power to the military representatives at Versailles. They decided to establish a General Reserve of British and French divisions, which would be under the command of a committee consisting of the Allied military representatives at Versailles, under Generals Foch and Wilson. This intention evoked a crisis. Robertson detested the Versailles Committee. He suspected that this new arrangement would in fact make Wilson a sort of second CIGS, with the power to move British troops independently of Haig and Robertson. The two British generals concerned, particularly Robertson, regarded this as intolerable.[67]

The question of the creation of a General Reserve was discussed at the third session of the SWC at Versailles from January 30 to February 2, 1918. On the final day, the council accepted a proposal to appoint General Foch president of the committee to deal with the General Reserve, to issue orders to the commanders in chief concerning when and where it would be used, and to determine its strength in consultation with the C in Cs. Haig noted in his diary that to some extent it made Foch a "Generalissimo." He added that he and Pétain, the French C in C, had a good relationship and that no coordinating authority was necessary.[68] In fact, this indicates that at this juncture, the General Reserve was still an illusion. This state of affairs is also reflected by Palmer, author of the biography of the U.S. Secretary of War:

Meanwhile, the Allied whispering galleries had an idea that the reserve actually existed. Warning had been sent to all the Allied censorships that no mention must be made of the size, location, and composition of that reserve—which actually consisted of one Ferdinand Foch, a bow-legged little French general aged sixty-six, and his faithful right-hand man, General Weygand, with their orderlies.[69]

The fourth session of the council, which was convened in London in mid-March, dealt primarily with the question of the requisition of Dutch ships. Since Holland was a neutral country, such a step had implications under international law. The assumption was that it would not bring Holland into the war on Germany's side. However, there was still a question whether the Allies should bring Holland into the war on their side. General Bliss maintained that the proposed Allied action would certainly become known to Germany, which would then declare war on Holland. He questioned whether the Allies could render immediate assistance to Holland. This became the central issue of the fourth council session. This dilemma illustrates that the council was forced to deal with compromises involving military expediency, laws and ethical standards. The sixth session of the SWC, which was in Versailles on June 3, 1918, agreed not to try to get Holland into the war secretly.[70]

On March 21, 1918, the long-expected German Spring Offensive began, resulting in a breakthrough on the British Fifth Army's thinly held front. It soon became apparent that the General Reserve was nonexistent, and the arrangements between the two C in Cs—Haig and Pétain—were worthless. Moreover, on March 24, Pétain indicated to Haig both that he could not render any assistance to the British and that he intended to fall back on Paris, regardless of the need to preserve contact with the British army. Haig reported the situation to the British war minister and General Wilson, the CIGS, who had succeeded Robertson. They rushed to the front in France and on March 26 a conference of Allied leaders convened at Doullens, where a resolution was drawn up and signed, charging General Foch with coordinating the actions of the Allied armies on the western front. He was to come to an understanding with the generals in chief, who were invited to furnish him with all necessary information.

In General Bliss's article, he observed that many persons thought that this action made General Foch the Allied commander in chief. But this was not the case. His functions were limited to the British and French armies and did not extend to the American army. No American attended the conference at Doullens. No control was given over the Belgian or the Italian armies. Moreover, he was not given any power of command. He could only consult and advise. Little wonder that the result was what might have been expected. He was forced to waste precious time in traveling from one headquarters to another, trying to persuade commanders to do what he should have been empowered to order.[71] Lloyd George's criticism of the Doullens Resolution was identical.[72]

A week later, on April 3, another conference at Beauvais was called to remedy the shortcomings of the Doullens Resolution. This time the Americans attended, represented by Pershing and Bliss. They signed the following agreement:

General Foch is charged by the British, French and American Governments with the duty of co-ordinating the action of the Allied armies on the Western Front; and with this object in view there is conferred upon him all the powers necessary for its effective accomplishment. For this purpose the British, French and American Governments entrust to General Foch the strategic direction of military operations. The Commanders-in-Chief of the British, French and American Armies shall exercise in full the tactical conduct of their armies. Each Commander-in-Chief shall have the right to appeal to his Government if, in his opinion, his army finds itself placed in danger by any instructions received from General Foch.[73]

General Bliss again drew attention to the weak points of this resolution. First, the document refrained from giving General Foch the title of Allied commander in chief. Second, it gave him no control over the Italian army. At the next session of the Supreme War Council, held at Abbeville on May 1 and 2, 1918, Italian Premier Vittorio Emanuele Orlando asked on behalf of the Italian army, as Lloyd George reported in his memoirs, whether General Foch's function as commander in chief should also extend to the Italian army. Although he was prepared to accept the application of the Beauvais arrangement to the Italian troops that were in France at that time, he claimed that the Doullens agreement alone was applicable to the army in Italy, since that gave Foch the right to coordinate but not to command.[74]

Whereas Foch's biographer maintained that "on 14th April, 1918, General Foch had been appointed 'General Officer Commanding in Chief the Allied Armies in France' [and] at the Abbeville Conference his powers were extended to cover the Italian front,"[75] Bliss added: "All that could be agreed upon was that 'the powers of co-ordination conferred on General Foch by the agreement of Doullens are extended to the Italian front.' "[76] But Bliss went on to say that these powers were ineffective and illusory. In fact, when, in the crisis of the campaign of 1918, General Foch wanted the Italians to make a move that might relieve some of the pressure against the western front, he could only beg—and beg in vain.[77]

Even at this trying time for the Allied cause, it was not easy to overcome antagonism between the coalition partners, as is evident from Foch's biography and Haig's memoirs, as well as from the comments given by Bliss to his biographer. Bliss's witty remark concerning the sixth session of the SWC at Versailles on June 1, 1918, characterizes this fact. He recalled that even in this crisis, the Supreme War Council discussed general subjects and policies for the future. The successful German drive was not even mentioned specifically. On the other hand, the Italian representatives were able to fight the proposal for unity of command and a unified combined fleet in the Adriatic with their old-time fervor and for the same old reasons, and the British representatives were expending much energy trying to get the Siberian expedition launched.[78]

The problems in connection with the termination of the war and the resulting Peace Conference are the basis for Chapter 9.

INTER-ALLIED COMMITTEES

The conduct of such a huge coalition,[79] which embraced continents and included millions of soldiers, was fraught with difficulties. These included complicated transportation problems, maintaining the supply of raw materials for industry and food for the armies and the civilian population, the recruitment of the required labor force, propaganda and problems of morale among the soldiers and on the home front, medical care, assistance to neutral countries, and so forth. Handling these considerations demanded the establishment of inter-Allied committees. They were gradually formed as the need for coordination in a particular field became evident. Twenty-five such committees are listed in Appendix C.[80] However, it is quite possible that there may have been others.

NOTES

1. Supra, p. 9.

2. Winston S. Churchill, *The World Crisis 1911–1918*, London, 1964, pp. 333–34.

3. Lord Maurice Hankey, *The Supreme Command 1914–18*, vol. 1, London, 1961, p. 140.

4. See pp. 49–50 of this volume.

5. Ferdinand Foch, *The Memoirs of Marshal Foch*, New York, 1931, pp. 162–63.

6. Maurice Paléologue, *Am Zarenhof während des Weltkrieges*, vol. 1, München, 1925, p. 106; Jurij N. Danilov, *Rußland im Weltkriege 1914–1915*, Jena, Germany, 1925, p. 107.

7. Hankey, vol. 1, p. 274.

8. David Lloyd George, *War Memoirs of David Lloyd George*, vol. 1, London, 1936, p. 240.

9. Ibid., pp. 240–41.

10. Lady Algeron Gordon Lennox, ed., *Diary of Lord Bertie of Thames 1914–1918*, vol. 1, London, 1924, p. 107; Raymond Poincaré, *The Memoirs of Raymond Poincaré*, vol. 4, New York, 1931, pp. 26–30 passim.

11. Sir Charles Edward Callwell, *Experiences of a Dug-Out, 1914–1918*, London, 1921, pp. 222–23.

12. Lloyd George, vol. 1, pp. 328–30 passim.

13. Hankey, vol. 1, p. 347.

14. Hankey, vol. 1, pp. 347–48; Poincaré, vol. 4, p. 182; Charles Bugnet, *Foch Speaks*, New York, 1929, p. 225; Danilov, pp. 530–34; Sir Frederick Maurice, *Lessons of Allied Cooperation: Naval, Military and Air 1914–1918*, London, 1942, p. 20; Joseph Jacques Césaire Joffre, *The Personal Memoirs of Joffre, Field Marshal of the French Army*, vol. 1, New York, 1932, pp. 380–81.

15. Paléologue, vol. 1, pp. 370–71.

16. Sir Charles Edward Callwell, *Field-Marshal Sir Henry Wilson*, vol. 1, New York, 1927, p. 258.

17. Hankey, vol. 2, p. 440; also Poincaré, vol. 4, pp. 290–91.

18. Hankey, vol. 2, pp. 448–49.

19. Ibid., p. 411.

20. Douglas Haig, *The Private Papers of Douglas Haig, 1914–1918*, London, 1952, p. 112. Entry of November 7, 1915.

21. Hankey, vol. 2, p. 451.

22. On the Chantilly Conference, vide: Joffre, pp. 411, 414; Keith Neilson, *Strategy and Supply*, London, 1984, pp. 122–25 passim.

23. Poincaré, vol. 4, p. 332.

24. Maurice, p. 26; William Robertson, *Soldiers and Statesmen 1914–1918*, vol. 1, London, 1926, p. 210.

25. Robertson, vol. 1, pp. 211–12.

26. Hankey, vol. 2, p. 502.

27. Alfred W. Knox, *With the Russian Army, 1914–1917*, vol. 2, New York, 1921, p. 417.

28. Ibid., p. 419.

29. George Arthur, *Life of Lord Kitchener*, vol. 3, London, 1920, p. 349.

30. Knox, vol. 2, pp. 419–20; Arthur, vol. 3, pp. 349–51; Samuel Hoare, *Das vierte Siegel, das Ende eines russischen Kapitels: Meine Mission in Rußland 1916/17*, Berlin, 1936, pp. 205–6.

31. Lloyd George, vol. 1, pp. 554–55.

32. Joffre, pp. 512–13; Haig, pp. 179–80; Lloyd George, vol. 1, pp. 567–78; Maurice, p. 32.

33. Callwell, *Wilson*, vol. 1, p. 299.

34. Churchill, p. 795.

35. Sir Roger Keyes, *The Naval Memoirs of Admiral of the Fleet Sir Roger Keyes*, vol. 2, London, 1934/1935, pp. 25–29.

36. William Robertson, *From Private to Fieldmarshal*, London, 1921, pp. 292–93.

37. Vassilij Iasifovic Gurko, *Rußland 1914–1917*, Berlin, 1921, p. 194.

38. Hoare, pp. 207–8.

39. George William Buchanan, *My Mission to Russia and Other Diplomatic Memories*, vol. 2, London, 1923, pp. 52–54 passim; Gurko, pp. 189–94 passim; Paléologue, vol. 2, pp. 343–44; Neilson, pp. 166, 235; Aldrovandi Luigi Marescotti, *Der Krieg der Diplomaten*, München, 1940, ch. 3; Callwell, *Wilson*, vol. 1, pp. 310ff.

40. Callwell, *Wilson*, vol. 1, p. 308.

41. Ibid., vol. 1, pp. 308–9; Marescotti, p. 130; Churchill, p. 796; Lloyd George, vol. 1, p. 855.

42. Lloyd George, vol. 1, p. 855.

43. Churchill, p. 796.

44. Haig, pp. 192–95 passim.

45. Churchill, p. 797.

46. Ibid.

47. Supra, p. 54.

48. As for the Calais Conference, vide: Haig, ch. 10; Callwell, *Wilson*, vol. 1, p. 324; Edward L. Spears, *Prelude to Victory*, London, 1939, ch. 9; Churchill, pp. 797–98; Lloyd George, vol. 1, pp. 893–96; Hankey, vol. 2, p. 617.

49. Churchill, p. 798.

50. Spears, pp. 194–95, 575–77; Hankey, vol. 2, p. 620.

51. Spears, p. 577.

52. Vide: Appendix A, p. 177.

53. Supra, p. 21.

54. Tasker H. Bliss, "The Evolution of the Unified Command," *Foreign Affairs* 1, December 15, 1922, p. 1.

55. Lloyd George, vol. 2, pp. 1411–1412.

56. Ibid., pp. 1413–1414.

57. Ibid., p. 1431.

58. Ibid., p. 1438.

59. Ibid., pp. 1439–40.

60. Charles Seymour, ed., *The Intimate Papers of Colonel House*, vol. 3, New York, 1926–28, p. 184.

61. Ibid., vol. 3, p. 198.

62. Frederick Palmer, *Bliss, Peacemaker*, New York, 1934, pp. 192–93.

63. John J. Pershing, *My Experience in the World War*, vol. 1, New York, 1931, p. 216.

64. Ibid.

65. Vide: Appendix B, p. 179. Also Minutes of the SWC, M 923, 10-36-2, File No. 376, National Archives, Washington, D.C.

66. Frederick Palmer, *Newton D. Baker*, vol. 1, New York, 1931, p. 392. (Emphasis added.)

67. Haig, pp. 46–48 passim.

68. Ibid., p. 282.

69. Palmer, *Baker*, vol. 2, p. 130.

70. Palmer, *Bliss*, p. 278.

71. Bliss, p. 28; Pershing, vol. 2, pp. 362–63.

72. Lloyd George, vol. 2, pp. 1743–44.

73. Ibid., vol. 2, p. 1749.

74. Ibid.

75. Bugnet, p. 244, n.1.

76. Bliss, p. 29.

77. Ibid.

78. Palmer, *Bliss*, p. 271. As for the frictions between Haig and Foch, vide: Bugnet, pp. 324–25; Haig, pp. 314–19 passim; on naval controversies, see Palmer, *Bliss*, pp. 272–73.

79. Vide: Appendix A, p. 177.

80. Vide: Appendix C, pp. 181–82.

6

GENERAL RESERVE AND UNIFIED COMMAND

The chain of events described in Chapter 5 clearly shows that all the coalition partners tried to derive frameworks for coordinating the joint war effort, but only in their hour of peril did they reluctantly adopt the means of unified command. Lord Hankey, who was a close observer of the Allies' coordination efforts, remarked bluntly: "No Power engaged in the war had thought out the problem of the Supreme Command and everyone blundered in this respect."[1] In spite of this observation, in the memoirs of all the personalities involved, statesmen and soldiers, the term "unified command" or "unity of command" runs like a golden thread from the outbreak of the war until the very end, in almost identical definitions, independent of nationality and profession.

This phenomenon of the absolute need for a unified command on the one hand, and the reluctance to adopt it on the other, is rather complicated, but an explanation is to be found in the previous chapters. Although all parties involved were convinced that a coalition should be conducted by a single authority (bear in mind Lloyd George's aphorism that "one General is better than two"),[2] in fact all the national-particularistic and personal conditions hampered the application of an obviously necessary principle. Foch, who, after four unfortunate years of trial and error, was finally appointed generalissimo, said to his biographer: "They [the coalition partners] saw things in a different light from ourselves [the French]. They agreed with reluctance to the unified command."[3] He even used the term of "duality of command" when referring to the situation on the French and Belgian fronts at the beginning of the war.[4]

In fact, this state of affairs began with the instructions given by the

British government to the commander in chief of the British Expeditionary Force. Subsequently, similar instructions were given to the commander in chief of the American forces in Europe by the U.S. administration. Early in the war, Field Marshal Sir John French wrote in his diary: "We suffer terribly from lack of 'unity of command.' " He seemed resigned to the outcome: "Allies must always suffer so."[5] This fatalistic sigh is probably intended to excuse the fact that during Sir John's entire tenure as head of the BEF, he insisted on his right, given to him by the governmental instructions, not to accept orders from the C in C of the front in France. Little wonder, therefore, that the commander in chief, General Joffre, in his account of the first months of the war, stressed the fact that the British government had laid down most categorically that Field Marshal French was not subordinate to him and that he was responsible only to his own government. In the course of his memoirs, Joffre would often refer to the absence of a Supreme Command, which was one of the major causes of the Allied weakness.[6]

The "unhealthy" relations between the partners on the same front can be gleaned from the memoirs of the liaison officers exchanged between the two armies: Huguet and Spears.[7]

The situation was even more complicated in connection with the co-ordination of military operations on the Russian and Serbian fronts. As a matter of fact, on these fronts, there was never any arrangement that came near a unified command, a fact that is emphasized in the memoirs of all the Russian generals.

THE MILITARY STATUS OF KINGS

When the war began, France was the only republic. All the remaining coalition partners were monarchies. In some cases, the king was not only the nominal head of the armed forces but also the commander of his forces in the field. For instance, Albert I, King of the Belgians, was the commander in chief of the Belgian army, but shortly after the war began, the army was one of the only components of his kingdom that remained at his disposal. At the end of 1914 and in the spring of 1915, when the French decided to form an army group, which included Belgian and British forces in addition to the French, on the northern wing of the western front under the command of General Foch, the King of the Belgians was subordinated to a French general, creating a rather delicate situation. With much tact and insight, General Foch abstained from issuing explicit orders, but rather made suggestions, and the king correctly understood that for all intents and purposes, they were orders.

The existence of royalty as an issue in the coalition was also demonstrated in 1917 at the peak of Field Marshal Haig's controversy with Lloyd George and Nivelle over the question of his subordination to the French C in C, when Haig appealed directly to his king.[8]

After the final appointment of General Foch as commander in chief of the Allied forces, the question of giving orders to the King of the Belgians arose again. Foch again disguised the orders he gave to other C in Cs as suggestions. In return the king understood that they were orders to be carried out. The same problem emerged when Foch's authority was extended to the Italian front, where King Victor Emmanuel III of Italy was the commander in chief of his army.

PROPOSALS FOR UNIFIED COMMAND

In spite of the particularistic interests of all the coalition partners, in all the memoirs one senses an uneasiness concerning the common war effort. Little wonder, then, that suggestions to remedy this situation were soon forthcoming.

It was natural that General Joffre, who suffered the most from this unlucky state of affairs, was eager to find a remedy. What Joffre had in mind in early 1915 was a unified command. General Wilson's biographer points out that one evening in March 1915, Joffre suddenly announced his intention of raising the question of the command in France and Belgium. He proposed that this command should be under his control and that he should be placed in a position to give orders to Sir John French. "Wilson realized that the raising of such a question under the circumstances then existing would be in the highest degree inopportune, that the British Government would be unlikely to assent to such an arrangement, and that the matter being even mentioned was to be deprecated."[9]

In order to convince Joffre to drop his proposal, Wilson used a rather odd argument. He pointed out that "if Joffre were to be granted the power to give orders to the BEF, he must also possess the power to discard any commanders in that force with whose handling of the troops under their orders he felt dissatisfied."[10] Wilson's diary makes it clear that Joffre was convinced, and he dropped the matter. Wilson continued to hold the view that this question of a generalissimo being by his position empowered to deprive subordinate commanders of their appointments effectively disposed of the idea of such a post being created, and he held it almost till March 1918. His biographer added that although this plea may sound more like an excuse than a justification for deprecating unity of command, in practice it would not seem to have given rise to any difficulty, neither during the brief space of time when Sir D. Haig was placed under the orders of General Nivelle nor during the closing months of the war when General Foch was appointed commander in chief of the Allied armies on the western front.[11] Callwell's verdict seems to be correct.

The information provided in Wilson's biography is confirmed by an entry in Poincaré's diary on March 21, 1915. He indicated that Joffre considered it necessary that Sir John should come under his orders and this was a point to be discussed with Kitchener as soon as he came to Paris.[12] Alluding to the tense relations between Joffre and Field Marshal French, Poincaré mentioned that at his request, the French ministers negotiating with the British government should try to obtain unity of command under Joffre in France, the more so since French troops would come under British command in the Dardanelles.[13] This remark also indicated that matters of national prestige were involved in such a vital issue for the Allied cause. A month later, in connection with the Allied meetings, Poincaré recorded in his memoirs that there was a consensus of opinion that there must be one directing brain and that that brain could only be in France. He added that unfortunately the Allies did not seem to see this in the same light. Until something better could be evolved, Poincaré asked if it were possible to convene the generals delegated by the Allied powers—England, Belgium, Italy, Serbia and if possible Russia— to receive general directions from the French commander in chief.[14]

In one of Joffre's letters to the war minister, he elaborated that the different armies were acting without effective coordination. Moreover, there was a growing impression that the war was not being well managed by the Allies. In consequence, Joffre suggested that the French government should propose to the Allied powers the centralization of the supreme control of the war in the French GQG in order to work out concerted plans and instructions for operations. For this purpose the French commander in chief should have with him a general officer duly credited by each power, whose duty it would be to give the French GQG exact information as to the army that he represents; this officer would speak in the name of the commander in chief whom he represented, and he would convey to him the plans and instructions drawn up by the French command. He added that if the English and Belgian armies would not go so far as to say that the French commander in chief should issue orders, it was at least imperative in order to win the war that the English and Belgian commanders in chief should follow his instructions. Poincaré commented on this letter that Joffre was quite right, but it still remained to convince the Allied governments and their commanders in chief; whether it was a matter of orders or instructions, they did not seem inclined to receive any other than their own.[15]

After the establishment of an Allied front at Salonika, where French, British and Serbian troops were deployed and the participation of Greek troops was anticipated, the British and French agreed to a unified command under a French general. Although this was a step in the right direction, the very fact that this theater of war was, and remained during the whole course of the war, merely a side show neither influenced the process in the main theater nor provided a solution for the overall Allied conduct of the war.

Robertson, who, as is already evident, was one of the main obstacles on the way to unity of command, in his capacity as CIGS pretended innocence when reporting on the final command arrangement, and wrote in connection with the situation in 1915: "As early as the autumn of 1915 various proposals were put forward, both by ministers and soldiers, for setting up some form of Allied body charged with ensuring more unified action and wholehearted co-operation, but for reasons unknown to me they failed to materialise."[16]

In Joffre's memoirs it is clear that toward the end of 1915, Aristide Briand, the new French prime minister, in his effort to find a solution for the delicate problem of Allied unified command, found a happy definition for the policy of the new government, namely, "a united front." Joffre added that it was not possible to arrive at such a unity without concerted action on the part of the Allies. But this action was dependent upon the establishment of a general plan. He stressed that the prime minister knew that all his efforts were directed to this end.[17] Winston Churchill was impressed by Briand's slogan, "unity of front," which in his opinion expressed the first great and obvious need of the Allies. He explained that nevertheless unity of front did not meant unity of command. Although this idea had dawned on many minds, it was not within the bounds of possibility. He explained that unity of front, or "only one front," meant that the whole great circle of fire and steel within which the Allies were gripping the Central Powers should be treated and organized as if it were the line of a single army or a single nation. Moreover, everything planned on one part of the front should be related to everything planned on every other part of the front, and instead of a succession of disconnected offensives, one combined and simultaneous effort should be made by the three Allies to overpower and beat down the barriers of hostile resistance. He added that in these broad and sound conceptions, Mr. Asquith, Mr. Lloyd George, Lord Kitchener, Monsieur Briand, General Joffre, General Cadorna, the czar and General Alexeieff, all four governments and all four General Staffs, were in full accord.[18] Even if this last statement is true, it still took almost three years to become reality.

The first real attempt to establish unified command was made with the approach of the so-called Nivelle Offensive in 1917. It was an utter failure. In retrospect, Foch told his biographer, "The unified command is only a word. It was tried in 1917 under Nivelle, and it did not work."[19] He saw the root of the failure in Nivelle's unsuccessful human relations, and made it clear that his interpersonal relations were more appropriate.[20]

After the disastrous outcome of the 1917 offensive, General Wilson discussed the problem of joint conduct of the war with General Smuts and suggested the creation of an inter-Allied staff "composed of three soldiers, English, French and Italian, with suitable staffs and full knowledge, who would be empowered to draw up plans of attack and defence along the whole line from Nieuport to Egypt."[21] This seems to be a kind of "instant unified command" or even "command by committee." Such an attempt may not be surprising, because a few months later, after the creation of the Supreme War Council at the Rapallo Conference of November 7, 1917, Wilson displayed his aversion to the idea of unified command. He reported that Clemenceau talked about unity of command but did not seem to know quite what he wanted. It was an impossible thing, in Wilson's opinion. He asked Clemenceau what he meant by unity of command, and his reply was that only two men should run the whole thing—a Frenchman (himself) and an Englishman (he meant, in fact, Wilson). He wanted the Supreme Council to have much more power than it had then.[22]

On the other hand, among Haig's papers there is a letter from Robertson dated August 1917 that sheds some light on the mood of the CIGS toward proposals for improving the Allied command structure. He wrote that Foch had proposed to set up an Allied Staff, at Paris, to study and prepare arrangements. And he added that he would have nothing to do with an Allied Staff, although he had heard since that the French ministers were very sick in consequence. Haig knew the meaning of this Allied Staff without Robertson's explanation. But since Lloyd George was keen on the Italian project for the time being and knew that Robertson was against it while the French were for it, and since the French kept rubbing in that it was necessary to have a central staff at Paris, Robertson suspected that Lloyd George wanted in the future to agree to such an organization in order to put the matter in French hands and to take it out of Robertson's. His game would be to put the "useless" Foch against Robertson as he had put Nivelle against Haig in the spring.[23]

In another letter the following month, Robertson wrote to Haig that Lloyd George and Painlevé (who was now prime minister in Paris) were desirous of forming an Allied General Staff in Paris to direct operations. He felt certain that this could not work. It seemed to be an effort of the French to retain control of operations, notwithstanding that their army had ceased to be the main factor in the military problems.[24]

It is hard to believe that these letters could have been written just a short time before the Caporetto disaster that triggered the Rapallo Resolution. Not only was Robertson averse to the idea of creating some inter-Allied mechanism, but this was also Haig's attitude, and it continued after Caporetto. He wrote in his diary on October 30, 1917, that H. Wilson advised the formation of an "inter-Allied Council" with presumably himself as head of the British staff section. Two days later, the entry of November 1 reads that Pétain had shown him a short note that he had written on the question of an Allied commander in chief (à la Hindenburg). This, however, was possible amongst allies only when one army was really the dominant one, as in the case of the Central Powers. He remarked that the Allied case was different. Three days later—three days before the Rapallo Conference—Haig had a meeting with Lloyd George. He reported that the prime minister first made a few remarks regarding the necessity for forming an inter-Allied Supreme War Council and Staff and asked Haig's views. Haig replied that this proposal had been considered for three years and each time had been rejected as unworkable. He gave several reasons why it could not work, and said that having such a body would add to the Allied difficulties.[25]

Enter a new factor: the United States joined the Allied camp. General Bliss prepared a note on December 18, 1917, in which he maintained that the Allies' crisis was not only due to the collapse of Russia as a military factor but was also largely due to lack of military coordination, the lack of unity of control on the part of the Allied forces in the field. In his detailed note, he analyzed the situation from the American point of view. He stressed that the lack of unity of control resulted from military jealousies and suspicion as to ultimate national aims. The Allies urged the Americans to profit by their experience in three and a half years of war: to adopt the organization, the types of artillery, tanks and so forth that the test of war had proved satisfactory. But the Americans should go further. In making the great military effort now demanded of them they should demand as a prior condition that their Allies should also profit by the experience of three and a half years of war in the matter of absolute unity of military control. National jealousies had to be put aside in favor of this unified control; otherwise, the American dead and their own might have died in vain. Securing this unified control was within the power of the president if it was in anyone's power. Moreover, the military men of the Allies admitted its necessity and were ready for it. They objected to Mr. Lloyd George's plan devised in Rapallo (which, however, Bliss was prepared to accept if nothing better could be done) for the reason that in the final analysis, it provided political and not military control. Bliss recalled that he had asked Sir Douglas Haig and General Robertson what would happen if the military advisers of the Supreme War Council recommended and the prime ministers accepted a military plan that the British commander in chief in the field and the chief of staff would not approve. Their answer was that it would be impossible to carry it into execution without their approval, that they would have to be relieved and the advisers of the Supreme War Council put in control. Bliss added that given the present temper of the English people, such an issue could not be forced without the probable defeat of the government. In general, the people held that the problem at that time was a military one and that in some way unity of control had to be obtained through an unhampered military council.

Initially Bliss thought that the commanders in chief of the armies should compose the Supreme War Council. But on reflection, he determined that political control was the most practical. He continued in his report that the difficulty would come with the political men. They had a feeling that military men, uncontrolled, might direct military movements counter to ultimate political interests. Relating to the fear that a unified command might deploy troops of any nation contrary to basic national interests, he considered it not merely a political necessity but also a military one that any commander in chief had to recognize, namely, that the English army had to fight with its back to the Channel, the French army had to fight with its back to Paris, the Italian army had to continue to fight Austria in the only direction by which it could reach her. However, this would not prevent troops of any of the four—English, French, Americans, Italians— being detached in accord with some coordinated plan from their main army where they were less needed to operate on another part of the front where they were more needed.[26]

It was not only Bliss who thought that the U.S. president should play a role in imposing unity. This was also the view of his Secretary of War, Newton D. Baker. In addition, the Counsellor of the American Embassy in Paris wrote in October 1917 that in the fourth year of the war, with everyone rather weary of the whole thing, he seemed to notice more signs of lack of harmony between the Allies than ever before. As America was the most disinterested nation engaged and as the Americans had the confidence of all the Allies to a greater extent than any other country, he believed it to be the logical role of America to unite the Allies in concerted action and to act as a general harmonizing influence.[27]

In fact, President Wilson issued a message indicating that he was in complete agreement with the action taken by the Allied governments in Rapallo, and that he was prepared not just to associate himself with the newly created Supreme War Council but also to take an official part in its deliberations. Lloyd George announced to the House of Commons on November 19 that Colonel House, head of the American mission and special representative of President Wilson in Europe, had received a cable from the president stating emphatically that the government of the United States considered that unity of plan and control between all the Allies and the United States was essential in order to achieve a just and permanent peace. He added that the president emphasized the fact that this unity had to be accomplished if the great resources of the United States were to be used to the best advantage, and he requested Colonel House to confer with the heads of the Allied governments with a view to achieving the closest possible cooperation.[28]

Lloyd George introduced a new slogan, "unity of strategy," into the debate over the unity of command in addition to "unified command," "unity of front" and "unity of plan." He asked the hypothetical question: Why did the British Government concentrate on unity of strategy rather than on unity of command? He answered that unity of command had already been attempted in this year's campaign on the western front: In the spring offensive the combined French and British attack had been placed under the general control of General Nivelle. In the Flanders offensive the French contingent was under the direction of Sir Douglas Haig. In neither operation did the arrangement work satisfactorily. In the first instance the explanation was largely personal. The two commanders did not hit it off—consequent lack of zeal on one side and lack of tact on the other led to misunderstandings, and the misunderstandings led to delays, where rapidity of action was of the essence of the strategy. He added that whatever the reasons might be, in neither offensive was there any unity or agreement on policy. Thus the result was that, although there was apparent cooperation, it was not real and wholehearted in either case. Therefore the unity of command was for the time being discredited by the failure of the two experiments made in 1917—one with a French generalissimo and the other with a British. Lloyd George reasoned that they had failed partly because there was no joint staff to work out the basis of united action. Therefore, the first steps in the attainment of unity of command should be to secure real agreement on strategy and to have an inter-Allied staff directly responsible to the commander in chief and not thwarted by the staffs attached to and dependent upon the ideas of the commander in chief of each national army. Thus a genuine unity of command ultimately would evolve out of this move. But even then, so great were the prejudices to be overcome that it had to be achieved by two separate steps and as a necessity arising out of the consequences of overwhelming disaster. It thus happened that at Doullens, Foch was called upon to coordinate the efforts of the two armies. However, he was not given the authority to command. Therefore, this did not constitute a united leadership and in practice it failed to achieve one common direction. As a matter of fact, unity of command was only established later on at Beauvais, where Foch was made General en Chef of the two armies. Lloyd George stressed that Versailles was but the first step; Doullens was the second, and Beauvais was the final achievement of Allied unity on the western front.[29]

However, on the way to this final achievement, there was still one grave obstacle to be overcome: the problem of a General Reserve.

GENERAL RESERVE

Although the need for the existence of a reserve is taught on every level of officer's training, the translation of this principle into reality in a coalition war is difficult. The first apparent reference to the issue was in a letter from General Smuts to Lloyd George dated May 24, 1917, in connection with the future deployment of the American forces expected to arrive in France:

If the war goes on till America can come in in 1918, she will become a factor of decisive military importance. The most careful forethought should therefore be given as to the form her military effort should take and where her army, which will be *our fresh strategical reserve*, could be utilized to best advantage. For this it may be necessary to review our whole military and naval strategy for the future, as it may be found that none of the existing fronts should be allowed to absorb this our *final reserve force*.[30]

A similar idea is expressed in Baker's biography. In connection with America's entry into the war, Baker reasoned that the Allies should have a reserve army ready to prevent a breach wherever the attack came. He believed that the French and British armies had this in mind for their own fronts. The remaining question was who would maintain a General Reserve. The Americans assumed that their representatives had the advantage of an uninvolved overview, especially since their country's borders were not being threatened by the anticipated German offensive. Consequently, General Bliss was an ardent supporter of the plan for an Allied reserve.[31]

On February 2, 1918, after the Russian collapse released a considerable number of German forces from the East, resulting in the anticipation of a massive Central Powers offensive, the Supreme War Council, meeting in its third session at Versailles, approved the following resolution, proposed by Lloyd George:

1. The Supreme War Council [SWC] decides on the creation of a General Reserve for the whole of the Armies on the Western, Italian, and Balkan Fronts.

2. The Supreme War Council delegates to an executive composed of the Permanent Military Representatives of Great Britain, Italy and the United States, with General Foch for France, the following powers to be exercised in consultation with the Commanders-in-Chief of the Armies concerned:

(a) to determine the strength in all arms and composition of the General Reserve, and the contribution of each national army thereto;

(b) to select the localities in which the General Reserve is normally to be stationed;

(c) to make arrangements for transportation and concentration of the General Reserve in the different areas;

(d) to decide and issue orders as to the time, place and period of employment of the General Reserve; the orders of the Executive Committee for the movement of the General Reserve shall be transmitted in the manner and by the persons who shall be designated by the Supreme War Council for that purpose in each particular case;

(e) to determine the time, place and strength of the counteroffensive, and then to hand over to one or more of the commanders-in-chief the necessary troops for the operation. The moment this movement of the General Reserve, or of any part of it, shall have begun, it will come under the orders of the commander-in-chief to whose assistance it is consigned;

(f) Until the movement of the General Reserve begins, it will for all purposes of discipline, instruction and administration, be under the orders of the respective commanders-in-chief, but no movement can be ordered except by the Executive Committee.

3. In case of irreconcilable differences of opinion on a point of importance connected with the General Reserve, any Military Representative has the right to appeal to the Supreme War Council.

4. In order to facilitate its decisions, the Executive Committee has the right to visit any theatre of war.

5. The Supreme War Council will nominate the President of the Executive Committee from among the members of the Committee.[32]

In accordance with paragraph 5 of this resolution, the SWC appointed General Foch as the president of the Executive Committee. Maurice criticized the whole arrangement as being a clumsy and impracticable arrangement. He argued that command by committee had never succeeded in war, even when the members of the committee had all come from one army, and therefore a committee composed of generals from four different countries was not likely to be an exception.[33]

In retrospect, General Bliss asked in his *Foreign Affairs* essay in 1922, How could there by an Allied reserve without an Allied commander in chief? He reasoned that the control of a General Reserve, the ability to order it hither and yon without let or hindrance from anyone, was the supreme function of a commander in chief. He should decide the point of danger, to meet it, if he could, by first stripping his line of disposable local reserves; he had to decide when and to what extent to send in his General Reserve; and, above all, if he could defeat the enemy while still leaving his own General Reserve intact, it was for him to decide whether with it he could change his defense into an offensive that might win ultimate and supreme victory. Bliss concluded that this was the intimate connection between the creation of an Allied General Reserve and the question of unified command. Its commander would become, for one all-important purpose, an ipso facto commander in chief.[34]

General Pershing argued along the same lines. In his opinion, in theory, the plan for a General Reserve appeared to be a reasonable method of avoiding the difficulties inherent in any plan for mutual support between the French and British armies. However, upon analysis, one could not escape the conclusion that its application would result in the senior officer of the Executive Board assuming supreme control of the joint action of the two armies. As a matter of fact, with thirty reserve divisions at his command, he would be in a position to dictate what should be done.[35]

This was also the posture adopted by Foch during the SWC deliberations. Comprehending the complicated situation of the coalition, he was prepared to compromise. In response to Lloyd George's question, Who will command the General Reserve? Foch replied that there had to be one authority, able to create, conserve, and prepare for the employment of the General Reserve by the various armies, but in agreement with the commanders. When the moment arrived to make use of the reserve, this very same authority had to decide on its use, arrange for its transport, and feed the battle line in which the reserve was to be engaged. Foch added that since the reserve might be used to support any of the Allies, this central authority must be inter-Allied in character and must be able to make all the necessary preparations. Above all, this inter-Allied organ must be required to make decisions if the governments were not in session at Versailles. It therefore had to be an inter-Allied organ of execution. Foch suggested bringing together the chiefs of the staff who advise their governments on the different questions, in order that they might carry out their duties in agreement. Moreover, to these principal members of the central organ there should be added representatives of the American and the Belgian armies.[36]

From Trask's account it is clear that at the preliminary discussion of the military representatives, General Weygand argued that the reserve could not function without a specific commander in chief, while General Wilson refused to approve such an appointment. Thus the representatives proposed a General Reserve, leaving the difficult problems of composition and command to the Supreme War Council. Trask also explained that the reaction to the General Reserve reflected the military jealousies both within and between countries, "which disturbed inter-Allied relationships."[37]

A skeptical Churchill summarized that this decision, like many others of the Supreme War Council, remained a dead letter; events moved forward without the British army receiving either the reinforcements for which Haig had pleaded or the reserves that Lloyd George had labored to supply. Although the thirty divisions were nonexistent, the Executive Committee to control them at Versailles was nevertheless created.[38]

Palmer's cynical remark about the reserve, that it actually consisted of "one . . . bow-legged little French general," has been quoted previously.[39] In a more optimistic vein, General Pershing concluded that the failure of the plan to become operative for lack of divisions to constitute the General Reserve led fortunately to the selection of an Allied commander in chief, which was probably the object sought by some of its farsighted advocates.[40]

STEEPLECHASE TOWARD UNIFIED COMMAND

A month after the decision to form one, the General Reserve still existed only on paper. Instead of assigning the divisions, Haig and Pétain raised objections to the control plan. Consequently, Foch's committee reported that under these circumstances the Executive War Board found itself unable to continue its work and, therefore, was unable to organize the inter-Allied General Reserve, as the Supreme War Council at its sitting of February 2 had instructed it to do, and therefore the Executive War Board had decided that each military representative should so inform his own government and ask for instructions.[41]

In fact, it was General Ludendorff, whose Spring Offensive began on March 21, 1918, who forced the Allies to end the stalemate over the problem of a central command. After the Germans broke through the thin lines held by the British Fifth Army, on March 24, Haig was informed by Pétain, the French commander in chief, that he intended to fall back on

Paris rather than dispatch the reserve divisions they had agreed on and he had promised. Haig, who was concerned, reported to his war minister and the CIGS simultaneously. As Foch reported, Haig telephoned Foch to ask for someone to take charge of the war.[42] The result was the Doullens Conference on March 26, which was described in the previous chapter.[43] On March 26, Haig recorded in his diary that Clemenceau proposed that Foch should be appointed to coordinate the operations of an Allied force to cover Amiens and ensure that the French and British flanks remained united. Haig thought this proposal was worthless, as Foch would be in a subordinate position to Pétain and to himself. He held the opinion that it was essential to success that Foch control Pétain. He therefore recommended at once that Foch should coordinate the action of all the Allied armies on the western front.[44] Both governments agreed.

However, the Doullens agreement proved unsatisfactory. Therefore, on April 3, another inter-Allied conference was convened in Beauvais. In contrast to the Doullens Conference, this time the Americans participated. Pershing recalled in his memoirs that Clemenceau stated that the purpose of the meeting was to settle the simple question regarding the functions of General Foch. He thought that all agreed as to the coordination of Allied action, but there was some difference in the understanding of General Foch's powers as conferred upon him at the Doullens Conference of March 26. General Foch then explained his difficulties. He drew attention to the fact that the powers conferred upon him by the Doullens Conference were limited to the coordination of action between the Allies. They were conferred while the action was on. This meant that the power to coordinate was limited to the time the Allies were in action. That was the case on March 26 at Doullens. But now it was April 3. The two opposing armies were no longer in action but had stopped and were facing each other, and there was no more need for coordination. At this time there should be the authority to prepare for action and direct it. Thus the alliance was right back where it was before, and nothing could be done until action started again.

Pershing's account continued, recalling that Lloyd George entered the discussion, saying basically that more than three years of this war had passed and there had been two kinds of strategy: one by Haig and another by Pétain; they were different, but nothing had been gained. The only thing that was achieved was by General Nivelle when he was in supreme command. The Supreme War Council that met in February had adopted a plan for handling a General Reserve, but through the action of those concerned, nothing had come out of it. It was worthless. He continued that what had happened recently had stirred the British people very much and must by no means happen again, as the people would demand to know why it had happened, and somebody would be called to account. The people wanted some sort of unity of command. Although General Foch was now empowered to coordinate the action of the Allied armies, this did not go far enough, as he had no authority to control except by conferring with the respective commanders in chief. He needed authority to prepare for action. Lloyd George thought that the resolution made at Doullens should be modified so that better understanding could be reached. He then solicited the opinion of the American generals. Bliss read the Doullens Resolution and interpreted it to mean that General Foch was given no authority to act except in concert with the two commanders in chief. He continued his analysis of the resolution, suggesting that in order to meet all situations, the powers conferred upon General Foch should be enlarged. General Pershing then read aloud a memorandum he had prepared during the meeting, pointing out that the principle of unity of command was undoubtedly the correct one for the Allies to follow. He did not believe that it was possible to have unity of action without a supreme commander. There was already enough experience in trying to coordinate the operations of the Allied armies without success. But there had never been real unity of action. Any coordination of this kind between two or three armies was impossible, no matter who the commanders in chief might be, since each commander in chief was interested in his own army and could not get the other commander's point of view or grasp the problem as a whole. Pershing was therefore in favor of a supreme commander and believed that the success of the Allied cause depended upon this. He was in favor of conferring the supreme command upon General Foch.

Lloyd George was delighted by Pershing's presentation, and asked to hear Field Marshal Haig, who said the Allies had practically had complete unity of action. He had always cooperated with the French, whom he regarded as in control of the strategical questions of the war. He was placed directly under the command of General Nivelle, and General Pétain and he had always worked well together. He agreed with General Pershing's general idea that there should be unity of command, but he thought that the Allies had had it.

General Pétain's views were identical to Haig's. After further discussion, and the explicit demand of the American generals to include the American forces in the new resolution, the Beauvais Resolution was signed.[45]

These events have been described in great detail because they reflect the birth pangs of unified command. Once these problems were settled, a new one emerged: General Foch's title. General Wilson, already the CIGS, revealed in his diary that Foch wanted a title for himself. Obviously, the matter was discussed. Wilson objected to Clemenceau's suggestion of Commander in Chief of the Allied Forces, pointing out that Foch's authority was confined to France, and he proposed instead Commander in Chief of Allied Forces in France.[46] This title was approved by all concerned, including President Wilson. From Pershing's memoirs, however, it is evident that British public opinion was decidedly opposed. He quoted an article published in *The Globe*, which at the time was supposed to represent the views of the British High Command in the field, that objected to the appointment of a generalissimo. These objections were not so much military but political, since any generalissimo was the servant of the state that appointed him. Consequently, such an office involved the possibility that the Allied army might pass under the control of foreign politicians.[47] In fact, entries in Haig's diary during the entire month of June 1918 reveal that the field marshal was not pleased with Foch's appointment and tried through various channels to ensure that it should only be temporary.[48]

At the meeting of the SWC held in Abbeville in early May, Foch's authority was also expanded to the Italian front. However, Hankey's report shows that the expansion of authority to both the Italian and Belgian fronts was discussed at meetings of the Supreme War Council, but the representatives of both countries asked that the decision be deferred, because of the constitutional difficulties arising from the fact that in each case, the king was head of the armed forces. Finally, on November 8, 1918, Foch was granted strategic direction of all the forces against Germany.[49] Thus the problem concerning royalty was also settled.

Although the unified ground command was finally created, the Allies never managed to establish a unified naval command. Even the attempt to appoint an admiralissimo in the Mediterranean was cancelled, because the Italians opposed such a measure.[50]

In retrospect, Lloyd George pondered the mistakes that the Allies committed during the war. In connection with the problems of General Reserve and unified command, he wrote that the last opportunity missed was over the establishment of a real unity of command. He maintained that a unity that depended upon prolonged argument between two rival and independent staffs was a sham. Even the unity that was supposed to have been established during the spring offensive of 1917 was not much better, since it never operated with goodwill. The delay caused by bickerings between two commanders—not one of whom had the power to give a peremptory order to the other—was responsible for converting an appreciable victory into a disastrous failure. It was the Germans who recognized that the real unity arranged between French and British when

Foch was made commander in chief on the whole front was largely responsible for the failure of their Spring Offensive in 1918. Lloyd George concluded that had a General Reserve been set up under central command before the March offensive, the defeats of March and April would never have occurred.[51]

In his study, Sir Frederick Maurice drew attention to another problematic facet of the unified command, arguing that Foch began his task of coordinating the action of the Allied armies on the western front with a small staff of about one dozen officers solely concerned with military operations. But later, when French, British, and American troops became intermingled, the problems of coordinating different systems of supply and administration became acute, and an administrative staff was added. At first two British officers were appointed as liaison officers with General Foch, but by the middle of July a regular British mission headed by a senior British general was established at his headquarters. Maurice observed that French military methods and practice were different from British and that it took time for the new machinery to run smoothly. Foch used to issue his instructions to his armies in the form of directives, and their meaning and his intentions were not always grasped at once by the British generals, who were used to receiving orders of a different kind and in different form.[52]

The problems of logistics in a wartime coalition will be discussed in Chapter 8.

NOTES

1. Lord Maurice Hankey, *The Supreme Command 1914–18*, vol. 1, London, 1961, p. 140.

2. Supra, p. 87. Quoted by Winston S. Churchill, *The World Crisis 1911–1918*, London, 1964, p. 797.

3. Charles Bugnet, *Foch Speaks*, New York, 1929, p. 250.

4. Ibid., p. 221.

5. Gerald French, *The Life of Field-Marshal Sir John French*, London, 1931, p. 245.

6. Joseph Jacques Césaire Joffre, *The Personal Memoirs of Joffre*, vol. 1, New York, 1932, p. 357.

7. Vide: Charles Julien Huguet, *Britain and the War*, London, 1928; and Edward L. Spears, *Liaison 1914*, London, 1930.

8. Supra, p. 54.

9. Sir Charles Edward Callwell, *Field-Marshal Sir Henry Wilson*, vol. 1, New York, 1927, p. 217.

10. Ibid.

11. Ibid., pp. 217–18.

12. Raymond Poincaré, *The Memoirs of Raymond Poincaré*, vol. 4, New York, 1931, p. 68.

13. Ibid., p. 51.

14. Ibid., p. 144.

15. Ibid., pp. 149–50.

16. William Robertson, *From Private to Field Marshal*, London, 1921, p. 327.

17. Joffre, p. 399.

18. Churchill, pp. 669–70.

19. Bugnet, p. 250.

20. Ibid., pp. 250–52.

21. Callwell, vol. 2, p. 7.

22. Ibid., pp. 30–31.

23. Field Marshal Sir Douglas Haig, *The Private Papers of Douglas Haig, 1914–1919*, London, 1952, p. 251.

24. Ibid., p. 255.

25. Ibid., pp. 262–63.

26. Frederick Palmer, *Bliss, Peacemaker*, New York, 1934, pp. 205–7 passim.

27. Frederick Palmer, *Newton D. Baker*, vol. 1, New York, 1931, pp. 373–76.

28. David Lloyd George, *War Memoirs of David Lloyd George*, vol. 2, London, 1936, pp. 1445–46.

29. Ibid., p. 1449.

30. W. K. Hancock and Jean van der Poel, eds., *Selections from the Smuts Papers*, vol. 3, Cambridge, England, 1966, p. 523. (Emphasis added.)

31. Palmer, *Baker*, vol. 2, p. 128.

32. Sir Frederick Maurice, *Lessons of Allied Cooperation: Naval, Military and Air 1914–1918*, London, 1942, pp. 122–23.

33. Ibid., p. 123.

34. General Tasker H. Bliss, "The Evolution of the Unified Command," *Foreign Affairs* 1, Dec. 15, 1922, p. 13.

35. John J. Pershing, *My Experience in the World War*, vol. 2, New York, 1931, p. 366.

36. Bliss, p. 13.

37. David S. Trask, *The United States in the Supreme War Council*, Middleton, Conn., 1961, p. 56.

38. Churchill, p. 856.

39. Supra, p. 94.

40. Pershing, vol. 2, p. 366.

41. Bliss, p. 22.

42. Haig, pp. 296–300 passim; Bugnet, p. 233.

43. Supra, p. 95.

44. Haig, p. 298.

45. Pershing, vol. 2, pp. 373–77.

46. Callwell, vol. 2, p. 89.

47. Pershing, vol. 2, p. 379.

48. Haig, pp. 314–15.

49. Hankey, vol. 2, p. 797.

50. Vide: Haig, p. 313; Callwell, vol. 2, p. 104.

51. Lloyd George, vol. 2, p. 2002.

52. Maurice, p. 135.

7

AMALGAMATION OF FORCES

It is well known in military circles that a coalition, or a mixture of forces from different countries in a joint venture, invites disaster. Such a situation was vividly illuminated in a report from the British liaison officer with the French army in August 1914. Spears recalled the difficulties of combined action. He reported that an attack had been planned in which a Belgian brigade from the field army was to cooperate with the French cavalry corps on the left and the garrison of Namur on the right. It resulted in the Belgians on the left mistaking the French for Germans and firing at them. In the sequel, this contretemps had hardly been adjusted when the Belgians vanished completely and were not seen again until the autumn in Flanders. Whereas this disappearance seemed incomprehensible at the time, it was due to the fact that during the engagement they had received the general order to retire that had been issued to the whole of their army, and had obeyed it without informing the French.[1]

From the viewpoint of the stronger or more senior partner, the most desired remedy to avoid incidents of this kind was the amalgamation of forces, which in fact meant the incorporation of the forces of the minor partner into the forces of the senior partner. In the most narrow sense, amalgamation is "the action of combining into one uniform whole" or "a homogeneous union."[2] This is precisely what the advocates of amalgamation of forces had in mind.

THE BELGIAN ARMY

From the memoirs of Albert I, King of the Belgians, it is obvious that by mid-November 1914, the French intended to distribute Belgian units among the French forces in the Ypres sector, in the proportion of one Belgian brigade per French division. But the king would neither agree to being deprived of his constitutional prerogatives as the commander in chief of his armed forces nor let his army be split up. He said that he would not agree to "deliver the fate of his soldiers to decisions of foreign authorities beyond his control."[3] A few days after this attempt by General Foch, who was at that time the CO of the Allied Northern Army Group, Field Marshal John French, the commander in chief of the BEF, transmitted a message to the Belgians stating that on the next arrival of British reinforcements, the British, with the cooperation of the Belgian army, would take over the whole line. Field Marshal French therefore asked whether the Belgian army intended to stand fast and would be able to take the offensive. If the answer were in the affirmative, a sector would be given to the Belgian army; if in the negative, the Belgian army would be incorporated into the British army, one brigade per British division.

As expected, this demand was rejected by the king, who stressed that he wanted divisions on which one could count, adding that the existence of his country depended upon it.

However, in his memoirs, he reported that since the English were short of artillery, they asked for a regiment to be placed at their disposal for the defense of the Ypres salient. This request was immediately granted.[4]

In his memoirs, Field Marshal French recounted that at the end of December 1914, he had devised a scheme to amalgamate the Belgian and British armies. He wanted Belgian brigades of infantry to be embodied in the British army corps at convenient sections in the line, and he wanted to apply the same process to the cavalry and artillery. He admitted that this apparent surrender of independence was no doubt a heavy trial to impose upon the Belgian General Staff, but he nevertheless believed it to be the surest and best method to adopt, if one wished to get the highest efforts out of the two armies. As a justification for this infringement on Belgian sovereignty, he argued that the standard of training and war efficiency was higher in the British army than in the Belgian. This applied, above all, to the leaders and the staff. Summing up his ideas for the amalgamation of Belgian and British troops, he reasoned that it could hardly be doubted that a division composed of two British infantry brigades and one Belgian would probably have done more, either in attack or defense, than such a unit composed entirely of Belgian troops. He concluded that no doubt this scheme that he proposed would have ensured a much greater unity of effort.[5]

It is already clear that this scheme was opposed by both the Belgians and the French General Staff. On January 2, 1915, General Wilson lamented in his diary that all the plans for incorporating the Belgian army into the British by brigades had fallen to the ground because the Belgian king wouldn't have it.[6] It is also obvious that at that time General Joffre would not agree to place even a French cavalry division and two reserve divisions, which were echeloned in reserve, behind the BEF directly under the orders of the British commander in chief.

THE BRITISH EXPEDITIONARY FORCES

At a certain point in 1916, the British liaison officer with the French recalled that he began to hear gossip from Paris. Although it was concerned mainly with developments in the French political sphere, it also contained hints of the impact of domestic affairs on military matters. In his memoirs, he reported that one suggestion, which was put forward with the idea of husbanding the dwindling French manpower, amazed him. He discovered that in influential French circles, both military and political, a plan was on foot whose object was to create mixed corps of one British and two French divisions under a French general. This project was called the *amalgame*. He added that although there had already been newspaper articles on the subject in the autumn of 1916, no soldier had taken them seriously so far. Spears's criticism was that the idea was preposterous to anyone who had ever had the task of supplying a mixed Anglo-French force. He maintained that the material difficulties were insuperable, not to mention at all the far greater ones of attempting to fuse the unmixable British with the insoluble French. As a result, both the French and the British would very probably have starved, the guns would never have received their shells, and the picture of a dapper French general giving orders that would be accepted literally, if understood at all, by the British and on the other hand be interpreted anything but literally by the French, was so ludicrous that one would almost forget to be angry at such suggestion. Certainly the plan would have disrupted the British army, which was by now at least the equal of the French. In addition to this intentionally rather comic presentation, Spears tacked on another bit of gossip: he had gathered quite definitely that a scheme was afoot in Paris to get rid of General Robertson because he would not support this scheme.[7] From a note in Spears's book, it is clear that during the winter of 1915 the *amalgame* had been the object of studies by the then French Minister of War, General Gallieni.

There also seems to have been an exchange of views between Gallieni and his British counterpart, Lord Kitchener. After the death of General Gallieni in May 1916 the concept lay dormant, and was only revived in early October 1916, when it was again written about in the French press, which gave rise to a controversy between *Le Figaro* in Paris and the London *Times*. At that time the French view, which was reflected in the newspapers, was that the *amalgame* would have been possible if it had been requested in time, when the English had only a few divisions on the French front. But it was considered very unlikely in 1916.[8]

Among Haig's papers is a letter from Lord Esher dated July 22, 1916, that stated that there was a group of silly soldiers that was pushing what they called the "amalgam," an idea, which they fathered quite falsely on to Gallieni, for amalgamating the armies by brigades, and so forth, under one chief. Esher had warned Briand that the mere discussion of such a plan—apart from its inherent idiocy—would only do harm, by rousing suspicion and mistrust.[9]

It is interesting to note that two years later, in 1918, the recollection of this attempt still poisoned the atmosphere. An entry in Haig's diary on April 19, 1918, recalled in this context that he had said that he would do anything necessary to help to win the battle, but that it was desirable to tell Foch that any idea of a permanent amalgam must be dismissed from his mind at once, because that would never work. From the same entry it is obvious that the British Secretary of State for War, Sir Alfred Milner, was entirely opposed to mixing up units of the French and British. He admitted that the needs of this great battle had made intermingling of units necessary for a time, but he would never approve of a permanent amalgam.[10]

THE AMERICAN EXPEDITIONARY FORCE

The urgent need for American manpower was stressed at the inter-Allied conference in November 1917. At that time, the military leaders of the Entente suggested to Colonel House, President Wilson's representative, that instead of waiting to form a complete and independent American army, as was the American intention, General Pershing should permit his troops to be incorporated as individuals or by small units into the British and French armies. On December 6, 1917, General Pétain submitted to Colonel House a memorandum called "Training of the American Army." The opening paragraph read: "It is necessary to hasten the training of the American army, both in the United States and in France, for the purpose of rendering its co-operation more rapid."[11] In more detail, this document advised that practice could rapidly be obtained at good advantage if the

American army would, for a short time, waive their feeling of national pride and depend completely upon the experience of the French army. The method suggested by Pétain was to place the American army in a sector, not all at once in large units but by fractions composed of regiments of infantry and groups of artillery, in the frame of a large French unit. This military document also contained a political warning, in case the French proposal was rejected by the Americans, namely, that the French public, in spite of its great admiration for the effort of the United States, would understand only with difficulty why the effective manifestation of this effort should be so long in coming.[12]

House's papers make it clear that he referred the issue to the president, who was eager to do everything in his power to meet the wishes of his new allies. On the other hand, he was determined that General Pershing, the commander of the American Expeditionary Force (AEF), have a free hand and use his own military judgment. On December 18, 1917, by order of the president, House drafted a cablegram to the commander of the AEF, mentioning that both English and French were pressing upon the president their desire to have the American forces amalgamated with theirs by regiments and companies and that both expressed their belief in an impending heavy drive by the Germans. Although the Americans did not want to lose the identity of their forces, the president regarded that as secondary to the meeting of any critical situation by the most helpful use possible of the troops at Pershing's command. But House added that this suggestion was not pressed beyond whatever merit it had in Pershing's judgment. The president's sole purpose was to acquaint Pershing with the representations made by the Allies and to authorize him to act with entire freedom in making the best disposition and use of his forces possible to accomplish the main purpose in view. It was hoped that complete unity and coordination of action could be secured in this matter by conferences with the French and British commanders.[13]

It is obvious that there were differing points of view between the French and British commanders on the one hand and the American C in C in France on the other. The former regarded the American troops as a reservoir of manpower to supplement their own depleted ranks and wanted to provide the Americans with actual battle experience alongside their seasoned veterans. However, such a procedure would have prevented the formation of an American army in France. Nevertheless, in the opinion of the Entente leaders, the method they proposed was the most effective means by which the Americans could render the fastest service. After a meeting of the SWC on January 30, 1918, the American Embassy reported to Colonel House that General Foch, General Pétain, and General Haig agreed that the American armies, if taken as an autonomous unit, could not be counted upon for effective aid during the present year and that the only method of rendering them useful at the earliest possible moment would be to amalgamate American regiments or battalions into French or British divisions. Little wonder that the posture of the commander in chief of the AEF was diametrically opposite. He was against American soldiers serving under a foreign flag.[14]

In his memoirs, General Pershing recalled that the French politicians put pressure on him in the direction of amalgamation of American troops with the other Allied armies. Clemenceau, for instance, said that after America had been in the war for several months, the French people were wondering when Americans could be expected to take an active part. He pointed to the fact that the French army was exhausted by the war. Nevertheless, Clemenceau argued that it was not so much a question of troops being ready as it was of giving relief to the Allies. Pershing remarked in his memoirs that it was obviously quite out of place for M. Clemenceau to make any such demand. But he commented that there was little doubt that he gave expression to a very general sentiment among the French people at that moment: they simply wanted to see American troops in the trenches. And he added that M. Clemenceau's visit left the impression that the French were inclined to dictate what disposition the Americans should make of their units. Moreover, in many of their suggestions it was easy to see the possibility of amalgamation lurking in the background.[15]

With this suspicion constantly in the back of his mind, Pershing was at serious loggerheads with Clemenceau, and the latter contacted the American president behind his back. In his memoirs, Pershing wrote that the French were dead set on getting the American troops under their control. It was clear that the prime minister, feeling that the American plans were not working out, sought to create some doubts in the minds of the administration at Washington regarding the wisdom of Pershing's management of things. Clemenceau obviously thought that Pershing's opposition to amalgamation could thus be overcome.[16]

The French were not alone in vying for American troops. They were joined by the British. In the biography of the American Secretary of War, it is stated that on December 2, 1917, Lloyd George appealed to Colonel House to integrate American troops into British divisions, arguing that even half-trained American companies or battalions could fight well if mixed with two- or three-year veterans. A short time later, Field Marshal Haig approached Pershing with a plan to attach American battalions or regiments under their own flags, one to a British brigade, for trench training purposes. The idea was that at the same time, American division and brigade commands would be learning their roles in cooperation with British commands who had had three years' combat experience. As soon as an American division staff had been organized and indoctrinated by actual contact with the enemy, the regiments would be withdrawn into American divisions under their own command and assigned to the American army. On January 3, 1918, Secretary Baker wrote to the president that it seemed to him entirely clear that if American regiments were integrated with either French or British divisions, the difficulty of getting them back when wanted would be very great. He reasoned that the ultimate effect of such a course would be practically to put American troops in French and British divisions under the command of French and British commanders, which would weaken the forces under General Pershing's command for independent operations. Pershing also raised an additional argument against the incorporation of American regiments into French divisions: the language barrier.[17]

It is interesting to find in General Bliss's biography a remark that in December 1917 the American general, who played an important role in inter-Allied affairs in France, was inclined to endorse a rather strange British idea. Bliss reported as follows: "We must take note of the deep, growing and already very strong conviction on the part of Englishmen, both military and civil, that the war must finally be fought out by an Anglo-Saxon combination."[18] Later he added that General Robertson and Sir Douglas Haig were so earnest in this matter that in an interview he had with them they had urged amalgamating American troops with theirs. Bliss reported that Sir Douglas Haig had even said that he would give command of these mixed organizations to American officers.[19] It was obvious that the common language made training with the British easier than with the French.

Palmer also remarked that experience had proven that it was fatal for military efficiency to mix small American units with the French. On the other hand, this had not yet been proven with the British. An additional argument in favor of the British was that since the British command had given the Canadians and Australians independent corps, which were very distinct entities, it could hardly refuse to turn the American divisions back to Pershing when any defensive crisis was over.[20] Pershing also stressed the fact that there was no accord in ideas of organization or battle tactics between the British and the French and each sought to impress the Americans with the superiority of their respective systems. He admitted that the British methods of teaching trench warfare appealed to him more strongly.[21] He could not rid himself of the suspicion that the French were really hoping to have the American units amalgamated for service with theirs, and this with the special object in mind of avoiding having to reduce the number of their divisions. He suspected that this was hidden away under the insistence upon taking over training.[22] He also introduced an additional argument, namely, that it was unnecessary to say that when the war ended, the American position would be stronger if their army acting as such had played a distinct and definite part.[23]

It is appropriate to view this issue from the perspective of André Tardieu, the French representative in the United States, who was well acquainted with the American scene. He revealed that the French generals did not believe it possible to create a great American army in a few months. Foch told him to urge the Americans to send regiments to be incorporated into French brigades. Pétain suggested recruiting American volunteers to replace French losses. The French air service begged Tardieu not to let the Americans try to build airplanes and motors, feeling that they should specialize on raw materials and parts. In fact, as Tardieu put it, "Every one looked upon the United States as a vast reservoir from which European forces and supplies could be fed. No one believed it capable of creating a new army to be added to those already fighting."[24] However, Tardieu argued that the creation of an American army was the only thing that could key America up to the necessary pitch and that the passive role that Europe expected the United States to play would have discouraged its enthusiasm. He claimed: "When a nation of one hundred and ten millions goes to war, to so distant a war, it cannot consent to be merely a recruiting depot for others. If it goes to war, it must be its own war, with its own army and under its own flag." Tardieu concluded: "If we had refused to recognize the military autonomy of the United States, if we had insisted upon amalgamation, co-operation would have been a failure."[25] On January 8, 1918, he warned the French government:

If your aim is really amalgamation, that is, the enlistment of the American army by small units on our front, you will fail. It is not only the American High Command which will oppose such a policy, but the Government, public opinion, and events. You could not get the English to consent to any such thing when their army was quite small; and you will not get the Americans to consent.[26]

As a matter of fact, General Pershing never stopped insisting on the creation of an independent American army in France, and rejected any French or British attempt at amalgamation. After the initial German success in their Spring Offensive in March 1918, and in particular after the heavy blows the Fifth British Army endured, the British nourished the hope that President Wilson might become startled into a more compliant mood and agree to the amalgamation of American troops with the Allied armies.[27] However, Pershing remained adamant, though offering and rendering any assistance to the other armies.

In May, during the next crisis of the war, the issue was discussed again at the Abbeville Conference of the SWC. On this occasion Lloyd George leveled a rather sharp accusation against the United States: "If France and Great Britain should have to yield, their defeat would be honorable, for they would have fought to their last man, while the United States would have to stop without having put into line more men than little Belgium."[28] In his memoirs, General Pershing mentioned his reaction. He spoke in the name of the American army and in the name of the American people, and wished to express their earnest desire to take their full part in this battle, and to share the burden of the war to the fullest extent. However, although all desired the same thing, the American means of attaining it were different from those of the others. America had declared war independently of the Allies and intended to face it as soon as possible with a powerful army. He laid stress on one important point, namely, that the morale of the American soldiers depended upon their fighting under their own flag. Pershing emphasized that the American soldier had his own pride, and the time would soon come when the American troops as well as the American government would demand an autonomous army under the American High Command.

It is obvious that the Supreme War Council had no other choice but to accept General Pershing's view, as he informed his Secretary of War in a cablegram, indicating that it was the opinion of the Supreme War Council that, in order to carry the war to a successful conclusion, an American army should be formed as early as possible under its own commander and its own flag.[29] Nevertheless, even after this resolution, the commander in chief of the AEF still harbored some suspicions. He had at the same time reached the impression, as did many of the American officers familiar with the arguments on both sides, that the Allies, though greatly in need of assistance, were nevertheless inclined to press the plea for amalgamation as a means of keeping the Americans in a subordinate role.[30]

As late in the war as the beginning of October 1918, Secretary of War Newton D. Baker, surveying the American cooperation and contribution in the war to the other coalition partners, stressed that he had no intention of feeding American soldiers into the French or British army. He wanted to have an American army in exactly the very same sense that Great Britain had a British army and France a French army. However, he recognized the right of Marshal Foch, as commander in chief of the Allied forces, to send

divisions of Americans or French or British from one part of the line to
another for particular operations or to create a composite reserve that
would have troops of all three nations ready for use. However, he made it
absolutely clear that the American troops in France were as completely
under General Pershing's control as the British troops in France were
under the control of Sir Douglas Haig. In a conversation with Lloyd
George, Baker stressed that Lloyd George ought to expect the American
army as such to exist in the same sense as the British army and that it
should be used there as a whole or by detachment of divisions wherever
the largest good could be accomplished for the cause in the judgment of
the commander in chief as he considered the problem from time to time.[31]

In Baker's biography an argument is quoted that was used by the
secretary to justify America's insistence on an independent American
army in France. He argued that no commander had better reasons than
Haig, out of his own experience, to appreciate the mistake of infiltrating
troops of another nation into his army. Baker mentioned that the British
army included the rivalries of the English, the Scotch, the Welsh and the
Irish. In addition, troops came from the Dominions: the high-spirited
Canadians, Australians, New Zealanders, and South Africans, who regarded themselves as belonging to distinctive, self-governing common-
wealths, or even nations, within the Empire. As a matter of fact, the
Canadians and Australians had their own separate army corps under their
own commanders, and the New Zealanders had their own division. It was
well known that the Canadians or the Australians did not always see eye
to eye with a cockney in their relations in action or behind the lines.
Moreover, the rivalries between the Canadians and Australians approached a feud. And in addition to these elements, Haig had at one time
under him native Indian regiments of antipathetic races and customs.[32]

Pershing recalled a negative experience of his own as the result of his
readiness to compromise. In order to meet the need for replacements in
French units, he had consented to send temporarily to the French four
"colored" infantry regiments of the 93rd Division with the provision that
they were to be returned for the formation of the 93rd Division when called
for. But unfortunately, these regiments soon became identified with the
French, and there was no opportunity to assemble them as an American
division.[33]

In conclusion, it is obvious that during the course of World War I, the
efforts for amalgamation of different national contingents never ceased.
Unfortunately, it is also an established fact that none of these attempts
succeeded.

NOTES

1. Edward L. Spears, *Liaison 1914*, London, 1930, pp. 96–97.

2. *The Shorter Oxford English Dictionary*, 1962 ed., S. V. "Amalgamation."

3. Albert I, *The War Diaries of Albert I*, London, 1954, p. 25.

4. Ibid., pp. 25–28.

5. John French, *1914*, Boston, 1919, pp. 350–52; also Charles Julien Huguet, *Britain and the War*, London, 1928, p. 160.

6. Sir Charles Edward Callwell, *Field-Marshal Sir Henry Wilson*, vol. 1, New York, 1927, p. 199.

7. Edward L. Spears, *Prelude to Victory*, London, 1939, pp. 110–11.

8. Ibid., p. 540.

9. Field Marshal Sir Douglas Haig, *The Private Papers of Douglas Haig*, London, 1952, p. 156.

10. Ibid., p. 304.

11. Quoted in Charles Seymour, *The Intimate Papers of Colonel House*, vol. 3, New York, 1926–28, p. 286.

12. Ibid., pp. 286–87.

13. Ibid., pp. 428–29.

14. Ibid., pp. 429–30.

15. General John J. Pershing, *My Experience in the World War*, vol. 1, New York, 1931, pp. 158–59.

16. Ibid., pp. 271ff.

17. Frederick Palmer, *Newton D. Baker*, vol. 2, New York, 1931, pp. 106–16 passim.

18. Frederick Palmer, *Bliss, Peacemaker*, New York, 1934, p. 207.

19. Ibid., p. 207.

20. Ibid., p. 208.

21. Pershing, vol. 1, p. 151.

22. Ibid., p. 294.

23. Ibid., p. 295.

24. André Tardieu, *France and America*, Boston, 1927, p. 218.

25. Ibid., p. 218.

26. Ibid., p. 219, n.1.

27. W. B. Fowler, *British-American Relations 1917–1918*, Princeton, N.J., 1969, pp. 136–37.

28. Pershing, vol. 2, p. 31.

29. Ibid., vol. 2, pp. 31–35 passim.

30. Ibid., p. 35.

31. Ibid., pp. 316–17.

32. Palmer, *Baker*, vol. 2, pp. 109–10.

33. Pershing, vol. 1, p. 291.

8

LOGISTICS AND WAR FINANCES

In the framework of military activities, the term logistics is loosely applied to a wide range of noncombat activities. This includes, for example, supply, distribution and storage, transportation, and construction, as well as care and evacuation of the sick and wounded. Also included are support services to the armed forces, such as repair and maintenance of weapons and equipment, and general administration, which includes organizing, coordinating and managing military activities. Although prewar planning, as surveyed in Chapter 2, assumed that the armies of different nations would wage war jointly against a common foe, in different theaters of war, it will become clear that not only was detailed strategic planning almost entirely lacking but absolutely no thought was given to any survey of the imminent logistic problems.

PROBLEMS OF INTER-ALLIED TRANSPORTATION

The impact of these problems on the Allied conduct of the war was felt right from the beginning. The rather vaguely coordinated French and British prewar planning made it clear that upon its arrival on the Continent, the British Expeditionary Force would have to be transported by French railways, and would thus come into conflict with the transportation schedules of the French army. General Joffre's memoirs discuss the impact of the British mobilization on the movement and deployment of his own troops. He recalled that when the British government decided to enter the struggle, August 5, 1914, was fixed upon as the first day of mobilization.

Consequently, and in accordance with the arrangements that had been made in time of peace, the concentration transports of the British Expeditionary Corps would commence on the French railways on August 11. Therefore, the first day of operations would be August 21. However, due to various delays in the mobilization, the first day of British mobilization had to be fixed for August 9. Thus it was impossible to hope that the British forces arriving on the Continent could be ready to move forward before August 26.[1]

Moreover, the British government decided to change the BEF's concentration area in France. Joffre was annoyed because this not only confused the railway timetable but also completely upset the general dispositions of the Allied forces at the most sensitive point of the battle, and presented the danger of delaying the probable date when the British troops would be ready to go into action, and, as Joffre put it, at the very moment when the Belgians were urging the French to come to their aid. However, on August 13, Joffre learned that Lord Kitchener, the new British Secretary of State for War, had decided to stick to the original arrangement.[2]

In September and October, the commander in chief of the BEF wanted to shift his forces and concentrate them on the left (northern) wing of the Allied forces. As already explained, for mainly particularistic British reasons, this movement of troops again interfered with the general transportation schedules of the French railways. The British demands, as Joffre admitted, "were well-founded." But he added, with much justification, "Where we differed was as to the suitability of making the change immediately."[3] He tried to explain to his British colleague that while in his capacity as commander in chief of the whole front in France, he had considered the possibility of withdrawing a certain number of corps without modifying his front, but certainly he had never contemplated transporting an entire army, the removal of which would create a gap in the front line. Moreover, the movement contemplated by Field Marshal John French would entail grave complications not only in the position of the troops but also in those of supply trains, and so forth.

Joffre, however, concluded his report of this controversy by pointing an accusing finger at his British Allies, charging that the precipitation with which the British army got itself relieved from the Aisne front caused, as could have been predicted when the question arose, an almost complete interruption of ten days of the transport of the French troops toward the northern theater of operations. Moreover, Joffre stressed that the definite loss of the rich region centering in Lille was due to this operation, to which he had consented only with the greatest regret.[4]

Field Marshal Haig also recalled that the British financial adviser on his staff in France "assisted in the adjustment of financial questions connected with the use of French railways and harbors."[5] From the memoirs of General Robertson, relating to his service as chief of staff of the BEF, it is clear that the French Mission at the British headquarters comprised a considerable number of officers, "as there were daily many questions in regard to civil administration, the use of railways, etc."[6]

As might be expected, transportation problems concerning Russia were mainly related to shipping. Kitchener's suggestion to dispatch some regiments of cossacks (and later, a Russian infantry brigade) to England was based on the assumption that Great Britain would provide the necessary ships. This was not to be.[7] In his capacity as CIGS, Robertson complained of the lack of close contact with the Russian General Staff. He recalled that General Alexeieff had pressed for more British divisions to be sent to the eastern theaters, including some to cooperate with the Russian forces in Armenia. But Robertson censured his Russian counterpart by remarking in his memoirs that he never seemed able to appreciate the tax imposed by long-distance operations on overstrained British naval and shipping resources.[8]

America's entry into the war further complicated Allied transportation problems. At the same time that the U.S. military establishment began considering the participation of American troops in the war in Europe, the U.S. War College carried out a study of such an eventuality. Bliss's biography makes it clear that the estimation was that for each 100,000 men abroad, 700,000 tons of shipping would be required, or 3.5 million tons for the 500,000 American soldiers contemplated for the AEF. However, at that time, just a week before Congress declared war on Germany, the means of transportation for the first group of 100,000 American soldiers to be dispatched was inadequate.[9] It is well established that by the time of the signing of the armistice in 1918, more than one million American soldiers had crossed the Atlantic in British ships.[10] Tardieu, who was sent to the United States to arrange for France's needs, realized that with the appearance of American troops on French soil, it had become necessary to create a framework to look after the things the American army needed in France. This required the creation of a government department in Paris called the General Commissariat of American Affairs.[11]

After his arrival in France, Pershing surveyed the problem of lines of communication on the western front. He reported in his memoirs that the French system of lines running from the base at Paris to the front was bearing maximum burden. If the Americans wanted to have independent and flexible lines of communication, their army could not be tied to the railways the French were using. Therefore, the American rail communications should be carefully chosen in order to avoid any increase in the load that had to be carried by the systems already in use by the two other Allied armies.

Since the Americans had to take into account their overseas communications, they were compelled to investigate what French ports would best serve their purpose. Pershing reached the conclusion that the only ports on the west coast of France that would accommodate vessels of more than moderate draft and were more or less free were St. Nazaire, Bassens and La Pallice, while Nantes, Bordeaux and Pauillac were only capable of taking light draft shipping. However, these ports had the advantage of being somewhat beyond the patrolling area of the German submarines that tried to blockade the British Isles. Moreover, the main railroad routes from these ports toward northeastern France were not included in the service of the rear for the other Allied armies, and hence were more available for handling materiel and supplies for the American armies. It was also estimated that these lines could be improved to meet all the American needs.[12] From Pershing's memoirs, however, it is obvious that from the beginning to the very end of American participation in the war, there was constant tension between the French bureau officials and the American officers who became their counterparts. He mentioned as an example that the French had been repeatedly urged to turn over certain docks and facilities for exclusive American use. But while some concessions had been made, this was always done grudgingly and in piecemeal fashion, and the Americans were never certain of more than temporary occupancy.[13]

There was one special feature connected with transportation problems that was caused by the arrival of American troops in Europe. In this premotorized era, the Americans had to be supplied with a sufficient number of horses for their artillery and trains. In February 1918, Pershing made preliminary arrangements for the purchase of 50,000 horses from the French government at the rate of 10,000 per month. There was the possibility that the total might be increased to 150,000 animals. Meanwhile, Pershing was also trying to get 20,000 to 30,000 horses from neutral Spain, and was promised about 14,000 from England. In the end, during the course of the war, the Americans bought 105,000 horses from the French. Some of the animals were sold at rather high prices.[14] In his memoirs, Tardieu revealed the French version. In order "to obtain every available ounce of tonnage, it was necessary to impose fresh sacrifices on France in the matter of supplies. Old men, women, and children, whose unrelenting labour had saved our crops, saw their last horses taken from them."[15]

Another transportation problem was stranger still: the recruitment of the so-called Chinese Auxiliary Corps. Lloyd George estimated that 15,000 Chinese laborers were brought to work in France. Of this total, about 6,000 were required for work on the railroads and 1,000 for inland water transport, with the remainder employed on road construction and other projects.[16] In her study, which is more recent, historian Madelaine Chi-Sung-Chun claims that 200,000 Chinese coolies were toiling in Europe during World War I.[17] The explanation for this great discrepancy remains unsolved. However, Chi-Sung-Chun's study makes it clear that

the Chinese government was . . . willing to contribute more than just laborers. . . . The Chinese government would be ready to furnish the [A]llies with as many men as desired provided the United States would give financial assistance. . . . The French government . . . was most enthusiastic in its support. The French Ambassador in Washington . . . stated that France could transport Chinese troops to Europe upon completion of four steamers which she had ordered from Japan. It was largely due to French insistence and the French promise of being able to provide transport that the question of sending Chinese troops to Europe was approved by the Supreme War Council in January 1918.[18]

The British government viewed this project with disdain. Moreover, the Admiralty warned the foreign office "that no encouragement should be given to the project owing to the shortage of tonnage."[19] A junior member of the foreign office maintained that "it is impossible to imagine a greater waste of time, trouble, equipment, money and tonnage" than sending Chinese soldiers to Europe.[20] Foreign Minister Balfour considered the scheme "idiotic" and "insane."[21] Finally, as Chi-Sung-Chun reports, "the project was dropped in April 1918, because France could not provide the transport as she had hoped, and there was no other shipping available."[22]

In Bliss's biography it is stated that in 1917 the Allies were faced with an additional transportation problem: with the end of the Russian Revolution, Czech soldiers, who had been Russian prisoners of war, were gathering in Vladivostok, and were considered another source of recruits for the Allied cause. The possibility of bringing them across Canada to the western front was discussed. Lloyd George argued that their transportation would mean so many fewer Americans and Canadians in France. But the Italians stressed that the Czechs, who had been their adversaries when they were in the Austro-Hungarian army, were good fighters, while Clemenceau made the point they were battle-trained veterans, while the

Americans were not. It was decided to bring the Czechs on available ships. However, no one knew for certain how many Czechs there were in Vladivostok.[23]

RUSSIA: A SERIOUS LOGISTIC PROBLEM

The memoirs of the statesmen and soldiers of the Western partners of the Entente reveal their great hopes for the impact of the Russian "steamroller" on their mutual enemy. Indeed, the invasion of East Prussia by Russian troops immediately after the outbreak of the war seemed to have justified these expectations. It came as quite a shock when they realized that the Russians were short of all kinds of weapons and ammunition. General Gurko's memoirs make it clear that even before the war, Russia could not rely solely on its own arms production and had to purchase from abroad. These purchases were not limited to Russia's allies.

As a result, it should have been clear that in the event of war, the imperial arms industries would not be able to cover the anticipated losses in rifles with their own production. Gurko accused the Russian War Ministry of starting to look for foreign weapons' suppliers only after the outbreak of the war. There was no lack of offers, especially from the United States, which was originally neutral. Since this meant a shift to a new type of rifle, however, large sums of money would be required if standardization was desired. Gurko also complained that instead of boosting the local production capacity of artillery, the ministry ordered them from Creusot in France. Thus, when war broke out, the production of these plants became harnessed to the French war effort. As far as the American factories were concerned, they had to develop their new production lines before they could increase their output for mass production. Therefore, it was not assured whether they could meet the promised delivery dates on the contracts they had signed. Gurko suspected that from the beginning, they had not intended to meet the delivery schedules they had agreed on.[24]

George W. Buchanan, the British ambassador in St. Petersburg, recalled that on September 25, 1914, General Joffre inquired whether Russia's supply of ammunition was sufficient to meet its high rate of consumption. He was assured that there was no cause for alarm. But suddenly on December 18, he and the French ambassador, Maurice Paléologue, were informed by the chief of staff at the Ministry for War that, although Russia had in its depots enough men, it had no rifles to arm them with, and its ammunition reserves were exhausted. For Buchanan, "this announcement came as a bolt from the blue."[25] In his diary, Paléologue provided alarming statistics showing the discrepancy between the consumption and production of ammunition, in addition to the fact that rifles that the General Staff was believed to have in its warehouses did not exist.[26]

The British liaison officer with the Russian army provided even more shocking information: the French military attaché discovered that the output of the Russian factories amounted to only 35,000 shells a month, but the rate of consumption at the front averaged 45,000 shells a day.[27] On December 4, Field Marshal French recorded in his diary that it was obvious that the Allied generals found it difficult to comprehend this new situation the Russian forces found themselves in. He assumed that the Russian message was "only a piece of 'bluff' to get the most they can out of us and to induce us to take all possible pressure off of them."[28] French's assumption was bolstered by a message he received from Lord Kitchener on December 26:

I am inclined to think Russians have been bluffing to a certain extent. I cannot get answers to my questions from Petrograd which would clear up the situation. For instance, the amount of reserve ammunition in hand, which, according to [the] Military Attaché here, who is kept entirely in the dark by his Government, ought to be very considerable. A reason for a certain amount of bluff on this part might be that they are now negotiating to obtain from us a loan of forty millions.[29]

It is apparent from French's memoirs that at the same time, General Foch "felt sure that the Russians were exaggerating their deficiencies in ammunitions, rifles, etc., in their presentation both to the British and French Governments." However, Foch's explanation was "that they were afraid that the troops in the West were not displaying sufficient energy, and their idea was to stimulate this."[30]

In early 1915, Kitchener became fully aware of the gravity of the ammunition situation in Russia. His biographer reports that

Kitchener, negotiating with the Russian Government, had committed himself to serious responsibilities as to procuring rifles, machine-guns and artillery—with their complement of ammunition—from the United States and Japan. . . . Huge contracts were placed in America and the Far East . . . and placed in the first instance almost entirely on the security of the British War Minister's name.[31]

The biographer also admitted that

the results of these healthy reforms were not fully apparent for many months, but before the close of the campaign of 1916 a very marked change had taken place. The output from America and Japan started slowly, and it was not until the winter of 1916–1917 that shipment of war material—for which Kitchener had contracted eighteen months earlier—poured across the Atlantic and the Pacific to fit out the Russian armies for their great effort timed for the summer of 1917.[32]

This delay in delivery is confirmed by Russian General C. Shumsky-Solomonov, who wrote:

1915 is the year of Russia's single-handed fight against Germany, Austria and Turkey. This year was the hardest for Russia not only because all attention and all efforts of the three enemy powers were directed against Russia alone, but also because in 1915, Russian was less than ever before prepared for the struggle—being without arms, shells and munitions.[33]

The memoirs of Russian Minister for War Aleksey A. Poliwanow underscore the gravity of the situation: "Rifles are more valuable than gold. The delivery of 12,000–15,000 rifles of foreign types fit only for replacement battalions so that the men shall not be trained with sticks."[34]

In his memoirs, Russian General Jurij Nikiforovich Danilov wrote that among other items, Japan had supplied Russia with heavy artillery, although, as he stressed, "of an obsolete type."[35] Gurko admitted that "our Japanese Ally" had supplied a useful type of infantry rifles.[36] However, Chi-Sung-Chun's study reveals that Japanese support also had a political price:

In order to secure large supplies of rifles, guns, and ammunition—the most urgent needs felt by Russia—Russia had to offer Japan the portion of the Chinese-Eastern railway from Changchung to Harbin as compensation. This was a branch of the Trans-Siberian railway laid in South Manchuria, which lay within the Japanese sphere of interest.[37]

In addition, when the British Dardanelles Committee discussed the issue of Russian rifles, the problem was whether the 300,000 rifles should consist entirely of Italian rifles or a mixed batch of Japanese and British types. Kitchener favored sending Italian rifles, since the others were required for defense at home. Lloyd George demurred, arguing that the limited amount of ammunition available for the Italian rifles made them useless to the Russians, and pressed the committee to take a gamble on home defense.[38]

At the same time as the Russian arms and munition shortage, the Allies were occupied with other problems. Hoare's memoirs suggest that one was the need to ship the heavy machinery for the weapons industry to Russia. This was difficult, because most of the sea lanes to Russia were closed.[39] Another problem that demanded Allied intervention was that from the beginning of the war, the Russian search for ammunition led to unchecked competition on the neutral American market.[40]

It has already been mentioned that Lord Kitchener's planned visit to Russia, as well as the Petrograd Conference in 1917, were closely connected with the Allies' efforts to ascertain Russia's real situation and to find solutions, inter alia, for the armament and ammunition crisis. Indeed, the Allied efforts until then had improved the situation, as Shumsky-Solomonov admitted: "That year [1917] was the first year that the Russian Army had at last obtained sufficient armaments and supplies."[41]

THE AEF: THOUSANDS OF MILES FROM ITS BASES

In addition to the transportation problems encountered by the American Expeditionary Force, its very presence in Europe, thousands of miles from its home bases, presented difficulties that the Alliance was compelled to solve. Some of the solutions were to come from the General Commissariat of American Affairs established in Paris by the French government. It included the services of the general secretariat and the military, financial and transport services in addition to administrative and legal affairs, a press and information service, the mission to the American General Headquarters, and a mission for the service of supplies in the ports.[42]

Although this seemed to be a logical arrangement, General Pershing, who should have been the main benefactor, had his doubts. He thought that it would be more expeditious to utilize the French officers then on duty at his headquarters and to develop a workable system through experience. He explained his views to M. Painlevé and arranged for the officers of the American supply departments to confer directly with the chiefs of the corresponding bureaus of the French organization. Pershing maintained that in the beginning it looked as though there would be easy sailing, but he soon discovered that the Americans still had much to learn in dealing with French bureaus, either directly or indirectly.[43] Pershing complained about the quality of these contacts, stressing that the American efforts to arrange for the procurement in France of munitions, aviation, various classes of equipment and supply, and the use of facilities brought the American officers in close contact with bureaus of the French government. In the beginning the Americans were largely dependent upon these bureaus to make up deficiencies in many things necessary to complete their preparations. But the failure of the French to realize the necessity of hearty cooperation became evident early in the relations with them. The higher authorities apparently understood and gave promises of assistance, but when the Americans got down to actual details they encountered difficulties. This was above all true of the granting of docking facilities, the allotment of rail transportation, and the assignment of forests for lumber procurement.[44]

Pershing maintained that this uneasy situation, which prevailed for the three years of the American presence in France, was due to the lack of a clear division between bureaus and departments. His verdict, reflected in his memoirs, was rather damaging: In dealings with French bureaus many obstacles had to be overcome. He observed that the subordinate one might happen to encounter at the start was usually impressed with his own importance and would undertake to make decisions, which would lead one to think the matter practically settled—only to find that this official had little if any authority and that his action was not approved by the senior next above him. Then, when much time was already lost, it would be learned that this was not the proper office after all. When at last the responsible bureau was reached, one was likely to be told that the thing could not be done, no reason being apparent except that it never had been done. Therefore, frequently throughout the war, it was necessary for Pershing to make a personal appeal to the minister concerned that orders be given for supplies or services that were already promised and that there was every reason to expect would be furnished. In exasperation, Pershing stated that after a few contacts with their system one marvelled that the French had managed to get along so well in supplying their armies during three years of war. He observed that the French were very intelligent and had a highly organized government, but from the practical viewpoint they often became deeply involved in nonessential details and lost sight of the main objective.[45]

Tardieu tried to explain the difficulties in cultural terms: "On the one side, French logic; on the other Anglo-Saxon empiricism."[46] One may wonder whether this sociological and psychological explanation is precise, or whether this is a basic phenomenon inherent in a wartime coalition.

On the British side, Bliss's biography suggests that one of the problems discussed with the Allies—the French as well as the British—was whether the AEF should be equipped with American-made artillery, thus waiting for the American manufacturers and placing an additional burden on shipping facilities from the United States to France. The alternative, of course, was to use materiel furnished by England and France. It was decided not to wait for the production of guns at home, but to rely on the provision of artillery equipment and ammunition for the troops as they arrived in France.[47]

Pershing mentioned that on his arrival in England, he had discussed this problem with Winston Churchill, then Minister of Munitions, and found him ready to provide British artillery. However, the Americans had already decided to use French equipment.[48] He recalled in his memoirs that he learned definitely that, although not fully supplied themselves, the French could increase the output of their factories provided they could get steel from the United States. The main reason for deciding in favor of French artillery pieces was that it seemed probable that the American troops would operate in proximity to French armies and sought their assistance in obtaining the guns needed, at least for the first two years. Pershing secured an agreement that his troops, as they came along, would be provided with French guns and ammunition, including not only the 75s and 155s but 37-millimeter guns and 58-millimeter trench mortars as well.[49] In addition to steel, another item that the French and British requested in order to secure the ammunition for the guns supplied to the Americans was American-made propellants.[50] William J. Snow's memoirs indicate that the Americans bought a total of 1,828 75-millimeter guns from the French government.[51]

In addition to artillery, the AEF badly needed tanks. The British promised Pershing a certain number of heavy tanks, but when he tried to requisition them, the British claimed that they had none to spare. Foch, on the other hand, said the French would let the Americans have five battalions of light tanks, three with French personnel and two to be manned by Americans. Additional American efforts to obtain an equitable allotment of heavy tanks from the British were in vain. Meanwhile, the Inter-Allied Tank Commission was formed. Pershing reported that as the French decided to take no active part, the British proposed that the Americans should undertake the manufacture of heavy tanks jointly with them. It was understood that the British would build the hulls, the United States would furnish the motors and chassis, and the assembling would be done in France.[52]

The supply of aircraft for the Americans was no less complicated. The French had suggested that they would increase their output of various types of airplane bodies and that the Americans should confine themselves to the production of Liberty engines. Pershing, who was "once burned, twice shy," explained that the American experience so far had not been such as to give confidence in the French fulfillment of an agreement of this sort. Therefore, this suggestion was politely rejected. A short time later, the British also sought joint cooperation with the Americans. They proposed that the Americans should limit their construction to long-range strategic aircraft and the manufacture of Liberty engines, while the British would supply the AEF with the aircraft necessary for purely American operations. The British claimed that this project was coordinated with the French.

Pershing discovered that this was not the case. Quite perplexed, Pershing concluded in his memoirs that such incidents showed the tendency to gain particular advantage and caused the Americans to doubt the sincerity of proposals for cooperation in such matters.[53] Nevertheless, it is obvious that the Americans had furnished the French with 4,200 mechanics, mainly to assist in the manufacture of planes, and the eight American air squadrons deployed on May 15, 1918, over the front lines were all equipped with French airplanes.[54]

Summing up the assistance France rendered to the AEF, Tardieu provided the following data: all the 75mm and 155mm guns, all the tanks, 81 percent of the airplanes, 57 percent of the heavy artillery and 65 million shells fired by the artillery.[55]

Medical services became the most serious problem Pershing was forced to deal with, because the Americans had no civilian hospitals at their disposal. As a result, provisions had to be made for hospital accommodations in France, as only convalescents unfit for further service could be returned to the United States. Early estimates, submitted in August 1917, suggested that the initial force of 300,000 men needed 73,000 beds in permanent, semipermanent, or temporary hospitals. However, all facilities throughout France were nearly full with the French sick and wounded. Thus the AEF was forced to plan new facilities, which called for additional labor and materials, both of which were scarce. In addition, as Pershing recorded, the French used the ordinary railroad facilities for the transportation of their wounded, but the distances from the AEF probable front to the zone of available hospital accommodations, and thence to the American base ports, made it advisable to have the most advanced rail equipment. Thus, negotiations were at once started in England to obtain hospital trains, which began to arrive early in February. Nineteen trains of fifteen cars each were in operation at the time of the armistice.[56]

Grave problems often produce unexpected solutions. Pershing disclosed in his memoirs that due to the gloomy outlook regarding tonnage losses, the question of supplies appeared precarious enough for Washington to send him for comment a suggestion that had been received regarding the possibility of augmenting the food supply for the American armies through increased cultivation of the soil in France and northern Spain by American farmers. One has to bear in mind that Spain was a neutral country. Pershing had already discussed this possibility at his headquarters, and reached the conclusion that it would be much wiser to increase the U.S. military forces more rapidly and thus relieve the older classes of French soldiers from the front to enable them to return to their farms.[57]

Strange as this may seem, it must be taken into account that in 1918, it was predicted that there would be an estimated shortfall of 284,000 tons of oats for the animals of the armies in France.[58]

In his memoirs, Pershing shed some light on the American view of the darker side of coalition relations. He observed that among the Allies, especially the French, there was a tendency to exaggerate the urgency of their requests for materiel. It often happened that upon investigation, their estimates could be substantially reduced and in some instances ignored altogether. He stressed the point that so faulty was the organization and management of the government's business that at times the French lost track of considerable amounts of raw materials they actually had received from abroad.[59]

POOLING OF LOGISTICS

On being appointed the American military representative in Versailles, Bliss pressed the pooling of Allied supplies. His efforts succeeded, and during the third session of the Supreme War Council meeting in Versailles at the end of January 1918, the Inter-Allied Committee for Pooling of Supplies was established for the unification of supplies and utilities.[60]

However, just as with the beginning of "unity of command," making the "pooling of supplies" a reality was also a long, drawn-out process. Only a crisis in procurement, which resulted mainly from a lack of tonnage, forced the supply agencies of the different governments to consider this solution seriously. Thus, as late as April 19, 1918, General Pershing sent a memorandum to Clemenceau concerned almost entirely with this issue. He referred to a conversation he had had the day before and suggested that all supplies and war materials that were used in common by the Allied armies be pooled and that the principle be extended as far as possible also to the civil populations of the Allies in Europe. He drew attention to the defects of the present methods of handling supplies. Nevertheless, each of the Allied armies continued to think only in terms of its own requirements independently of the other armies. It should be realized that there were many classes of supplies used by all the Allies that could be pooled and issued to a particular army as required, but still no practical solution to the problem had yet been reached. Some attempts had been made already through coordinating Allied committees—including the Supreme War Council—but these bodies were only advisory. The authority to order the allotment and distribution of supplies to the different armies did not yet exist. Pershing suggested that the following classes of supplies should be included in the arrangement: aviation material, munitions as far as practicable, horses, oats, hay, meat, flour, coal, gasoline, wagons, harnesses, motor transport, depots, warehouses, lumber and timber. This concentration or control of supplies would no doubt result in economy of port construction and especially of storage facility use. Pershing proposed to Clemenceau that in order to meet the situation in question, somebody should be designated who would occupy a position regarding supplies and material similar to that of General Foch in military operations, someone who would have authority to decide just what supplies and materials should be brought to France by the Allies and to determine their disposition.[61]

In spite of Pershing's final paragraph, he soon had second thoughts about the idea of appointing a supreme head for supplies, and when approached by Marshal Foch on the matter, Pershing explained that he did not think this step was practical.[62] He explained his change of opinion to Clemenceau, concluding that the best solution to this difficult problem would be an inter-Allied committee whose decisions should be unanimous.

In a further conference with Clemenceau, General Pershing presented a draft for an agreement that they eventually both signed. They agreed that the Allied governments should subscribe to the principle of unification of military supplies and utilities for the use of the Allied armies. Further, they agreed that a board consisting of representatives of all the Allied armies should be constituted at once in order to apply this principle and so far as possible coordinate the use of utilities and the distribution of supplies among the Allied armies. Moreover, the unanimous decision of this board regarding the allotment of material and supplies should have the force of orders and be carried out by the respective supply agencies. Further details of the organization by which this plan would be carried out should be left to the board, subject to such approval by the respective governments as might at any time seem advisable. Clemenceau and Pershing expressed their desire to submit this plan immediately to the British and Italian governments.[63] Pershing explained to Foch that whereas the strategical use of the armies had been placed in the hands of the Allied commander in chief, the responsibility for their tactical direction still remained in the hands of their respective commanders. If, however, there had been a general mingling of units regardless of national integrity, then a general supply system applicable to the entire front under a single head might have been logical. But no commander in chief would forego control of his supplies any more than he would yield the military command over his army, and it was therefore only by establishing the principle of unification that even the inter-Allied board could be made acceptable. Pershing concluded that the system already gave excellent service, and he maintained that it was more satisfactory than any plan of arbitrary control could be.[64]

THE IMPACT ON LOGISTICS OF OPENING
ADDITIONAL THEATERS OF WAR

Even the militarily inexperienced understand that the shift of troops into new or additional theaters of war involves the need to maintain these troops in their new location. This implies not only their transportation, but also supplying them with ammunition, food and clothing, while planning for medical care and evacuation of the sick and wounded. As a result of changes, transportation and munitions have to be diverted from other fronts.

In the framework of World War I, it is evident that logistic changes were required for the Dardanelles campaign, the opening of the Macedonian front, the diversion of troops for the Mesopotamian front, the Sinai and Palestine front, the Alpine front in Italy and the smaller campaigns in Africa. Each new effort necessitated logistic planning. The decision makers had to weigh not just the operative aspects, but also the pros and cons from a logistic point of view.

While concluding the investigation of logistic problems, it should be mentioned that Portugal was added as a partner in the Entente mainly because of logistic considerations. British Foreign Minister Edward Grey's memoirs made it clear:

It seemed unreasonable to us to expose Portugal to the risks of war, unless our military or naval authorities considered that action on her part could be of material assistance to us. . . . For some weeks therefore, after the outbreak of war, it seemed better that Portugal should remain neutral. . . . In the autumn, however, both the British and French Armies came to be in urgent need of field-artillery. The Portuguese had some excellent guns, and Kitchener told us that it was essential to get these for use on the French front immediately. It became my business to get the guns. The Portuguese were willing that we should have the guns, but they belonged to the Government, and for a Government, as distinct from a private firm, to supply guns to a belligerent is an unneutral act. If Portugal departed from neutrality she wished to do it with the full status of an Ally at our request.[65]

Grey recalled that the request was made, and as a result Portugal entered the war. While this may sound rather exaggerated, it is true.

WAR FINANCES

Even a superficial glance at the list of members of the Alliance[66] reveals a grave disparity in economic and financial power among the twenty-eight (or thirty-four) nations involved.

First and foremost, the Russian Empire was seriously weak financially, due not only to its inherent social structure but also to the military defeats it sustained during the previous decades and, above all, during the Russo-Japanese War of 1905. Thus the French, when concluding the Franco-Russian Convention of 1892, discussed in Chapter 2, were already aware that in order to encourage their new ally and to enable it to fulfill its part in a future war against Germany, substantial financial support would be required. This was accomplished by providing French loans for the development of the heavy Russian industry and for the extension of the Russian railway network.[67] Nevertheless, Danilov argued that immediately after the outbreak of the war, severe financial difficulties developed.[68] Anticipated additional financial burdens led him to oppose the entry of smaller partners into the Alliance.[69]

In order to find proper solutions for the Russian financial plight, the three Allied finance ministers met in Paris in February 1915. Poincaré reported in his diary that the French finance minister, Ribot, had had a financial talk with the Russian finance minister, Bark, and the British Chancellor of the Exchequer, Lloyd George. But the Chancellor of the Exchequer would not hear of a collective loan to be issued for the benefit of the three Allied nations, and preferred that the reserve bullion in the Bank of France should be put at the service of England if her reserve of gold were to fall low. Ribot was very reasonably opposed to an arrangement that might depreciate the French standard, and thought that at the most, if any danger were to arise, France might lend England a fixed sum, say 150 million. However, he felt that in return England should consent to open her market to France or, at any rate, not to forbid her banks to accept French national defense bonds. Moreover Poincaré reported that Ribot would also have liked the Triple Entente to agree to issue jointly the loans necessary for Belgium, Serbia, Greece and Romania, or at least to guarantee them. Concerning these last points nothing was yet decided, but certain principles had been laid down and some measures were adopted. Poincaré's report continued that on the initiative of Mr. Lloyd George, the conference had proclaimed the financial and economic solidarity of the Allies, and consequently, until circumstances permitted Russia to borrow money on the French and English markets, the two governments had promised that each of them would make advances to Petrograd of up to

25 million sterling. Thus the first credit to be opened by France in favor of Russia in 1915 was fixed at a maximum sum of 625 million francs. Poincaré concluded that up to now Mr. Lloyd George's solidarity had only operated against France. He asked whether France could ever invoke it in her own favor.

The following day, Poincaré gave another reference to this conference in his diary, indicating that the press had published a very optimistic official communiqué on the ministerial conference in which it stated that "the three Powers are resolved to combine their financial, no less than their military, resources so as to prosecute the war to final victory."[70] President Poincaré continued by writing that in spite of this note, very difficult negotiations had been going on all day and some pretty sharp words had been exchanged. Bark again insisted that either the French and English markets should be opened for a large loan or that upwards of $2.5 billion should be advanced to Russia. But he finished on a more reasonable note. Lloyd George then asked for a sort of pool of reserves of bullion, but it was only agreed that the Banks of France and Russia should each send 150,000,000 francs worth of gold to the Bank of England if the reserve in London were to fall below a certain figure. Poincaré concluded that in the end everything was settled, but the uncompromising attitude of Bark had had a very bad effect on Ribot, who spoke of the Russian minister with curled lips.[71]

On may wonder how financial aid to Russia was perceived by British generals in October 1914. In Field Marshal French's memoirs appeared the question, How can the Russian people successfully withstand the strain of the clash of arms, when the immense foreign loans and the placing of enormous contracts brought grist to the mills of that corrupt mass of financiers whose business was only to fatten on the misfortunes of their fellow creatures?[72]

Some 5½ months after the meeting of the three finance ministers, the issues discussed in February 1915 were still not settled, as is clear from Poincaré's diary. He reported that Ribot still had serious difficulties not only with the Russian finance minister, who was asking for a renewal of the advance of 625 million, but also with the Bank of England and the English banks, who were not willing to offer trade credits to the French bankers and were therefore not facilitating French purchases of raw materials and manufactured goods in Great Britain. Poincaré mentioned that Ribot had appealed to the Chancellor of the Exchequer. He concluded that there was still a great distance from that perfect financial entente that had been so cheerfully announced.[73]

Among the subjects on Lord Kitchener's agenda for his planned visit to Russia in 1916 were financial considerations, which were still a serious issue among the Allies.[74] In Field Marshal Haig's diary also, there are references to inter-Allied financial problems. In an entry dated April 14, 1916, he mentioned that Asquith had told him that Ribot, on behalf of the French government, had come to arrange for giving France a big loan and that unless they received the money they would have to make terms with the enemy, or at any rate the French government would be defeated. Moreover, Leo Rothschild told him about the demands of the French government for a loan due to the fact that they were afraid to tax their people. He concluded that it appeared that the French people would rather make peace with the Germans than submit to war taxes.[75] The following day, after a meeting of the Army Council with a subcommittee of the cabinet, Haig reported in his diary that in fact Britain bore the burden of the expense of all the Allies. He mentioned that recently the French had said that they were unable to meet their share of the subsidy that France and Great Britain had jointly undertaken to pay to Russia (some 300 million sterling). In addition to this, France the previous week had asked England for 60 million and would probably ask for more. He lamented that in order to keep the war going, Great Britain had to subsidize the Allies.[76]

About seven months later, Haig recorded in his diary that England gave France and Russia each 300 million a year. To Italy, Romania, Portugal, and so forth, England gave another 200 million, making a total of 800 million pounds a year handed over by England to its Allies in addition to its own expenses![77]

Haig's claim was to a certain extent confirmed by U.S. Colonel Edward M. House:

Just as vital to Allied success as British tonnage, was the maintenance of British credit, which in the preceding years had, to a large extent, been providing for the purchasing of necessary supplies for the Entente. British gold and credit had paid for the mass of food supplies, munitions, and various manufactured products which the United States exported to the Allied countries; Great Britain not merely financed its own war trade, but advanced large credits to France and Italy and the smaller Allies. But the spring of 1917 brought British finances to the verge of collapse. British balances in the United States were at the point of exhaustion. Without immediate financial assistance from the United States Government, it seemed certain that the trade between America and the Allies would cease, the war needs of the Allies could not be met, and Allied credit would collapse.[78]

This last statement is supported in General Bliss's biography, where it is stated that the first concern of the British and French missions to the

United States after obtaining an American declaration of war on Germany was loans for their depleted war chests.[79] According to Bliss, this was also the reason the Italians asked for American troops to be diverted to Italy. They had heard of the large sums the Americans were spending in France, and Italian politicians were being blamed for not getting their share.[80]

Even the Chinese were vying for American money during the war. Chi-Sung-Chun's study reveals that the Chinese government was ready to furnish the Allies with as many men as they desired, provided the United States would give financial assistance.[81]

Finally, in order to regulate the financial problems, the Inter-Allied Council on Finances and War Purchases was appointed in mid-December 1917.[82]

It seems that when discussing the problems of war financing in the context of the coalition partners, the relations can best be summed up by the proverb, He who pays the piper calls the tune.

NOTES

1. Joseph Jacques Césaire Joffre, *The Personal Memoirs of Joffre*, vol. 1, London, 1932, pp. 149–50.

2. Ibid., pp. 154–55.

3. Ibid., p. 300.

4. Ibid., pp. 299–304 passim; also: John French, *1914*, Boston, 1919, pp. 167–77 passim.

5. Field Marshal Sir Douglas Haig, *Features of the War*, Washington, D.C., 1919, p. 20.

6. William Robertson, *From Private to Field-marshal*, London, 1921, p. 227.

7. Jurij N. Danilov, *Rußland im Weltkriege 1914–1915*, Jena, Germany, 1925, p. 103.

8. Robertson, p. 252.

9. Frederick Palmer, *Bliss, Peacemaker*, New York, 1934, p. 135.

10. André Tardieu, *France and America*, Boston, 1927, p. 216.

11. Ibid., p. 223.

12. Gen. John J. Pershing, *My Experience in the World War*, vol. 1, New York, 1931, pp. 81–83.

13. Ibid., pp. 328–29; also: ibid., pp. 72, 144–45.

14. William J. Snow, *Signposts of Experience: World War Memoirs*, Washington, D.C., 1941, pp. 185–86, 187, n.5.

15. Tardieu, p. 223.

16. David Lloyd George, *War Memoirs of David Lloyd George*, vol. 1, London, 1936, p. 478.

17. Madelaine Chi-Sung-Chun, *The Chinese Question during the First World War*, Ann Arbor, Mich., 1977, p. 329.

18. Ibid., p. 330.

19. Ibid., p. 331.

20. Ibid.
21. Ibid.
22. Ibid., p. 330.
23. Palmer, pp. 277–78.
24. Vassilij Iasifovic Gurko, *Rußland 1914–1917*, Berlin, 1921, pp. 86–88.
25. George William Buchanan, *My Mission to Russia and Other Diplomatic Memories*, vol. 1, London, 1923, pp. 219–20.
26. Maurice Paléologue, *Am Zarenhof während des Weltkrieges*, vol. 1, München, 1925, pp. 217–19.
27. Alfred W. Knox, *With the Russian Army, 1914–1917*, New York, 1921, p. 220.
28. Gerald French, *The Life of Field-Marshal Sir John French*, London, 1931, p. 264.
29. John French, p. 342.
30. Ibid., p. 334.
31. George Arthur, *Life of Lord Kitchener*, vol. 3, London, 1920, pp. 346–47.
32. Arthur, p. 347; Sir Charles Edward Callwell, *Field-Marshal Sir Henry Wilson*, vol. 1, New York, 1927, pp. 302–3.
33. C. Shumsky-Solomonov, *Russia's Part in the World War*, New York, 1920, pp. 18–19.
34. Günther Frantz, *Rußland auf dem Wege zur Katastrophe: Tagebücher des Großfürsten Andrej und des Kriegsminister Poliwanow: Briefe des Großfürsten an den Zaren*, Berlin, 1926, p. 276.
35. Danilov, p. 105.
36. Gurko, p. 88.
37. Chi-Sung-Chun, p. 224.
38. Keith Neilson, *Strategy and Supply*, London, 1984, p. 117.
39. Samuel Hoare, *Das vierte Siegel, das Ende eines russischen Kapitels: Meine Mission in Rußland 1916/17*, Berlin, 1936, p. 224.
40. Neilson, p. 52.
41. Shumsky-Solomonov, p. 29.
42. Tardieu, p. 223, n.1.
43. Pershing, vol. 1, p. 72.
44. Ibid., p. 144.
45. Ibid., p. 145.
46. Tardieu, p. 231.
47. Palmer, p. 204.
48. Pershing, vol. 1, p. 52.
49. Ibid., p. 107.
50. Frederick Palmer, *Newton D. Baker*, vol. 1, New York, 1931, p. 395.
51. Snow, p. 225.
52. Pershing, vol. 1, p. 232; also: vol. 2, p. 231.
53. Ibid., vol. 2, p. 18.
54. Ibid., p. 125.
55. Tardieu, pp. 176–77.
56. Pershing, vol. 1, pp. 176–77.
57. Ibid., pp. 122–23.
58. Palmer, *Bliss*, p. 278.
59. Pershing, vol. 1, p. 320.
60. Palmer, *Bliss*, p. 277.
61. Pershing, vol. 1, pp. 398–99.

62. Ibid., vol. 2, pp. 220–21.

63. Ibid., pp. 56–57.

64. Ibid., pp. 220–21.

65. Edward Grey, *Twenty-five Years 1892–1916*, vol. 2, New York, 1937, p. 233.

66. Vide: Appendix A, p. 177.

67. Vladimir Aleksandrovic Suchumlinov, *Die rußische Mobilmachung im Lichte amtlicher Urkunden und den Enthüllungen des Prozesses*, Bern, 1917, p. 241; Danilov, p. 113.

68. Danilov, p. 39.

69. Supra, pp. 31, 32.

70. Raymond Poincaré, *The Memoirs of Raymond Poincaré*, vol. 4, New York, 1931, p. 30.

71. Poincaré, vol. 4, pp. 28–30 passim; Danilov, p. 39.

72. John French, p. 198.

73. Poincaré, vol. 4, pp. 136–37.

74. Arthur, vol. 3, pp. 350–51.

75. Field Marshal Sir Douglas Haig, *Private Papers of Douglas Haig, 1914–1919*, London, 1952, p. 138.

76. Ibid., p. 139.

77. Ibid., p. 174.

78. Charles Seymour, ed., *The Intimate Papers of Colonel House*, vol. 3, New York, 1926–28, p. 4.

79. Palmer, *Bliss*, p. 145.

80. Ibid., p. 313.

81. Chi-Sung-Chun, p. 330.

82. W. B. Fowler, *British-American Relations 1917–1918*, Princeton, N.J., 1969, p. 106.

9

ALLIANCE ON THE PEACE PATH

With victory in sight, the Allies had to consider a new world order following the defeat of the Central Powers. At the same time, the pitfalls of a coalition emerged in the context of the termination of a war that was jointly conducted. Marshal Foch defined the problem succinctly: "One more disadvantage of coalitions: *the sharing of the plunder, the distribution of the assets!*"[1] It ultimately became necessary to survey the war aims of each partner, especially since there was a vast difference between the war aims of the veteran partners and those of the United States. In the summer of 1917, Colonel House drew attention to the fact that "coordination of war aims between the Allies and the United States was just as important, in a certain sense, as coordination of military and economic efforts."[2]

The atmosphere on the eve of the peace negotiations is vividly described in Bliss's biography. Palmer mentioned that the familiar faces of past meetings in days of stress and alarm were now there in this hour, when triumph was still touched with uncertainty: Lloyd George; Clemenceau; Orlando; Balfour; Pichon; Sonnino; Foch; Weygand; Sir Henry Wilson; Vesnetch, Serbian minister in Paris; Venizelos for Greece and in later meetings, Hymans for Belgium; Rodriguez, Portuguese minister in Paris; and Matsui, Japanese minister in Paris—while other emissaries of the Allies were hurrying to Paris or knocking at the door in order that they, too, might let their claims be known. Palmer drew attention to the fact that inevitably, humanly, nationally, with the sun of victory brightening the landscape in the distance, the Englishman was above all thinking of his empire, of Mesopotamia and India; the Frenchman, of course, of the Rhine again as a French river, and of Strasbourg as his own, and Syria; the Italian wanted Trieste, Fiume and the Adriatic as an Italian lake forever; the Serb longed for Bosnia and Herzegovina in a great Yugo-Slav nation with Fiume as its port; and the Greek wanted to expand as far as Constantinople. In addition, there appeared on the horizon the frantically gesturing hands of subject peoples who sought nationhood. Bliss clearly understood the position held by Lloyd George, Clemenceau and Orlando, who were, as he observed, deftly discarding President Wilson's Fourteen Points, and he understood their position as national leaders who sought national compensation for national sacrifices and loss of blood and money.[3]

As could have been expected, the question of the list of countries to be represented at the Peace Conference and the question of how many delegates each country should have were rather difficult issues. From Lord Hankey's account of the Peace Conference and its preliminaries, it is evident that the French proposed that each Great Power (Great Britain, the United States, France, Italy and Japan) should have five delegates. Small countries (Belgium, Greece, Portugal, Romania, Serbia, Siam), those with a "special interest" (China and Brazil) and already-recognized new states (Poland and Czechoslovakia) would each have two delegates. Small countries that were "theoretically belligerent" (Cuba, Panama, Liberia, Guatemala, Nicaragua, Costa Rica, Haiti, Honduras), those that severed diplomatic relations with the Central Powers (Bolivia, Peru, Uruguay, Ecuador), countries that remained neutral, and each new state-in-the-making, was to have one delegate.

The question of representatives from the British Dominions arose immediately, after it had been decided in London that their delegations should be admitted as additional small belligerent powers (two delegates each). Hankey reported that there was extended discussion on the list. For example, the allotment in the draft for Brazil was criticized on the grounds that it had not done much and had suffered little in the war. Compared to Belgium, which had fought hard and suffered greatly, Brazil's contribution was negligible. Balfour questioned why Brazil should have more representatives than Portugal, which had sent two divisions to the western front in Europe and had also taken part in the fighting in Africa. President Wilson took Brazil's side, stressing its size and power. Other disagreements centered around Serbia, which had suffered more than Belgium, and even after the German occupation had raised new divisions that played a decisive role in the final campaign in Macedonia.

Additional differences of opinion included Greece, Romania, Poland and Czechoslovakia. As was to be expected, Lloyd George maintained the

British claim for proper representation of Canada, which had lost more men than Belgium; Australia, which had lost more men than the United States; New Zealand, with an outstanding fighting record; South Africa, and India, whose native states alone had raised 180,000 men. He argued that all these countries should be represented. As was to be expected, these claims led to the question of overall British representation.

If, for instance, Canada, Australia, South Africa and India were to have two representatives and New Zealand either one or two, as the British demanded, the British Empire would have fourteen or fifteen representatives, while each of the other Great Powers would have five representatives. This would unbalance the conference. Hankey reported President Wilson's reaction that the question of representation was largely one of sentiment and psychology. The president declared that if the Dominions were given additional representation, the impression among those who did not know the full facts would be that they were merely additional British representatives. Above all, this impression would be strong among the small powers. He added that to put the matter brutally, the Great Powers would appear to be running the Peace Conference. Lloyd George countered that if five of the representatives from the Dominions were included in the British delegation, Great Britain would have no representation at all. Therefore, he maintained, the smaller powers should be satisfied with one representative each. He asked for the same representation for the Dominions and for India. He supported this claim with the fact that Australia, for example, had sent more men to the war than Belgium, Serbia or Romania.

After much wrangling, a compromise was reached that allotted two delegates each to Australia, Canada, India (including the native states) and South Africa, and one delegate to New Zealand. Newfoundland was not granted separate representation, but its delegate could be included in the British delegation. This decision satisfied all the Dominions except New Zealand.

The compromise on New Zealand created a difficult domestic problem, since it had intended to send both the prime minister and the leader of the other party in the coalition government to participate in the Peace Conference because a general election was scheduled immediately after the conference. In the end, New Zealand reached a gentleman's agreement that the two parties should have equal status at the conference. The problem was eventually solved by Lloyd George's consent to provide one of the five British seats for the second New Zealander.

With this problem solved, the other problems of representation of the smaller states were easily cleared up. President Wilson secured three seats for Brazil, while Montenegro and Costa Rica were excluded from the list.

The final list included seventy delegates. Russia was not represented in any form at the Peace Conference.[4]

The purpose of giving details of the preliminaries for the Peace Conference is to show that procedural considerations bore as much weight as substantial ones.

Another procedural issue concerned the official language of the conference. Lloyd George had instructed the British members on the administrative staff to insist from the outset that English be equal to French. Hankey reported that "the French officials objected strongly to the displacement of French from the privileged position it had occupied so long as the language of diplomacy."[5] They stressed its advantages in precision and nuance, and fought to secure it as the sole official text for the conference proceedings. However, the English-speaking countries— Great Britain, the Dominions and the United States—played a major role in the victory, and expected to have an equally important role in the peace process. Moreover, whereas in Europe, French perhaps still predominated, in many countries outside Europe, where there were numerous problems awaiting settlement, English was gaining in importance. In the midst of this debate, the issue became more complicated when the Italians insisted that if there was more than one official language, Italian must be added. They could accept French as the sole official language in case of dispute, but not two official languages. Lloyd George and President Wilson countered that if Italian was accepted as a third official language, then Japanese was to be admitted as a fourth. This issue was finally settled after prolonged discussions, and after the American delegation would not approve the "Protocol of the First Session" in French before receiving the English text. This proved to be decisive. Thereafter, all the proceedings were circulated simultaneously in French and English.[6]

THE LONG SHADOW OF RUSSIA

Even though Russia was not represented at the Peace Conference, the agreements concluded between Russia and the other members of the Entente, referred to in previous chapters, influenced the policy of the Alliance until the Russian Revolution. By late September 1914, the Russian foreign minister informed the French ambassador that Russia's intention was to create a situation in Europe that would lead to a lasting European peace. The French reply to this declaration of intent was that this ultimate Russian aim was in complete accordance with French aims.[7] At about the same time, Russian diplomatic contacts with Great Britain achieved British consent that in case of a German defeat, the question of the Straits and Constantinople would be settled in accordance with Russian intentions. In November 1914, the Russians also prepared a memorandum specifying their demands in connection with the Straits.[8]

After the Dardanelles campaign began, the Russians not only exchanged views with the other Allies concerning the possibility of Turkey withdrawing from the war and the conditions of a truce with the Ottoman Empire but also discussed the conditions for a future comprehensive peace.[9] A British aide-mémoire, dated February 27–March 12, 1915, was issued by the British Embassy in Petrograd in reply to a Russian memorandum the previous week. It stated that "in view of the fact that Constantinople will always remain a trade entrepôt for South-Eastern Europe and Asia Minor, His Majesty's Government will ask that Russia shall, when she comes in the possession of it, arrange for a free port for goods in transit to and from non-Russian territory." As far as the Dardanelles campaign was concerned, the British memorandum stated that "Russia alone will, if the war is successful, gather the direct fruits of these operations." However, the final passage of the memorandum stressed that "Sir E. Grey points out that it is most desirable that the understanding now arrived at between the Russian, French, and British governments should remain secret."[10] When the United States joined the coalition, they were not informed about the British and French agreement to the Russian demands. The letter from Grand Duke Nikolai Mikhailovitch to the czar in October 1916 was discussed in Chapter 3.[11] It detailed Russian aspirations if a peace agreement was dictated by the Allies.

In April 1917 General Henry Wilson recorded in his diary that he had had a talk with Smuts and Painlevé. Smuts wanted the English and French to come to a clear understanding as to what they wanted when peace began to be discussed, in particular with regard to Constantinople. However, Wilson pointed out that Constantinople could not be discussed in Russia's absence.[12] As soon as Russia dropped out of the war, it was no longer a party to the final peace arrangements. To the contrary, its former Allies, including the Americans, embarked on intervention into Russian territory.[13]

FRANCE AND PEACE NEGOTIATIONS

In Chapter 3, the reactions to peace by Huguet and Tardieu, two Frenchmen who were in close contact with the British and Americans, were quoted.[14] Both complained that their British partner was selfish in the face of peace and was completely ignorant of the severe sacrifices France had made toward the common goal. Therefore, it is not surprising that the French architect of the final victory, Prime Minister Clemenceau, was equally critical of the British. He maintained that England had, in many ways, returned to its former policy of raising conflicts in Europe. In addition, England was the only Ally that fiercely opposed the imposition of harsh armistice clauses on Germany. Clemenceau felt that England zealously tried to lighten Germany's fate, because it feared a shift of power in favor of its French "ally." Clemenceau also mentioned in his memoirs that Winston Churchill reported a conversation he had had with Lloyd George in which the latter was contemplating how England could best render aid to Germany. Sarcastically, Clemenceau pondered whether the English would not do better to contemplate how to assist France, which had been so brutally devastated by German soldiers.[15]

Clemenceau was no less critical of the United States. He accused it of having acquired great wealth during the war and then presenting France with the bill, revealing avarice rather than honor.[16] Tardieu, the Frenchman who was then best acquainted with American domestic affairs, agreed with the criticism of American economic policy leveled by his superior, while giving full credit to the American assistance rendered to France vis-à-vis Great Britain in the political sphere. He wrote that during the crises of the Peace Conference, President Wilson, except on one or two occasions, had proven himself a staunch supporter and honest friend of France. Without him, in April 1919, France could never have overcome Lloyd George's opposition to the occupation of the Rhine. It was thanks to President Wilson that in May France was able to save Upper Silesia from the grasp of Germany. Above all, it was his support which, in June 1919, enabled France to break down England's opposition to all the treaty clauses: territorial, military, political, and financial.[17]

In its hour of victory, French disappointment in its former ally is reflected in the epilogue to Huguet's memoirs. Pointing an accusing finger toward England, he stressed that victory had cost her dear: she was under a load of financial debt; in fact, the taxable were taxed more heavily than ever. Great Britain's industry, diverted from its normal channels of production by the needs of the war, was reviving only slowly; her overseas trade, which was half-paralyzed during the war, was faced everywhere with an America whose merchant marine had been enlarged incredibly during the last few years and whose coal was beginning to compete with hers. The number of England's unemployed grew to a disquieting figure. It was therefore of vital importance that this state of affairs should end as quickly as possible.

Huguet concluded that there was only one remedy, namely, to revive the old-time activity by reopening old markets and by creating new ones.

He condemned the British for denying their wartime vows that they would punish the guilty, oppress Germany, and ransack the very bottom of her purse to make Germany pay up to the last penny. Now there was no question of such activities. Huguet wrote that now the slogan reigned that peace, general peace, must be attained at all costs in order to allow, as quickly as possible, the resumption of business. This was, from then on, the sole aim of England, and to that she sacrificed every other consideration, including the critical position of France. She would not even admit, Huguet argued, the legality of French claims. While England was regarding France as an obstacle in the reestablishment of peace, Huguet maintained that from then on, France found England constantly in her way. Little wonder that he concluded that England always acted to France's detriment. He summed up by stating that one could almost say that the years gone by since peace was signed told the story of French differences with England.[18] One has to bear in mind that Huguet's book was published in 1928, ten years after the end of the war.

GREAT BRITAIN AND PEACE NEGOTIATIONS

On April 29, 1917, South African statesman Jan C. Smuts, who then had an important voice in the British war cabinet, submitted a memorandum entitled "The General Strategic and Military Situation." In this memorandum he defined four British war aims:

1. The destruction of the German colonial system with a particular view to the future security of all vital communications to the British Empire. Smuts argued that this had already been done, and stated that this achievement, which was of enormous value, ought not to be endangered at the peace negotiations.
2. All parts that might afford Germany opportunity of expansion to the Far East and would thus endanger Great Britain's position as an Asiatic power should be torn off from the Turkish Empire.
3. The enemy must evacuate Belgium, Northern France, Serbia, Montenegro and Romania, and must compensate Belgium and perhaps France and Serbia.
4. A settlement must be reached that will limit or destroy the military predominance of the Germanic powers in Europe, though Smuts was prepared to leave the actual details of such settlement open for the ensuing peace conference.[19]

In a different document also written in 1917, Smuts contemplated whether "Central Europe versus British Empire will be [the] real issue at peace." As far as America was concerned, his note read, "America (Monroe) may well prove [a] diplomatic embarrassment at end. Her objects [are] not ours. Unless our case [be] fair and moderate she will not support us."[20]

In his diary, published by his biographer in 1927, Field Marshal Sir Henry Wilson clarified British resentment about the diplomatic moves that President Wilson made without consulting his allies. In his entry of October 15, 1918, Sir Henry wrote: "It really is a complete usurpation of power of negotiation."[21]

Writing in his diary about the same events, Field Marshal Haig recorded a conversation with Prime Minister Lloyd George, who gave him the impression that he felt Great Britain might have to face both internal troubles and difficulties with some of her present allies.[22]

In the discussions held by the Imperial War Cabinet to resolve the issue of representation of the Dominions at the Peace Conference, Australian Prime Minister Hughes gave a caustic warning "that if we are not very careful we should find ourselves dragged quite unnecessarily behind the wheels of President Wilson's chariot."[23]

THE UNITED STATES: ON THE TRAIL OF PEACE

It is obvious that American war aims as well as plans for peace diverged from those projected by its European "associates." Tardieu, the sober French observer of the American scene, described the situation, hinting that from the first day the United States had insisted that it was not an Ally and that it would act only as an associate. The war aims of the others would not be its war aims; it would have its own war aims from which nothing would divert it. Tardieu concluded that the United States declared its own war, not the Allies' war. He quoted Colonel House and American newspaper columnist Walter Lippman, who said, "After all, we are not going to get mixed up in the future of Alsace-Lorraine and Constantinople."[24] Tardieu concluded that this state of mind remained unchanged. Even at the height of military enthusiasm there was always distrust of European politics. The war President Wilson declared on Germany was an American war, American in inception and American in spirit.[25]

In his memoirs, Trask stressed that it must be understood that "the United States entered the war without striking prior bargains with the Entente as Italy had done in 1915."[26] He also revealed that a short time after America entered the war, the president wrote to Colonel House and explained his reasons for avoiding discussion of war aims: England and France had not the same views with regard to peace that the United States had. When the war ended the United States could force them to its way of thinking because by that time they would, among other things, be financially in American hands, but they could not be forced at the time, and any attempt to speak for them would bring on disagreements that would inevitably come to the surface in public and rob the whole thing of its effect. U.S. peace terms, those upon which they would undoubtedly insist, were at that time not acceptable to either France or Italy. For the moment, Wilson left Great Britain out of consideration.

Trask maintained that "the President was under no illusions concerning the war aims of the Entente Powers." However, "he sought to adjourn discussion of the peace settlement until the Central Powers had been defeated and American power greatly enhanced."[27]

In August 1918, in a letter to Newton Baker, the Secretary of War, Bliss raised the possibility that while the Americans were striving for the termination of the war in 1919, the Allies might try to prolong it until 1920. Although they would say that they were interested in ending the war in 1919, Bliss assumed that in practice they might not be ready to do the things and to make the sacrifices that would be necessary to end the war at that time. He explained that all agreed that the war could be ended only by American troops, supplies, and money, but that when the end came, the Allies would want certain favorable military situations to have been created in different parts of the world that would warrant demands on the United States, which they thought perhaps would be the principal arbiter of peace terms. Bliss continued his argument, pointed out that if these sufficiently favorable military situations were not created on certain secondary theaters by the beginning of autumn of the next year, the Allies might want to continue through 1920, at the cost of United States troops and money, a war that possibly if not probably would have ended with complete success by operations on the western front in 1919.[28]

Continuing in this vein, Bliss wrote about American intention to bolster its forces in France to eighty divisions. If the proposed eighty-division program could be carried through, the United States would have in France before the middle of the next year more than the rifle strength of all its Allies on the western front combined. U.S. loss began at this time. Consequently, in the next year, instead of hearing of the losses of many hundreds of thousands of America's Allies on the western front, there would be hundreds of thousands of American losses and a constantly diminishing proportion of losses among its Allies. Although the Allies had lost frightfully in the past, the war did not need to be prolonged until the American losses equalled theirs. He added proudly that one could say that already the American troops had saved the situation. They had already saved France and Europe. Therefore, the United States had the right to demand that the hundreds of thousands of young American troops, the present hope of their country and the future hope of the world, should not be sacrificed unless it was an absolute necessity.

In fact, what Bliss had in mind was the suspicion that the Allies were prepared to continue the war for their own imperialistic ambitions. Five days after this letter was sent, he pressed the same points in a cable that read: "If sufficiently favorable military situations are not created in certain secondary theatres by beginning of autumn next year, the governments of our Allies may be willing to continue through 1920."[29] Little wonder that Secretary Baker suggested to the president a showdown on the subject. In the end, it was decided that Baker should go to Europe to oversee the coordination efforts for ending the war in 1919.[30]

When it became evident that the war might end unexpectedly in 1918, the Allies began discussions, first of the armistice terms, and immediately afterward, of peace terms. Marshal Foch consulted the other Allied military leaders about the terms of the armistice to be imposed on Germany. Pershing reported that he had a conversation with the marshal, who spoke of the notes that had been exchanged between the Germans and President Wilson. Foch expressed some apprehension about how far the president might commit the Allies, expressing his hope that the president would not become involved in protracted correspondence and allow himself to be duped by the Germans. Echoing Field Marshal Wilson, Foch complained that the president had not consulted the Allies. However, Pershing tried to placate Foch by telling him that the president would not act alone. Pershing ended the conversation with the impression that Foch favored the unconditional surrender of the German armies.

Pershing subsequently tried to ascertain British views, in particular those of Lord Milner, the Secretary of State for War, and General Henry Wilson, the CIGS. He understood that Lord Milner occupied a moderate position between those demanding unconditional surrender and those who wanted peace immediately on the best possible terms. In particular, he thought that an armistice should be granted only on the condition that Germany lay down its heavy guns and give a naval guarantee, such as the surrender of Heligoland. General Wilson, on the other hand, had his doubts as to whether it was possible to inflict a crushing victory on Germany before winter, although he thought that armistice conditions should make it impossible for Germany to resume operations. He was opposed to President Wilson's suggestion of German evacuation of Allied territory because he preferred to fight the Germans where they were rather than on their own frontiers with a much shortened line. Like his Secretary of State for War, General Wilson maintained that the Germans should abandon

their heavy guns, surrender Heligoland, forfeit some warships and submarines, and retire to the east bank of the Rhine.

From these discussions, Pershing received the impression that General
Wilson expressed the extreme British army viewpoint but that there were
more conservative circles within the British government that advised
against pushing Germany too far, for fear of having no government in
Germany strong enough to make peace. These circles feared that revolu-
tions in Germany might unsettle Allied countries and endanger constitutional monarchies. Pershing concluded: "These hints gave the general
attitude of the British as it was expressed later on when the time came to
dictate the terms."[31]

In the end, the military terms of the armistice with Germany were
drafted by Marshal Foch, after consultation with his colleagues, and were
finally approved by the political chiefs without any substantial changes.
The editor of Colonel House's papers reacted to the widespread "legend
that pictures the United States as pleading for softer terms," which in his
opinion "has no historical foundation."[32] He stressed that the president
sent Colonel House to the Supreme War Council with a free hand and
without any instructions. House made it clear that in all military matters,
the U.S. government was inclined to accept Foch's recommendations.
However, on October 29, 1918, Wilson sent a cable to House that made
his opinion clear. He declared that in his deliberate judgment, the whole
U.S. weight should be thrown behind an armistice that would not permit
a renewal of hostilities by Germany but, on the other hand, would be as
moderate and reasonable as possible within that condition. The president
was certain that too much severity on the part of the Allies would make a
genuine peace settlement exceedingly difficult, if not impossible. He
added that foresight was better than immediate advantage.

Colonel House sensed that there was no disagreement with this attitude
by either Clemenceau or Lloyd George. Moreover, he informed both prime
ministers that the president was quite willing to leave the terms of the
armistice to Marshal Foch, General Pershing, Field Marshal Haig, General
Diaz, and General Pétain.

Marshal Foch invited the generals to his headquarters on October 25 to
solicit their opinions. The chief difference between the French and the
British was that the French insisted on much more rigorous conditions than
the British. General Pétain proposed the disarming of German troops,
except for handguns, and the occupation of a broad strip of German
territory to serve as a pledge of compliance with Allied peace conditions.
He suggested a specific time for the German withdrawal that would
preclude their ability to carry away heavy equipment. In addition to the

undisputed evacuation of Alsace-Lorraine, Pétain suggested the Allied occupation not only of the left bank of the Rhine but of a zone fifty kilometers wide on the right bank. In comparison, Field Marshal Haig's conditions were much more moderate and seemed insufficient to the French as well as to the Americans.

On the whole, Pershing declared himself in accord with Pétain. Foch had not expressed his own views at this meeting, but in a draft of his terms that he sent to Clemenceau the following day, he deemed Haig's conditions insufficient. On the other hand, his demands were not as extreme as Pétain's. Foch also agreed with Pershing that it was necessary to occupy bridgeheads on the Rhine and to establish a neutral zone to the east. Whereas the British regarded these terms as unnecessarily severe, General Bliss believed that they would not fulfill the president's conditions. The president wanted to preclude the Germans from being able to resume the hostilities during the course of the peace negotiations. In Bliss's opinion, Foch's terms provided for the concentration of German armies within their own boundaries and left them with sufficient armaments to threaten a renewal of hostilities. Accordingly, his formula amounted to unconditional surrender: complete disarmament and demobilization.

Ten years later, answering the questions of Charles Seymour, the editor of House's papers, Bliss said "that no sooner was the Armistice signed [on Foch's terms] than the Allies became obsessed with a fear that Germany could rearm herself to such an extent, at least, as would make her very formidable, and for months this fear haunted the Peace Conference."[33] In order to support his own deviating position as far as the armistice terms were concerned, he explained: "It wasn't the partial disarmament of Germany that protected the Allies from this danger so much as it was the complete internal disruption of Germany following the signing of the armistice."[34]

Before the Peace Conference began, an additional procedural bone of contention with the Americans emerged. President Wilson wanted to attend the conference in person. The initial reaction in France and Great Britain was unfavorable, because the president was not only the head of government but also the head of state, and his presence might encourage other heads of states to attend. Hankey, who was intimately involved in the administrative aspects of the conference, argued that it might create precedents and problems, including the issue of who would be president of the conference. However, Wilson's desire to be present was so strong that he agreed to come as head of the American government and to accept Clemenceau as president of the conference.[35]

Thomas B. Mott, the U.S. military attaché in France, recalled that there was also tension between the Allies over the execution of the armistice clauses in connection with the three Allied bridgeheads on the Rhine. When these clauses were announced, it was discovered that the French alone were to occupy the Mainz bridgehead, while those at Cologne and Coblenz were to be staffed by combined British, American and French forces. The British protested and won their point. General Pershing ordered Mott to present his objections, but General Weygand was not convinced. Mott went to see Marshal Foch, who was equally firm in refusing to change. At the end of his heated discussion with Foch, Mott unleashed his anger: "Are you willing, for a matter which seems at best technical, to send two million American soldiers home with the feeling that they have not been treated altogether as your equals?"[36] In fact, as Mott recalled, he did not get immediate satisfaction, and the issue was settled later by a weak compromise. Mott's final verdict was:

There can be no doubt that a great majority of the American rank and file sailed away with a feeling of resentment against what they had grown to consider— justly or unjustly—as French tutelage. They felt somewhat the same about the British, but here the points of contact that might become irritating were fewer and the issues less important.[37]

In a similar context, Edward B. Parsons's study of Wilsonian diplomacy contains a reference to the Allied attitude to the American forces in Europe after the armistice. Wilson was aware of the fact that during the last few months of the war, the British had carried about 60 percent of Pershing's troops across the Atlantic. After the war, the American ships devoted to this task could not bring them home in less than eighteen months. If the British continued to refuse to help, as they had, the American forces in France would become "hostages" to the Entente if serious disagreements over the conditions arose between the United States and the Allies. The administration was concerned that if it pressed Britain for help, the British would demand that ships from the Americans be taken out of profitable trade traffic to help transport and supply Pershing's troops. The U.S. Secretary of Treasury pointed out that unless the British were persuaded to contribute shipping to take American troops home following the Armistice, the British would have additional cargo space to increase their trade at America's expense.[38]

As it turned out, economic differences developed as early as the summer of 1918 in connection with the postwar economic policy toward Germany.[39] There is evidence that the president was infuriated when he began to suspect that Britain was trying to ensure postwar domination of world markets to the detriment of the United States and other countries.[40] Parsons claims that "official Washington was taking the line that the war had been won by the United States' efforts; now Britain was seeking 'selfish gain' from a predominant American victory."[41]

ITALY AND JAPAN

It has been mentioned that the secret treaty that Britain, France and Russia concluded with Italy had not been published because it would have been bad propaganda in America.[42] Bliss's biography states that several copies of this pact were among his papers, and he apparently kept these as a reminder. Palmer believed that the treaty lay heavy on Bliss's mind throughout the Peace Conference. It was obvious that Italy entered the war in order to annex the territories specified in the pact. But, as Palmer wrote, it would have been an awkward note if President Wilson had supplemented his war cry "to make the world safe for democracy," in encouraging the American people and soldiers to put forth their utmost effort, with an appeal to make Trieste and the Trentino area Italian territory.[43] As a result, it was to be expected that the Americans were aware of the discrepancy between the principles on which the United States entered the war, characterized by Wilson's Fourteen Points as accepted by the Allies, and the Allies' commitments under their own treaties. The Anglo-Franco-Russo-Italian Pact of 1915 was the outstanding example, although there was a similar case with Japanese claims.[44] By the end of August 1918, Bliss's letter to Baker contained a hint that in the end, the Allies might be unwilling to grant Italy all that it was promised in the secret pact of April 26, 1915.[45] This is what happened at the Peace Conference, resulting in tragic consequences for the future of Europe and the world.

As for Japan, in February and March 1917 it received assurances from Great Britain, France, Russia and Italy that at the Peace Conference they would support its claims to inherit German rights in China and the German colonies in the Pacific north of the equator. Whereas Italy had no interests in the Far East, it took part in these secret agreements only because of its treaty relations with the Entente Powers. On the other hand, Britain, France and Russia maintained interests in China. Nevertheless, they acceded to this Japanese demand for expansion because of the pressing needs of the war at the time, and above all, because of the necessity to safeguard their own possessions in the East from Japanese molestation. In fact, this was the basis for the secret agreements with Japan.[46] One should not be surprised, however, that at the Peace Conference, the British Dominions in the Pacific and to some extent the United States were not prepared to accept all that had been promised to Japan.[47]

NOTES

1. Charles Bugnet, *Foch Speaks*, New York, 1929, p. 271. (Emphasis added.)
2. Charles Seymour, ed., *The Intimate Papers of Colonel House*, vol. 3, New York, 1926–28, p. 173.
3. Frederick Palmer, *Bliss, Peacemaker*, New York, 1934, pp. 348–49.
4. Lord Maurice Hankey, *The Supreme Control at the Paris Peace Conference 1919*, London, 1963, pp. 33–37.
5. Ibid., p. 30.
6. Ibid., pp. 30–31; also, p. 18.
7. Jurij N. Danilov, *Rußland im Weltkriege 1914–1915*, Jena, Germany, 1925, p. 292.
8. Ibid., p. 399.
9. Ibid., p. 475.
10. Frank Alfred Golder, *Documents of Russian History, 1914–1917*, New York, 1927, pp. 60–62.
11. Supra, pp. 32–33; Golder, pp. 74–77.
12. Sir Charles Callwell, *Field-Marshal Sir Henry Wilson*, vol. 1, New York, 1927, p. 336.
13. We shall not enter into a detailed investigation of the intervention in Russia. On the American participation, see David S. Trask, *The United States in the Supreme War Council*, Middleton, Conn., 1961, pp. 104–5, 118–28; Records of the American Section of the Supreme War Council, M 923, 10–36–2, National Archives, Washington, D.C.
14. Supra, pp. 23, 28.
15. Georges Clemenceau, *Größe und Tragik eines Sieges*, Stuttgart, 1930, p. 87 (Original French title: *Grandeurs et misères d'une victoire*, Paris, 1930).
16. Ibid., p. 81.
17. André Tardieu, *France and America*, Boston, 1927, p. 240.
18. Charles Julien Huguet, *Britain and the War*, London, 1928, pp. 210–11.
19. W. K. Hancock and Jean van der Poel, eds., *Selections from the Smuts Papers*, vol. 3, Cambridge, England, 1966, p. 482.
20. Ibid., p. 502.
21. Callwell, vol. 2, p. 136.
22. Field Marshal Sir Douglas Haig, *The Private Papers of Douglas Haig, 1914–1919*, London, 1952, p. 338.
23. Hankey, p. 18.
24. Tardieu, p. 157.
25. Ibid., p. 157.
26. Trask, p. 7.
27. Ibid., pp. 7–8.
28. Palmer, pp. 326–27.
29. Ibid., pp. 327–28.
30. Ibid., p. 329.
31. General John J. Pershing, *My Experience in the World War*, vol. 2, New York, 1931, pp. 348–49.

32. Seymour, vol. 4, p. 110.

33. Ibid., pp. 110–15; Bliss comment of June 14, 1928, ibid., p. 147.

34. Ibid., p. 115.

35. Hankey, p. 12.

36. Thomas Bentley Mott, *Twenty Years as Military Attaché*, New York, 1979, pp. 250–51.

37. Ibid., p. 251.

38. Edward B. Parsons, *Wilsonian Diplomacy: Allied-American Rivalries in War and Peace*, St. Louis, Mo., 1978, pp. 150–51.

39. Seymour, vol. 4, p. 61.

40. Trask, p. 144.

41. Parsons, p. 166.

42. Supra, p. 39.

43. Palmer, pp. 234–35.

44. Hankey, pp. 195–96.

45. Palmer, p. 330.

46. Madelaine Chi-Sung-Chun, *The Chinese Question during the First World War*, Ann Arbor, Mich., 1977, p. 208.

47. Supra, pp. 29–30.

10

CONCLUSIONS AND LESSONS

Having followed this investigation, the reader is undoubtedly aware of what an oversimplification it is to say that coalition warfare is a complicated matter. This is especially true if one takes into account that in modern times, the forces involved in war are huge, levied mainly on the basis of compulsory service of the entire population of the nations involved.

It was different prior to the French Revolution, when armies were quite small and mercenary and coalitions were rather limited in the number of participating partners. The wartime coalition of the Entente in World War I, including more than thirty coalition partners, was a new phenomenon, demanding new theoretical and practical approaches. In the opening chapter of this study, a typology of wartime coalitions was developed that distinguished between senior and junior partners. After having surveyed various facets of the war, it should be stressed that the supremacy of the senior partners in the coalition was based upon a number of facts.

The first is an abundance of manpower. As long as the British Expeditionary Force in France was a small contingent of four infantry and one cavalry divisions, it could not play any important part in the decision-making process on the battlefield and was forced to consent, *nolens volens*, to a subordinate role. This situation changed radically with the growth of the British forces. When the United States joined the coalition, its troops, though at first arriving in France slowly, nevertheless arrived at a time when the forces of the veteran partners were dwindling. The very promise of a huge American force gave these troops clout, in spite of the fact that they had no battle experience. An abundance of manpower alone was not sufficient to defeat the enemy. Russia could levy tremendous masses, but was unable to equip or supply them properly with the huge amount of ammunition that modern warfare required.

This leads to the second requirement for the supremacy of senior partners in a coalition: economic power. The highly developed industrial nations—England, France and the United States—became the suppliers for all the coalition partners. This included supplying fuel and coal, weapons of all kinds, means of transportation, and in many instances, food.

Hand in hand with economic power comes financial power. One of the assets of the senior partner is its wealth, which enables it to support the junior partners, even if these are striving concurrently to gain economic advantages. There are instances when this support is rendered without immediate financial gain, such as when it is important to prevent a particular nation from joining the opposing camp. Such a determination involves a certain price. Oddly enough, this very fact provides junior partners with a certain amount of bargaining power.

HANDICAPS OF COALITION WARFARE

It is obvious that waging war in the framework of a coalition has inherent weaknesses, as implied by the quotation from General Sarrail with which the book begins, to the effect that Napoleon was not a great general, but was lucky to fight against coalitions. This study is aimed at uncovering most of these weaknesses. Nevertheless, it is worthwhile to enumerate them again briefly.

Divergence of War Aims. Very seldom is there a complete identity of the aim(s) by the different coalition partners for waging a particular war. This divergence influences the conduct of the war on the whole and even affects the decisions for different operational steps. It becomes crucial at the termination of the war, at the stage that Foch called "the sharing of the plunder, the distribution of the assets."[1]

Political-Military Relationships. This is a touchy issue in the conduct of every war, even one waged by a single nation. It reaches complicated dimensions in a coalition because there is the need for coordination of many different, overlapping, inter-allied tendencies, both political and military. There are a multitude of possibilities for pitting soldiers or politicians from different nations against one another. To say that World War I supplied a multitude of examples to the detriment of its efficient conduct is an understatement.

Particularistic Interests. There was a manifest absence of unity of purpose on the part of members of the Entente. Although these nations fought against a common enemy, they were each guided by different particularistic interests, which influenced the formulation of separate war aims.

Impact of Public Opinion. This is a serious issue in every democratic country, whether at war or not. It takes on additional weight in a coalition, in particular against the background of many national war aims on which the partners are not always in full agreement. It is sufficient to mention the reaction of American public opinion in connection with the secret agreements to Italian territorial demands, Russian demands concerning the Straits and Constantinople, and Japanese expansion in the Far East.

Language Barrier. This factor is so obvious that it did not receive a special investigation. Its importance stems from its influence on the cooperation in battle of troops that speak different languages. Language differences had a disastrous impact on the first meetings between British and French generals early in the war,[2] resulting in almost irreparable damage. In many investigations this problem is combined with differences in national mentality, which also affect coalition warfare.

Role of Royalty. Today this factor plays a negligible role in prewar and wartime coalitions, but this investigation demonstrates that in World War I it was a factor that the leaders of the war effort had to take into account.[3]

Amalgamation of Forces. From a purely logical viewpoint, it seems advisable to combine the forces of a minor partner with those of a major one, or the forces of an inexperienced partner that entered late in the war with veteran forces. However, history has taught that many factors, above all national pride, counteract this attempt. All endeavors to amalgamate forces in World War I came to nought.

General Reserve. Although this is an axiom of military strategy, and no serious high-ranking commander can ignore its absolute necessity for the proper conduct of a military campaign, its creation in the context of a coalition is quite difficult. The disparate interests of the commanders in chief constitute a strange phenomenon that presents itself in direct disregard to the most basic rules of warfare. Each commander in chief wants to keep his forces united and has a deep aversion to allocating part of them to another commander. During World War I, the attempt to create an inter-Allied commission for the management of the General Reserve misfired badly, as was to be expected. Conduct of war by committee has never succeeded.

Unified Command. This is another maxim of warfare, but one that coalitions have traditionally found difficult to implement. During World War I, the Entente was almost defeated before a full-fledged Supreme Commander could be appointed with common consent of all coalition partners, and above all, with the consent of the military commanders of all national contingents.

Logistic Coordination. The lack of logistic coordination is one of the gravest handicaps of coalition warfare. The smooth conduct of military operations from the logistic standpoint demands standardization of equipment of all kinds, in particular ammunition and parts to repair equipment.

Another desirable logistic requirement is the pooling of supplies. This enables a central authority to distribute the logistic means in accordance with the necessities of the various theaters of war and fronts and prevents unnecessary waste. If nations from different continents form the coalition, as was the case in World War I, the pooling of transportation and above all of shipping is a must. However, the history of warfare in the twentieth century reveals that the standardization of equipment in nontotalitarian countries that form a prewar coalition is still an ideal. Too many domestic economic problems are involved in such an undertaking, which the situation in NATO shows. The only remedy for this impasse, which was tried in World War I, is the establishment of coordination boards. While these boards serve in an advisory capacity, not a directive one, their functioning depends on the goodwill of all participants, in addition to the recognition that they have no coercive power.

DOES A COALITION PROLONG A WAR?

Some of the civilian leaders of World War I believed that the Allied victory could have come much earlier than it actually did. This was the opinion of Winston Churchill and, above all, of Lloyd George. The latter expressed his feelings in his memoirs. He pondered that no one who dispassionately reviewed the events of the war could fail to discern opportunities that presented themselves, only to be snubbed by the military and political leaders of the Entente Powers. Above all, their most obvious and most costly blunder was their failure to treat the vast battlefield of the war as a single front. He stated that Russia had unlimited resources of superb manpower—in physique, courage and tenacity. These forces also had received sufficient training to constitute a formidable army on the defensive or offensive even against German troops; they were, no doubt, equal to if not better than the Austrians. But they lacked the necessary equipment to make the best use of this fine material. Lloyd George concluded that this was the only reason why Russia was beaten. He censured France and Britain for not having effected a wiser distribution of their financial and mechanical resources—at home as well as in America—between the armies fighting in the East and those in the West.

He believed that under the right conditions the German and Austrian attack on Russia would have failed with enormous losses, and thus would have crippled the Central Powers. Above all, it was Austria, with her large Slavonic population, that could have been defeated in 1916. This would have isolated Germany. Lloyd George was sure that Austria could not have withstood the onslaught of a well-equipped and numerically superior Russian army.[4]

There is no doubt that the cumbersome structure of a coalition, composed of free and democratic states, quite often results in a rather prolonged process of reaching decisions and executing them. It seems that this is probably the price people have to pay for their chosen regime. There can be no doubt that a coalition directed by a single, undisputed senior partner will be able to act more quickly. In the long run, however, this does not indicate in any way that it will be the final victor.

AFTER WORLD WAR I

From the memoirs of statesmen and soldiers published after World War I, it is evident that the lessons to be drawn from this traumatic experience remained with most of them. The most serious attempt was made by General Bliss, whose 1922 essay has been referred to repeatedly in this study.[5] Bliss managed to compress into thirty pages an analysis of "The Evolution of the Unified Command." However, this essay should be seen not only in its historical context but also as a blueprint for the future conduct of coalition wars.

World War II. In spite of Bliss's brilliant analysis, the outbreak of the next great war found the potential partners of the anti-Hitler coalition not just unprepared but in utter disarray. This caused disaster for many countries and a waste of precious time, which led to a tremendous number of unnecessary casualties and material sacrifices. However, a system was finally adopted, in line with Bliss's recommendations from 1922. SHAEF (Supreme Headquarters Allied Expeditionary Forces), under the command of General Dwight D. Eisenhower, was exactly what Bliss had suggested. Moreover, the dispute among various armchair strategists as to whether Eisenhower was a great military captain or a rather mediocre one misses the point. It is my contention that he was the right man in the right place at the right time. What was really required was not a brilliant strategist but an individual with the necessary ability to pilot the complicated efforts of the huge Alliance in accordance with one clearly defined plan. From the memoirs of all his contemporaries, it is evident that

Eisenhower had these abilities and applied methods similar to those proclaimed and adopted by General Foch as Supreme Commander.[6]

Statesmen also managed to improve the means of overall coordination of the war effort by refining the methods of contact between the partners and, above all, between the senior partners. The institution of summit conferences of the top leaders, who during World War II also included the Russian head of state, an individual excluded from the Supreme War Council of World War I, had a decisive impact on the conduct of the war. Improved means of communication between the Allies also played an important role.

Peacetime Coalitions and Future Wars. In the aftermath of World War II, the cold war led to the formation of two coalition blocs: NATO and the Warsaw Pact. These two alliances differed in structure because of their political orientations. The Warsaw Pact was dominated by the Soviet Union, which managed to standardize equipment. On the other hand, although the United States played the leading role in NATO, it was infected with all the characteristic maladies of democratic alliances: decisions had to be reached by consensus, particularistic tendencies had to be taken into account, and standardization was out of the question, so that NATO suffered from the use of a potpourri of weapons. In addition, there have been instances when national ambitions dictated command structure, weapons development, and so forth. Although the disintegration and disappearance of the Warsaw Pact has created a new situation, this does not necessarily herald the advent of world peace.

Wars under the U.N. Flag. The United Nations has succeeded where its predecessor, the League of Nations, failed. The League of Nations tried in vain to establish a coalition to oppose the Italian invasion of Ethiopia in 1935. In comparison, the United Nations has succeeded on two different occasions in creating an intervention force against aggression that was recognized by the Security Council. The first such occasion was the Korean War in 1950, which was waged by a United Nations force. At that time, U.S. General Douglas MacArthur was appointed commander in chief of the force, which was comprised of contingents from U.N. member nations, to fight against North Korean forces that had invaded South Korea. This precedent paved the way for the formation of the huge U.N. force that fought Iraqi aggression against Kuwait in the war in the Persian Gulf in 1991. Once again, an American general, Norman Schwarzkopf, was appointed commander in chief.

This ad hoc coalition was as complicated as its predecessor in World War I, and almost dissolved as the result of differences between the partners concerning war aims. Some commentators claimed the war ended too early. They ignore the fact that it terminated exactly at the moment the mandate given to the force by the U.N. Security Council was achieved: the liberation of Kuwait from hostile invasion forces. The anti-Iraq coalition had no mandate either to destroy Iraqi armed forces, to occupy Iraq, or to remove Saddam Hussein from power. Though these aims may have been cherished by the U.S. administration, and in particular by President George Bush, they were not included in the United Nations resolution, and any attempt by the commander in chief of the coalition force to extend the war would have been resented by some participating members, inevitably leading to the disintegration of the armed alliance.

This case in point conforms exactly to the findings of this study, and is therefore not surprising.

Vietnam War. From a purely theoretical standpoint, this war was without doubt a coalition war. One cannot ignore the fact that the United States played such a dominant role in the war and that the other partners were of no real significance.

Arab-Israeli Conflict. This armed conflict became a war when the nascent State of Israel, founded in 1948 as the result of a United Nations decision, was attacked by combined Arab armies, which formed a coalition of varying sizes in different phases of the war. In spite of the Arabs' superiority in numbers and equipment, Israel has emerged victorious from every round. This may serve as a confirmation of General Sarrail's remark, quoted by Lloyd George, that Napoleon was lucky because "he only fought a Coalition."[7]

FORECAST

An ancient Hebrew proverb suggests that "since the destruction of the Holy Temple, prophecy was given to fools." Therefore, it would be inappropriate to pretend to predict future developments in connection with the conduct of coalition warfare. It has been argued that since the collapse of the communist bloc and the dissolution of the Warsaw Pact, no future wars between coalitions are to be expected. This claim was immediately contradicted by the war in the Persian Gulf that began in January 1991. Moreover, the imbalance caused by the sudden disappearance of the communist world might create focuses of unrest, as already seems to be the case. It therefore seems appropriate not to dwell on illusions. The era of a world without war is still in the future. Should it nevertheless materialize, this study can be seen as an exercise in historical research and analysis.

NOTES

1. Supra, p. 153.
2. Supra, pp. 45, 46–47, 49.
3. Supra, pp. 102–3.
4. David Lloyd George, *War Memoirs of David Lloyd George*, vol. 2, London, 1936, p. 1998.
5. Vide: supra, p. 21.
6. Vide: supra, p. 58.
7. See epigraph at front of book.

MEMBERS OF THE ALLIANCE

1. Serbia	15. Greece
2. Russia	16. Siam
3. France	17. Liberia
4. Great Britain*	18. China
5. Belgium	19. Brazil
6. Montenegro	20. Guatemala
7. Japan	21. Nicaragua
8. Italy	22. Costa Rica
9. San Marino	23. Haiti
10. Portugal	24. Honduras
11. Romania	25. Bolivia
12. U.S.A.	26. Peru
13. Cuba	27. Uruguay
14. Panama	28. Ecuador

*Includes Canada, Australia, South Africa, New Zealand, Newfoundland, and India, for a total of 34 countries.

SESSIONS OF THE SUPREME WAR COUNCIL (SWC)

Session 1:   Rapallo, November 7, 1917
Session 2:   Versailles, December 1, 1917
Session 3:   Versailles, January 30–February 2, 1918
Session 4:   London, March 14–15, 1918
Session 5:   Abbeville, May 1–2, 1918
Session 6:   Versailles, June 1–2, 1918
Session 7:   Versailles, July 2–4, 1918
Session 8:   Versailles, October 31–November 2, 1918
Session 9:
Session 10:   Paris, January 12–13, 1919
Session 11:   Paris, January 22, 1919
Session 12:   Paris, January 24, 1919
Session 13:   Paris, February 7, 1919
Session 14:   Paris, February 14, 1919
Session 15:   Paris, February 17, 1919
Session 16:
Session 17:   Paris, March, 1919;
Session 18:   last session March 17, 1919

INTER-ALLIED COMMITTEES

1. Inter-Allied Transportation Council
2. Inter-Allied Aviation Council
3. Inter-Allied Tank Committee
4. Inter-Allied Committee on Manpower Statistics
5. Inter-Allied Naval Council
6. Inter-Allied Committee for Pooling of Supplies
7. Inter-Allied Council on Finance and War Purchases
8. Inter-Allied Maritime Transport Council
9. Belgian Relief Commission
10. Inter-Allied Surgical Commission
11. Central Office of French-American Relations
12. Sanitary Commission of Allied Forces
13. Inter-Allied Committee for War Timber
14. French-Italian Military Commission
15. Inter-Allied Statistical Bureau
16. Inter-Allied Committee on Inventions
17. Inter-Allied Purchasing Bureau in Spain
18. Anglo-French-Belgian International Commission for the Restoration of Belgian Ports
19. French-Romanian Committee
20. French-Anglo-Belgian Conference for the Revision of the Berlin and Brussels Conventions

21. Inter-Allied Radiotelegraph Commission
22. Commission for War Instruction
23. Permanent International Committee for Economic Action
24. Permanent International Committee of Supplies for Switzerland
25. Permanent Inter-Allied Committee for the Study of the Questions Concerning Invalids of War

BIBLIOGRAPHY

ARCHIVALIA

The National Archives of the United States, Washington, D.C., M 923, 10–36–2. Records
of the American Section of the Supreme War Council 1917–1919. Files No. 1,
31, 46, 115, 117, 148, 155, 168, 193, 196, 198, 201, 214, 259, 276, 299, 323, 327,
332, 334, 353, 355, 358, 366, 376.

PRINTED DOCUMENTS

Golder, Frank Alfred. *Documents of Russian History, 1914–1917*. New York, 1927.

BOOKS AND ESSAYS

Albert I. *The War Diaries of Albert I, King of the Belgians*. London, 1954.

Arthur, George. *Life of Lord Kitchener*, vol. 3. London, 1920.

Asquith, Earl of Oxford and. *Memoirs and Reflections*. 2 vols. London, 1927.

Bailey, Thomas Andrew. *The Policy of the United States toward the Neutrals, 1917–
1918*. Baltimore, 1942.

Beaverbrook, William Maxwell Aitken. *Politicians and the War 1914–1918*. London,
1960.

Bliss, General Tasker H. "The Evolution of the Unified Command." *Foreign Affairs* 1,
December 15, 1922, 1–30.

Bonwetsch, Bernd. *Kriegsallianz und Wirtschaftsinteressen: Rußland in den Wirt-
schaftsplänen Englands und Frankreichs 1914–1917*. Düsseldorf, 1973.

Brussilov, Aleksiei Aleksieevich. *A Soldier's Note Book*. London, 1930.

Buchanan, George William. *My Mission to Russia and Other Diplomatic Memories.* 2 vols. London, 1923.

Bugnet, Charles. *Foch Speaks.* New York, 1929.

Callwell, Sir Charles Edward. *Experiences of a Dug-Out, 1914–1918.* London, 1921.

———. *Field-Marshal Sir Henry Wilson: His Life and Diaries.* 2 vols. New York, 1927.

Chi-Sung-Chun, Madelaine. *The Chinese Question during the First World War.* Ann Arbor, Mich., 1977.

Churchill, Winston S. *The World Crisis 1911–1918.* London, 1964.

Clemenceau, Georges. *France Facing Germany.* New York, 1919.

———. *Größe und Tragik eines Sieges.* Stuttgart, 1930. (Trans. from French: *Grandeurs et misères d'une victoire.* Paris, 1930.)

Danilov, Jurij Nikiforovich. *Rußland im Weltkriege 1914–1915.* Jena, Germany, 1925.

Foch, Ferdinand. *The Memoirs of Marshal Foch.* New York, 1931.

Fowler, W. B. *British-American Relations 1917–1918: The Role of Sir William Wiseman.* Princeton, N.J., 1969.

Francis, David R. *Russia from the American Embassy, April 1916–November 1918.* New York, 1921.

Frantz, Günther. *Rußland auf dem Wege zur Katastrophe: Tagebücher des Großfürsten Andrej und des Kriegsminister Poliwanow: Briefe des Großfürsten an den Zaren.* Berlin, 1926.

French, Gerald. *French Replies to Haig.* London, 1936.

———. *The Life of Field-Marshal Sir John French, First Earl of Ypres.* London, 1931.

———. *Some War Diaries, Addresses and Correspondence of the Field-Marshal the Earl of Ypres.* London, 1937.

French, John. *1914.* Boston, 1919.

Grey, Edward. *Twenty-five Years 1892–1916.* 2 vols. New York, 1937.

Gurko, Vassilij Iasifovic. *Rußland 1914–1917: Erinnerungen an Krieg und Revolution.* Berlin, 1921.

Haig, Field Marshal Sir Douglas. *Features of the War.* Washington, D.C., 1919.

———. *The Private Papers of Douglas Haig, 1914–1919.* London, 1952.

———. *Sir Douglas Haig's Despatches (December 1915–April 1919).* London, 1919.

Hancock, W. K., and Jean van der Poel, eds. *Selections from the Smuts Papers,* vol. 3. Cambridge, England, 1966.

Hankey, Lord Maurice. *The Supreme Command 1914–18.* 2 vols. London, 1961.

———. *The Supreme Control at the Paris Peace Conference 1919: A Commentary.* London, 1963.

Hoare, Samuel. *Das vierte Siegel, das Ende eines russischen Kapitels: Meine Mission in Rußland 1916/17.* Berlin, 1936.

Huguet, Charles Julien. *Britain and the War: A French Indictment.* London, 1928.

Joffre, Joseph Jacques Césaire. *The Personal Memoirs of Joffre, Field Marshal of the French Army.* 2 vols. New York, 1932.

Kennedy, Paul. "Military Coalitions and Coalition Warfare over the Past Century." In Neilson, Keith, and Prete, Roy A., eds. *Coalition Warfare: An Uneasy Accord,* 1–15. Waterloo, Canada, 1983.

Keyes, Sir Roger. *The Naval Memoirs of Admiral of the Fleet Sir Roger Keyes.* 2 vols. London, 1934/1935.

King, Jere Clemens. *Generals and Politicians: Conflict between France's High Command, Parliament and Government, 1914–1918.* Berkeley, Calif., 1951.

Knox, Alfred W. *With the Russian Army, 1914–1917.* 2 vols. New York, 1921.

Lennox, Lady Algeron Gordon, ed. *Diary of Lord Bertie of Thames 1914–1918.* 2 vols. London, 1924.

Lloyd George, David. *War Memoirs of David Lloyd George.* 2 vols. London, 1936.

Magnus, Sir Philip. *Kitchener.* New York, 1959.

Marescotti, Aldrovandi Luigi. *Der Krieg der Diplomaten: Erinnerungen und Tagebuchauszüge, 1914–1919.* München, 1940.

Maurice, Frederick. *Governments and War.* London, 1926.

———. *Lessons of Allied Cooperation: Naval, Military and Air: 1914–1918.* London, 1942.

Monash, John. *The Australian Victories in France in 1918.* New York, n.d.

———. *War Letters of General Monash* [1914–1915]. Sydney, 1934.

Mott, Thomas Bentley. *Twenty Years as Military Attaché.* New York, 1979.

Neilson, Keith. *Strategy and Supply: The Anglo-Russian Alliance 1914–1917.* London, 1984.

Neilson, Keith, and Prete, Roy A., eds. *Coalition Warfare: An Uneasy Accord.* Waterloo, Canada, 1983.

Paléologue, Maurice. *Am Zarenhof während des Weltkrieges: Tagebücher und Betrachtungen.* 2 vols. München, 1925.

Palmer, Frederick. *Bliss, Peacemaker: The Life and Letters of General Tasker Howard Bliss.* New York, 1934.

———. *Newton D. Baker: America at War.* 2 vols. New York, 1931.

Parsons, Edward B. *Wilsonian Diplomacy: Allied-American Rivalries in War and Peace.* St. Louis, Mo., 1978.

Pershing, Gen. John J. *The Final Report of Gen. John J. Pershing Commander in Chief: American Expeditionary Forces.* Washington, D.C., 1919.

———. *My Experience in the World War.* 2 vols. New York, 1931.

Poincaré, Raymond. *The Memoirs of Raymond Poincaré,* vols. 3 and 4. New York, 1931.

Robertson, William. *From Private to Fieldmarshal.* London, 1921.

———. *Soldiers and Statesmen 1914–1918.* 2 vols. London, 1926.

Seymour, Charles, ed. *The Intimate Papers of Colonel House.* 4 vols. New York, 1926–28.

Shumsky-Solomonov, C. *Russia's Part in the World War.* New York, 1920.

Smith-Dorrien, Horace L. *Memoirs of Forty-eight Years' Service.* London, 1925.

Snow, William J. *Signposts of Experience: World War Memoirs.* Washington, D.C., 1941.

Spears, Edward L. *Liaison 1914: A Narrative of the Great Retreat.* London, 1930.

———. *Prelude to Victory.* London, 1939.

Suchumlinov, Vladimir Aleksandrovic. *Die rußische Mobilmachung im Lichte amtlicher Urkunden und den Enthüllungen des Prozesses.* Bern, 1917.

———. *Erinnerungen.* Berlin, 1924.

Tardieu, André. *France and America: Some Experience in Cooperation.* Boston, 1927.

Trask, David S. *The United States in the Supreme War Council: American War Aims and Inter-Allied Strategy 1917–1919.* Middletown, Conn., 1961.

Wallach, Jehuda L. "Suggestions for a Typology of Coalition Warfare." In Commission International d'Histoire Militaire, *Acta No. 6: Montpellier 2–6.IX.1981: Forces Armées et Systèmes d'Alliances,* vol. 1, 15–20. Montpellier, 1983.

INDEX

Siam, 154
Smuts, Jan Christian, South African
    statesman, 25, 56, 106, 110, 157, 159
Snow, William J., American soldier,
    141
Sonnino, Sidney, Italian statesman, 153
South Africa, 128, 155
South Pacific, 29
Spain, 134, 142
Spears, Edward L., British soldier, 15,
    22, 25, 47–48, 49–50, 54, 102, 119,
    121
Stavka (Russian General Staff), 30
Suchumlinov, Vladimir Aleksandrovic,
    Russian general and War Minister,
    10–11, 24–25
Summit conferences, 174
Supreme War Council (SWC), 36, 39,
    62, 67, 77, 90–92, 93, 94, 95, 96,
    106, 107, 108, 109, 111, 112, 113,
    114, 116, 123, 127, 135, 143, 163
Syria, 23, 154

Tardieu, André, French diplomat, 23,
    126, 133, 134, 140, 142, 157, 158,
    160
Third Reich, 3
Trask, David F., U.S. general, 21, 113,
    160, 161
Triple Alliance (Germany, Austria and
    Italy), 8, 9, 39
Triple Entente (Russia, France and
    Great Britain), 9, 76, 146, 156–57
Tunis, 23
Turkey. *See* Ottoman Empire

Unified Command, x, 36, 41, 52, 70,
    87, 93, 101–17, 143, 171–72, 173
United Nations, x, 174–75
United States, 3, 31, 37, 39, 40–41, 46,
    55–56, 67–70, 89, 92, 93, 95, 107,

108, 109, 111, 122, 123, 126, 127,
133, 135, 136, 137, 138, 140, 141.
142, 148, 149, 153, 154, 155, 156,
147, 158, 159–60, 160–66, 167, 169,
170, 171, 174, 175
Uruquay, 154

Venizélos, Eleutherios, Greek states-
    man, 69, 153
Victor Emmanuel III, King of Italy, 36,
    60, 103
Vietnam War, 175
Viviani, René, French statesman, 60

War aims, x, 22–41, 69, 153, 160, 161,
    170–71
War finances, x, 131–49, 170
Warsaw Pact, x, 174, 175
Waterloo, battle of, 1815, 64
Wemyss, Rosslyn E., British admiral, 40
Weygand, Maxime, French general, 76,
    94, 113, 153, 165
Wielemans, Belgian general, 80
Wilhelm II, German Emperor, 8
Wilson, Sir Henry, British Field Mar-
    shal, 15, 16, 25, 27, 40, 46–47, 49,
    52, 53, 63, 66, 79, 80, 84, 91, 92, 93,
    94, 95, 103–4, 106, 107, 113, 115–
    16, 121, 153, 157, 160, 162, 163
Wilson, Woodrow, U.S. President, 29–
    30, 56, 66–68, 69, 92, 107, 108, 109,
    116, 122, 123, 124, 125, 127, 154,
    155, 156, 158, 160–61, 162, 163,
    164, 165, 166
Wiseman, Sir William, British diplo-
    mat, 42 n.31, 68, 92
World War I, ix, x, 1, 2, 3, 8, 63–64,
    169–73, 174
World War II, 3, 173

Ypres, battles of, 26, 33, 120

About the Author

JEHUDA L. WALLACH is Professor Emeritus, Tel-Aviv University and President of the Israel Society for Military History. A widely recognized military historian, his earlier publications include *The Dogma of the Battle of Annihilation* (Greenwood Press, 1985).